GREEK THOUGHT, ARABIC CULTURE

With the accession of the Arab dynasty of the ʿAbbāsids to power and the foundation of Baghdad (762 AD), a Graeco-Arabic translation movement was initiated that lasted for well over two centuries. By the end of the tenth century, almost all scientific and philosophical secular Greek works that were available in late antiquity, including such diverse topics as astrology, alchemy, physics, mathematics, medicine, and philosophy, had been translated into Arabic.

Greek Thought, Arabic Culture explores the social, political, and ideological factors operative in early ʿAbbāsid society that occasioned and sustained the translation movement. It discusses the social groups that supported and benefited from the translation movement and studies the paramount role played by the incipient Arabic scientific and philosophical tradition in its symbiotic relationship with the translation movement. Finally, it traces the legacy of the translation movement in Islamic lands and abroad, suggesting a direct link with the ninth-century classical revival in Byzantium.

Greek Thought, Arabic Culture provides a stimulating, erudite and well-documented analysis of this key movement in the transmission of ancient Greek culture to the middle ages.

Dimitri Gutas is Professor of Arabic Language and Literature at Yale University. He is the author of *Greek Wisdom Literature in Arabic Translation* (1975), *Avicenna and the Aristotelian Tradition* (1988), and, with Gerhard Endress, *A Greek and Arabic Lexicon* (1992–).

GREEK THOUGHT, ARABIC CULTURE

The Graeco-Arabic Translation Movement in Baghdad and Early ʿAbbāsid Society (2nd–4th/8th–10th centuries)

Dimitri Gutas

ROUTLEDGE
Taylor & Francis Group

First Published 1998
by Routledge
2 Park Square, Milton Park, Abingdon, Oxon, OX14 4RN

Simultaneously published in the USA and Canada
by Routledge
270 Madison Ave, New York NY 10016

Routledge is an imprint of the Taylor and Francis Group

Reprinted 1999

Transferred to Digital Printing 2005

Typeset in Garamond by
Ponting–Green Publishing Services, Chesham, Buckinghamshire

British Library Cataloguing in Publication Data
A catalogue record for this book is available from the British Library

Library of Congress Cataloguing in Publication Data
Gutas, Dimitri.
Greek Thought, Arabic Culture: the Graeco-Arabic translation movement in Baghdad and early ʿAbbāsid society (2nd–4th/8th–10th c.) /
Dimitri Gutas
p. cm.
Includes bibliographical references and index.
1. Civilization, Arab–Greek influences. 2. Islamic Empire–Intellectual life. 3. Greek language–Translating into Arabic–History. 4. Translating and interpreting–Islamic Empire. 5. Islamic Empire–History–750–1258.
I. Title.
DS36.82.G7G88 1998 1998
909'.0974927–dc21 97–42761
CIP

ISBN 0–415–06132–6 (hbk)
ISBN 0–415–06133–4 (pbk)

To Athena, Smaragda, Platon,
and Ioanna

Partly because of empire, all cultures are involved in one another; none is single and pure, all are hybrid, heterogeneous, extraordinarily differentiated, and unmonolithic.

Edward W. Said, *Culture and Imperialism*, New York, Alfred A. Knopf, 1993, p. xxv.

CONTENTS

PREFACE

This is a study of the major social, political, and ideological factors that occasioned the unprecedented translation movement from Greek into Arabic in Baghdad, the newly founded capital of the Arab dynasty of the ʿAbbāsids, during the first two centuries of their rule (the eighth through the tenth centuries). It draws upon a long and distinguished line of historical and philological works on Graeco-Arabic studies, or the study of the medieval translations of secular Greek works into Arabic. It can thus gratefully dispense with the who, the what, and the when of the Graeco-Arabic translation movement and concentrate on the how and why, in an effort to understand and explain it as a social and historical phenomenon.

Graeco-Arabic studies has its formal origins (insofar as scholarly investigations of any subject can be said to have formal origins) in the wish expressed by the members of the Royal Society of Sciences in Göttingen, and recorded in the minutes of the session held in 1830, "that a collection be made of the references to Syriac, Arabic, Armenian, and Persian translations of Greek authors, an accurate account of which we are lacking to this day" ("Ut colligantur notitiae de versionibus auctorum Graecorum Syriacis, Arabicis, Armeniacis, Persicis, quarum versionum historiâ accuratâ adhuc caremus," as reported by Wenrich in his preface). Two scholars responded to this call, Gustav Flügel and Johann G. Wenrich, with essays, written in Latin, that appeared in 1841 and 1842 respectively. Flügel's "Dissertatio" is a modest survey of ninety-one Arabic *interpretes*, i.e., both translators and students of Greek works, while Wenrich's *Commentatio* is a more elaborate study following the specifications mentioned by the Royal Society: the first part contains a detailed account of the background and nature of the translations of secular Greek works into Syriac, Arabic, Armenian, and Persian, and the second lists the Greek authors and their works that had been so translated. The bibliographical survey of Arabic translations and translators was continued half a century later by Moritz Steinschneider who brought the work of Wenrich and Flügel up to date in a succession of articles published in various periodicals (1889–96) and reprinted jointly under separate cover only in 1960. Since Steinschneider's days much new information has been acquired, not least through the impressively comprehensive bibliographies of the Arabic sciences presented by Manfred Ullmann (*Medizin* [1970], *Geheimwissenschaften* [1972]) and Fuat Sezgin (*GAS* III–VII [1970–9]). These efforts culminated in the recent (1987–92) book-length article by Gerhard Endress, remarkable for its synthesis and historical contextualization. Published in two separate volumes of the collective work *Grundriss der Arabischen Philologie* (*GAP*), it offers the most extensive and up-to-date narrative and bibliographical survey of the translations, the translators, and the development in Arabic of each specialization.

Franz Rosenthal, who taught us all (and me in particular) as much by word as by example through his talent to identify and focus, in Graeco-Arabic studies as in other fields, on the truly significant, had compiled a reader of original sources from the translation literature and its aftermath in Arabic culture, or, as he called it, *The Classical Heritage in Islam* (1965, English 1975). This reader supplements and gives contour and substance to our perception of the translation movement and the Arabic philosophical and scientific tradition so masterfully surveyed by Endress. The just completed (1997) *maximum opus* of Josef van Ess, *Theologie und Gesellschaft im 2. und 3. Jahrhundert Hidschra*, adds immeasurable depth and breadth to our knowledge of the intellectual life of the society which produced the translation movement. It is a mine of apposite information and sagacious interpretation that will constitute, for generations to come, the starting point of all studies of ʿAbbāsid society. The incredibly rich and unique work of David Pingree, finally, on the medieval transmission of the sciences from and into Sanskrit, Pahlavi, Greek, Arabic, and Latin, has shed much light on the translation movement in concrete and specific details that are frequently our sole fixed points of chronological and geographical reference.

This study could not have been written without the work in print of these χαλκέντεροι predecessors and φιλόπονοι colleagues (or perhaps the adjectives should be reversed), my debt to whom will be amply apparent to the reader on every page. But I also benefited from informal talks with a number of individuals who shared with me their insight and knowledge. I remember a casual conversation with Muhsin Mahdi over a cup of coffee many years ago, when I had just completed my graduate studies. He hinted, very inconspicuously as is his wont, that there was no social and historical study of the translation movement to complement Steinschneider's bibliographical survey of translations (at that time the only one available) and the collection of readings in Rosenthal's *Classical Heritage*. I took notice, for a good reason: Ramsay MacMullen had taught me to ask why in historical analysis. More recently, the same subject came up in numerous stimulating talks with George Saliba, who urged me to write an article on it. Richard Stoneman of Routledge at about that time suggested a short book, and exhibited a rare combination of support, judiciousness, and patience thereafter. That the undertaking did not grow wildly beyond bounds and that it was finished at all is due, as always, to Ioanna, a true sister of Athena and my incessant source of prudence, insight, and strength. I am truly grateful to all of them. I hope that the final result is what each had originally in mind, but if not, I can only rephrase the famous Latin adage: books have a mind of their own, and after a certain point they tend to become assertive of their direction.

Dimitri Gutas
New Haven, September 1997

NOTE ON DATES, NAMES, AND TRANSLITERATION

Dates are given for the most part according to both the Muslim (Hiğra) and Christian calendars, in that order, and separated by a stroke or slant.

Medieval Arabic names frequently consist of compound words the discrete elements of which are not to be read separately. For the benefit of non-Arabists, in the transliteration of proper names all the words that form a unit of nomenclature are connected with a hyphen. Thus, Ḥunayn ibn-Isḥāq, Ibn-an-Nadīm, Abū-l-Farağ Ibn-aṭ-Ṭayyib.

In the transliteration of Arabic words and proper names I have used the standard system of transliteration in most German-language Arabist scholarship. The pronunciation of the few letters that are not immediately obvious to the non-specialist is the following:

ṯ	*th* as in 'think'
ğ	*j* as in 'jar'
ḏ	*th* as in 'that'
š	*sh* as in 'shout'
ʿ	strong guttural consonant
ġ	emphatic French *r*, as in the first letter of '*ramener*'
ʾ	aspirated glottal stop

The remaining diacritics do not seriously affect the value of the letter indicated.

In passages translated from the Arabic, words included in square brackets are my own explanatory additions to the text.

The ʿAbbāsid Caliphs During the Translation Movement

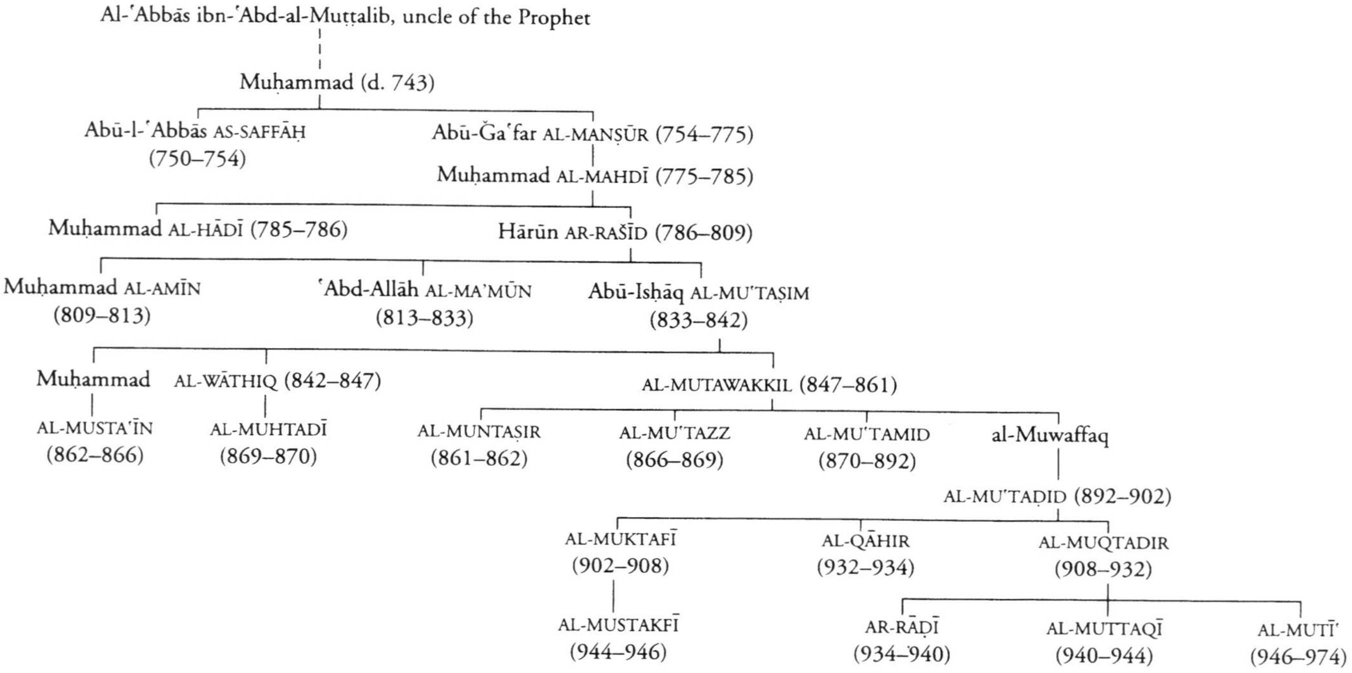
Al-ʿAbbās ibn-ʿAbd-al-Muṭṭalib, uncle of the Prophet
Muḥammad (d. 743)
Abū-l-ʿAbbās AS-SAFFĀḤ (750–754)
Abū-Ǧaʿfar AL-MANṢŪR (754–775)
Muḥammad AL-MAHDĪ (775–785)
Muḥammad AL-HĀDĪ (785–786)
Hārūn AR-RAŠĪD (786–809)
Muḥammad AL-AMĪN (809–813)
ʿAbd-Allāh AL-MAʾMŪN (813–833)
Abū-Isḥāq AL-MUʿTAṢIM (833–842)
Muḥammad
AL-WĀTHIQ (842–847)
AL-MUTAWAKKIL (847–861)
AL-MUSTAʿĪN (862–866)
AL-MUHTADĪ (869–870)
AL-MUNTAṢIR (861–862)
AL-MUʿTAZZ (866–869)
AL-MUʿTAMID (870–892)
al-Muwaffaq
AL-MUʿTAḌID (892–902)
AL-MUKTAFĪ (902–908)
AL-QĀHIR (932–934)
AL-MUQTADIR (908–932)
AL-MUSTAKFĪ (944–946)
AR-RĀḌĪ (934–940)
AL-MUTTAQĪ (940–944)
AL-MUṬĪʿ (946–974)

INTRODUCTION

The Graeco-Arabic Translation Movement as a Social and Historical Phenomenon

A century and a half of Graeco-Arabic scholarship has amply documented that from about the middle of the eighth century to the end of the tenth, almost *all* non-literary and non-historical secular Greek books that were available throughout the Eastern Byzantine Empire and the Near East were translated into Arabic. What this means is that all of the following Greek writings, other than the exceptions just noted, which have reached us from Hellenistic, Roman, and late antiquity times, and many more that have not survived in the original Greek, were subjected to the transformative magic of the translator's pen: astrology and alchemy and the rest of the occult sciences; the subjects of the quadrivium: arithmetic, geometry, astronomy, and theory of music; the entire field of Aristotelian philosophy throughout its history: metaphysics, ethics, physics, zoology, botany, and especially logic – the *Organon*; all the health sciences: medicine, pharmacology, and veterinary science; and various other marginal genres of writings, such as Byzantine handbooks on military science (the tactica), popular collections of wisdom sayings, and even books on falconry – all these subjects passed through the hands of the translators (cf. Appendix). In terms of the extent of the translated material, the enormity of the undertaking can best be grasped if one were to consider that the edition of Galen's complete works by Kühn, and the Berlin Academy edition of the Greek commentaries on Aristotle[1] – works that form only a small

1 C.G. Kühn, *Claudii Galeni opera omnia*, 20 vols, Leipzig, 1821–33; *Commentaria in Aristotelem graeca*, edita consilio et auctoritate academiae litterarum regiae Borussicae, Berlin, G. Reimer, 1882–1909; reviewed by K. Praechter in *Byzantinische Zeitschrift*, 1909, vol. 18, pp. 516–38; English translation of the review in R. Sorabji, *Aristotle Transformed*, London, Duckworth, 1990, pp. 31–54. Though not all Greek commentaries published

fraction of the books translated – comprise seventy-four large volumes. One can justly claim that the study of post-classical Greek secular writings can hardly proceed without the evidence in Arabic, which in this context becomes the second classical language, even before Latin.

The translation movement, which began with the accession of the ʿAbbāsids to power and took place primarily in Baghdad, represents an astounding achievement which, independently of its significance for Greek and Arabic philology and the history of philosophy and science (the aspects which have been overwhelmingly studied to this day), can hardly be grasped and accounted for otherwise than as a social phenomenon (the aspect which has been very little investigated). To elaborate: The Graeco-Arabic translation movement lasted, first of all, well over two centuries; it was no ephemeral phenomenon. Second, it was supported by the entire elite of ʿAbbāsid society: caliphs and princes, civil servants and military leaders, merchants and bankers, and scholars and scientists; it was not the pet project of any particular group in the furtherance of their restricted agenda. Third, it was subsidized by an enormous outlay of funds, both public and private; it was no eccentric whim of a Maecenas or the fashionable affectation of a few wealthy patrons seeking to invest in a philanthropic or self-aggrandizing cause. Finally, it was eventually conducted with rigorous scholarly methodology and strict philological exactitude – by the famous Ḥunayn ibn-Isḥāq and his associates – on the basis of a sustained program that spanned generations and which reflects, in the final analysis, a social attitude and the public culture of early ʿAbbāsid society; it was not the result of the haphazard and random research interests of a few eccentric individuals who, in any age or time, might indulge in arcane philological and textual pursuits that in historical terms are proven irrelevant.

For all these reasons, it is obvious that the translation movement was generated and sustained for a very long time by needs and tendencies in the nascent ʿAbbāsid society as reflected in its structure and consequent ideology; it can hardly be accounted for by the two theories that have been unreflectingly prevalent in most discussions

in this series are known to have been translated into Arabic, there are references by Arabic bibliographers to translations of other commentaries not extant in Greek; in terms of extent, they amply make up for the difference.

of the subject to this day. The first claims that the translation movement was the result of the scholarly zeal of a few Syriac-speaking Christians who, fluent in Greek (because of their particular education) and Arabic (because of their historical circumstances), decided to translate certain works out of altruistic motives for the improvement of society (or even, be it, the promotion of their own religion).[2] The second theory, rampant in much mainstream historiography, attributes it to the wisdom and open-mindedness of a few "enlightened rulers" who, conceived in a backward projection of European enlightenment ideology, promoted learning for its own sake.[3] Certainly the Syriac-speaking Christians played a fundamental role in the translation movement – the translators came overwhelmingly, though not exclusively, from within their ranks – and certainly without the active support of outstanding caliphs during the early ʿAbbāsid period – leaders like al-Manṣūr, Hārūn ar-Rašīd, and al-Maʾmūn – the translation movement would have turned out quite differently; and yet, why the Syriac Christians should have at all translated these books, or, to go a step farther, why patrons should have paid out good money to commission the translation of these books from the Syriac Christians, or even why caliphs, Arabs of Qurashité stock but a few generations away from the Prophet, should have been at all interested in Greek books in translation, are

2 See, for example, a statement such as that of Bénédicte Landron, written from a decidedly Christian perspective, who attributes to the Christian translators a sense of social responsibility and vocation: "Ces chrétiens [i.e., the translators] se sentirent une responsabilité, presque une vocation, dans la transmission de l'héritage philosophique antique;" in "Les chrétiens arabes et les disciplines philosophiques," *Proche Orient Chrétien*, 1986, vol. 36, p. 24. J.M. Fiey even wants today's eastern Christians to feel proud of the contribution of their ancestors (*Chrétiens syriaques sous les Abbassides, surtout à Bagdad (749–1258)*, Louvain, Secrétariat du Corpus SCO, 1980, p. 31). More recently, the same argument appears, though with a different focus, in Joel L. Kraemer's *Humanism in the Renaissance of Islam*, 2nd edn, Leiden, E.J. Brill, 1992, pp. 76–7.

3 For example, S. Ṭaha, "At-Taʿrīb wa-kibār al-muʿarribīn fi l-Islām," *Sumer*, 1976, vol. 32, pp. 345a and 346b, states that the factors that led to the translation movement were al-Manṣūr's sponsorship of scholars once he had established the ʿAbbāsid government and finished building Baghdad, and the promotion of translations by ar-Rašīd and some of his ministers and other lovers of the sciences. Fiey, *Chrétiens syriaques sous les Abbassides*, p. 31, attributes the development of the translation movement under al-Mahdī to his "curiosité." Similar statements could fill volumes. A corollary to this position in medieval Arabic sources is the ostensible reading of the simplistic account of al-Maʾmūn's Aristotle dream, of which more later (chapter 4.3).

questions that have been very little asked and even less answered.[4] The Graeco-Arabic translation movement was too complex and deep-rooted and too influential in a historical sense for its causes to fall under either of these categories – even assuming that these categories are at all valid for historical hermeneutics.

The scholarly consensus on the similar and equally far-reaching translation activity of Aristotelian and other ancient texts from Greek and Arabic into Latin in the twelfth century appears to be that it was due to the rise in western Europe of a new class of lay teachers. According to this explanation, which is essentially a corollary to the analysis of the rise of the bourgeoisie, this new class, because of its different socio-economic background, required a new kind of knowledge that was independent from and antagonistic to the traditional church learning of the clergy. Thus, "the works of Aristotle which were . . . made available by about the year 1200 did not gain the influence they had because they were fortuitously translated, but they were translated because the masters [i.e., lay teachers] wanted no longer simply to transmit, because they wanted to learn themselves."[5] The impetus for the translations is seen as coming from the shifting structure of western European society.

No similar analysis has been attempted or even suggested in connection with the Graeco-Arabic translation movement. The reasons for this vary, but the most relevant one is surely the lack of preparatory studies in this direction, which itself may be due to the

4 The cultural aspect, or question, of the entire translation movement has been raised but never really treated. See the set of questions posed by A.I. Sabra, "The Appropriation and Subsequent Naturalization of Greek Science in Medieval Islam: A Preliminary Statement," *History of Science*, 1987, vol. 25, p. 228; cf. H. Hugonnard-Roche, "Les traductions du grec au syriaque et du syriaque à l'arabe," *Rencontres de cultures dans la philosophie médiévale. Traductions et traducteurs de l'antiquité tardive au XIVe siècle*, Louvain-la-Neuve / Cassino, 1990, p. 132, note 4. F. Rosenthal gave a tantalizing hint but did not elaborate beyond the mere statement: "the ʿAbbāsid caliphs . . . sponsored and generously supported the translators and greatly encouraged their activities for personal as well as political motives"; *Classical Heritage*, p. 27. George Saliba raised the issue concretely and offered some general suggestions, but left the question open for a future study of "the social, economic, and political conditions during the latter part of the Umayyad times and the early Abbasid ones": "The Development of Astronomy in Medieval Islamic Society," *Arab Studies Quarterly*, 1982, vol. 4, pp. 212–13, reprinted in his *A History of Arabic Astronomy*, New York and London, New York University Press, 1994, pp. 52–3.

5 C.H. Lohr, "The Medieval Interpretation of Aristotle," in N. Kretzmann, A. Kenny, J. Pinborg (eds), *The Cambridge History of Later Medieval Philosophy*, Cambridge, Cambridge University Press, 1982, p. 84, with references to the work of J. Le Goff and L.M. de Rijk.

relative dearth of primary sources. There is, furthermore, a problem of method and appropriate analytical categories. The concept of bourgeoisie, or, in this case, lay teachers that spring from its midst, would appear to be a theoretical construct adequately representing the social reality of twelfth-century western Europe. The situation, however, was different in Baghdad in the second half of the eighth century, and it is doubtful that such an analytical category would apply in any meaningful way. The support for the translation movement cut across all lines of religious, sectarian, ethnic, tribal, and linguistic demarcation. Patrons were Arabs and non-Arabs, Muslims and non-Muslims, Sunnīs and Shīʿites, generals and civilians, merchants and land-owners, etc. It also lasted well into the Būyid era (945–1055), and thus saw support in a variety of social configurations with stratifications substantially different from each other; hence, what constituted a "class" in support of it in one configuration must also be explained in the next.[6] Finally, even the concept of *ʿulamāʾ*, or the learned elite, indigenous to Islamic societies, also tends to be not very helpful in this regard if only

6 There is a number of serious efforts by scholars to associate class differentiations with intellectual life in ʿAbbāsid society, but there is no corresponding consensus – or the semblance of one – about what constitutes a productive approach, let alone a theoretical orientation. In his numerous studies on early *kalām*, van Ess on occasion made use of the concept of the bourgeoisie to describe the social background of the theologians (see, e.g., his "Une lecture à rebours de l'histoire du muʿtazilisme," *Revue des Études Islamiques*, 1978, vol. 46, pp. 223–4); his approach, however, has been primarily descriptive. The final formulation that appeared in his *Theologie und Gesellschaft im 2. und 3. Jahrhundert Hidschra. Eine Geschichte des religiösen Denkens im frühen Islam*, Berlin, W. de Gruyter, 1997, IV, 731–7, is theoretically neutral and very useful in registering with precision the distinctions among the different class affiliations and professions of the theologians and other intellectuals. At a more theoretical level, and working with issues of immediate relevance to the subject of this study, S.D. Goitein saw the diffusion of the Greek sciences during the period of the translation movement as "due to the new middle class" ("Between Hellenism and Renaissance – Islam, the Intermediate Civilization," *Islamic Studies*, 1963, p. 227 and notes). All this is true enough and goes without saying; intellectual activities of a "middle class" or bourgeoisie presuppose literacy, which presupposes wealth and leisure, which presuppose urbanization and economic prosperity, which is precisely what happened in the Near East as a result of the initial Arab conquests, as briefly discussed in chapter 1.1. The problem is both to correlate causally such factors (and the attendant concept of class) with the translation movement in particular and to explain the absence of activities like the translation movement in other social situations where the same classes and social factors can also be observed. When the evidence from all such studies about all strata of society is in, an appropriate theoretical approach may suggest itself. Cf. the discussion in the Epilogue.

because it itself was being shaped during – and indeed largely as a result of – the translation movement.[7] It is thus difficult first to define a class as a meaningful analytical category in this context and then almost impossible to identify a specific one (or ones) as the supporters of the translation movement. I am not being disingenuous but, given the state of Arabic and Islamic studies in general, I would rather err on the side of naïveté than on that of theoretical obfuscation.

Let me be more precise. Because of the very nature of the subject of this book – the concrete social and historical roots of a major intellectual movement in human history – it is all too easy, indeed, according to some, necessary, to adopt a conscious theoretical standpoint from which to view and analyze the facts of the subject. One may either borrow a current theory or make up one's own, as, for example, Hamilton Gibb did in a lecture he once delivered on "The Influence of Islamic Culture on Medieval Europe," in which he came up with three "laws" which allegedly govern the way cultural influences operate.[8] There is quite an extensive literature on the transmission of Greek knowledge into Arabic which operates, mostly unconsciously, on the basis of such theoretical constructs. I find little benefit in spending time on them and with them if only because one has to come up with but one exception to such "laws" or "major ideas" that allegedly define a culture in order to invalidate them, and I seem to be coming across an awful lot of such exceptions. Furthermore, and perhaps more insidiously, it is frequently a small step from such a theoretical standpoint of defining "ideas" and "laws" to the adoption of assumptions about a culture which are essentialist and reificatory in nature and therefore quite ahistorical – assumptions such as the "Greek spirit" or the "Arab mind."[9] And because they tell us everything about the background and ideological orientation of the scholar using such theoretical constructs and nothing about the subject under discussion, they belong to the

7 See the informative discussion of this concept, and its potentialities and limitations for a study of Islamic societies, in R. Stephen Humphreys, *Islamic History. A Framework for Inquiry*, Princeton, Princeton University Press, 1991, pp. 187–208.

8 Published in the *Bulletin of the John Rylands Library*, 1955–6, vol. 38, pp. 82–98.

9 The essentialist nature of a host of such explanatory assumptions has been briefly discussed and documented, in a way that makes further comments superfluous, by A.I. Sabra, "Situating Arabic Science. Locality versus Essence," *Isis*, 1996, vol. 87, pp. 654–7, and especially p. 656 and note 2. For a concrete example of the confusion that such assumptions can cause in scholarly analysis see my review of M. Fakhry's *Ethical Theories in Islam* (Leiden, E.J. Brill, 1994) in *Journal of the American Oriental Society*, 1997, vol. 117, pp. 172a–3a.

sociology or history of knowledge in the nineteenth and twentieth centuries rather than to the historical investigation of the subject. As one can readily imagine, the transmission of Greek knowledge into Arabic has attracted an inordinate amount of such attention, but for the reasons stated I did not think it useful to allocate space to these discussions beyond what is absolutely necessary (see chapter 7.3). One section of the bibliography is devoted specifically to studies that discuss the cultural significance of Graeco-Arabic transmission. Quite a few of the more sonorous theories and ideas in these studies have been presented in some detail by Joel L. Kraemer in an article published fourteen years ago and recently reprinted; the interested reader will readily find them there.[10]

The Graeco-Arabic translation movement is a very complex social phenomenon and no single circumstance, set of events, or personality can be singled out as its cause. A variety of factors was instrumental in its development and sustention, and I have found no theory or set of theories that can comprehend its historical multiformity. What seems advisable at this preliminary stage of the study of early ʿAbbāsid society is to listen to and understand our sources as competently as possible, try to read them and interpret their semiotics as it was intended for the immediate audience to which they were addressed, and let them suggest the categories into which they would have the material break up; subsequent research may then be in a better position to develop more sophisticated analytical tools. Such an approach makes it relatively clear that the translation movement had very much to do, on the one hand, with the foundation of Baghdad and the establishment there of the ʿAbbāsid dynasty as the managers of a world empire, and, on the other, with the special needs of the society in Baghdad as it was forming itself both under the manipulation of the ʿAbbāsid dynasty and elite and through its own special and, in many ways, unprecedented configuration. Accordingly I have investigated these two aspects in Parts I and II of the book.

I am conscious of the difficulty of this undertaking both in terms of the intractable and complex source material, and in terms of the

10 "Humanism in the Renaissance of Islam: A Preliminary Study," *Journal of the American Oriental Society*, 1984, vol. 104, pp. 135–64; reprinted in his *Humanism* at the end of the book. Many of these ahistorical and essentializing views about "Islam" and "Hellenism" are the common fare of the majority of general essays written for public consumption; a relatively recent example is F.E. Peters, "Hellenism in Islam," in C.G. Thomas (ed.), *Paths from Ancient Greece*, Leiden, E.J. Brill, 1988, pp. 77–91.

relative novelty and delicacy of the subject. Nevertheless, the Graeco-Arabic translation movement of Baghdad constitutes a truly epoch-making stage, by any standard, in the course of human history. It is equal in significance to, and belongs to the same narrative as, I would claim, that of Pericles' Athens, the Italian Renaissance, or the scientific revolution of the sixteenth and seventeenth centuries, and it deserves so to be recognized and embedded in our historical consciousness. The formulation of a comprehensive and unitary account of the movement such as that attempted here seemed to be the best way to carry the discussion forward, which I hope this book will promote.

Part I

TRANSLATION AND EMPIRE

1

THE BACKGROUND OF THE TRANSLATION MOVEMENT

Material, Human, and Cultural Resources

1. THE HISTORICAL, ECONOMIC, AND CULTURAL SIGNIFICANCE OF THE ARAB CONQUESTS

Certain material conditions that prepared a background against which a translation movement could take place and flourish were established by two momentous historical events, the early Arab conquests through the Umayyad period and the ʿAbbāsid revolution that culminated in 134/750.

Less than thirty years after the death of the Prophet Muḥammad in 10/632, Arab armies had conquered in southwest Asia and north-east Africa the lands that a millennium earlier had fallen to Alexander the Great. They put an end to the Persian Sasanian empire (224–651), the successor to the Medes and the Parthians who had reclaimed from Alexander's empire the territories east of the Euphrates, and they rolled back irretrievably Alexander's conquests in the Fertile Crescent and Egypt, lands which had been ruled after him in succession by his epigones, by the Romans, and by the Byzantines. Although by 732 the new empire that was founded on and organized in accordance with the religion revealed to Muḥammad, Islam, was to extend yet further afield – from Central Asia and the Indian subcontinent to Spain and the Pyrenees – the heart of the new civilization which it generated lay in the centers of ancient civilization, from Persia through Meso-potamia and Syro-Palestine to Egypt.

The historical significance of the Arab conquests can hardly be overestimated. Egypt and the Fertile Crescent were reunited with Persia and India politically, administratively, and most important, economically, for the first time since Alexander the Great, and for a period that was to last significantly longer than his brief lifetime. The great economic and cultural divide that separated the civilized world for a thousand years prior to the rise of Islam, the frontier between the East and the West formed by the two great rivers that created antagonistic powers on either side, ceased to exist. This allowed for the free flow of raw materials and manufactured goods, agricultural products and luxury items, people and services, techniques and skills, and ideas, methods, and modes of thought. The salutary impact of this event was further magnified by the fact that it came in the wake of the disastrous Byzantino-Persian wars of 570–630 which devastated the area, decimated the local populations, and disrupted trade. These wars, like all the successive conflicts between Greeks, Romans, and Byzantines on the one hand and Persians on the other, were generated by the economic barriers raised by the political division of the Near East into East and West. Specifically, free access to the East–West trade routes would seem to have been at the heart of the conflict. Prior to the outbreak of renewed hostilities after Justinian's death in 565, his successor, Justin II (r. 565–78), well aware of the eventual effect of the war on trade, entered into negotiations with the Oghuz Turks in Central Asia in order for the Byzantines to gain access to the northern silk route, to the north of the Caspian Sea.

One particular aspect of the economic prosperity ushered by the reunion of East and West deserves special mention. Although, as one would expect, trade benefited particularly from the new conditions established by the "pax Islamica," it was agriculture that witnessed a revolution. The lifting of the barriers between India and the Eastern Mediterranean saw the systematic importation into Southwest Asia and the Mediterranean of numerous strains of plants, legumes, and fruits and the development of new ones, as well as agricultural techniques and a knowledge of intensive farming and full use of fallow lands. Thus, much more than trade, which enjoyed a continuity not seen before and a concomitant expansion, but whose benefits were necessarily restricted to the merchant classes, it was the agricultural revolution of the first centuries after the Arab conquests that provided much of the wealth of the early empire and benefited all social strata: the upper classes who owned the lands and appropriated the produce, the peasants who cultivated them, and the lower classes whose diets were inevitably enhanced.[1]

1 See the fundamental work by A.M. Watson, *Agricultural Innovation in the Early Islamic World*, Cambridge, Cambridge University Press, 1983. The effect of the agricultural

An equally significant result of the Arab conquests and arguably the most important factor for the spread of knowledge in general was the introduction of paper-making technology into the Islamic world by Chinese prisoners of war in 134/751. Paper quickly supplanted all other writing materials during the first decades of the ʿAbbāsid era, when its use was championed and even dictated by the ruling elite. It is interesting to note that the various kinds of paper that were developed during that time bear the names of some prominent patrons of the translation movement: *ǧaʿfarī*, named after Ǧaʿfar al-Barmakī, and *ṭalḥī* and *ṭāhirī* after two members of the Ṭāhirid clan.[2]

In addition to the introduction of paper, the lifting of the barriers after the Arab conquests between the East and the West of Mesopotamia also had an extremely beneficial, though obviously unintentional, cultural consequence. It united areas and peoples that for a millennium had been subject to Hellenization ever since Alexander the Great *while it isolated politically and geographically the Byzantines*, i.e., the Greek-speaking Chalcedonian Orthodox Christians. This is doubly significant. First, it was the exclusionary theological policies and practices of Constantinopolitan "Orthodoxy" that created religious schisms in the first place and drove Syriac-speaking Christians into religious fragmentation and, in the case of the Nestorians, into Persia. The effective removal from the Islamic polity (the *Dār al-Islām*) of this source of contention and cultural fragmentation, and their unification under a non-partisan overlord, the Islamic state, opened the way for greater cultural cooperation and intercourse. Second, the political and geographical isolation of the Byzantines also shielded these Christian communities under Muslim rule, and all other Hellenized peoples in the Islamic commonwealth, from the dark ages and aversion to Hellenism into which Byzantium slid in the seventh and eighth centuries.

While Chalcedonian Christians were quarreling over the icons and vying with each other in repudiating the pagan tradition, Syriac-

revolution on the diet of the people is sketched in the articles by E. Ashtor, "The Diet of Salaried Classes in the Medieval Near East," *Journal of Asian History*, 1970, vol. 4, pp. 1–24, reprinted in his *The Medieval Near East: Social and Economic History*, London, Variorum, 1978, no. III; and "An Essay on the Diet of the Various Classes in the Medieval Levant," in R. Forster and O. Ranum (eds), *Biology of Man in History. Selections from the Annales*, Baltimore, Johns Hopkins University Press, 1975, pp. 125–62.

2 See the article "Kāghad" by Huart and Grohmann in *EI* IV,419b. For these individuals see below, chapter 6.1c.

speaking Christians, who, after the Arab conquests, in addition to being doctrinally separate from the Chalcedonians were now also politically apart, developed along different cultural lines. Secular Greek learning was by this time thoroughly assimilated by Syriac speakers[3] and well entrenched in the major centers of Eastern Christianity throughout the Fertile Crescent, from Edessa and Qinnasrīn in the west, through Nisibis and Mosul in northern Mesopotamia, to Ǧundīsābūr well into western Persia, to mention only the most famous centers. The same atmosphere doubtless existed in Monophysite and Nestorian congregations thoughout the area, if we are to judge by scholars who appeared during the early ʿAbbāsid period with a solid background in Greek learning; witness Dayr Qunnā south of Baghdad on the Tigris [*EI* II,197], the site of a large and flourishing Nestorian monastery, where Abū-Bišr Mattā ibn-Yūnus [*EI* VI,844–5], the founder of the Aristotelian school in Baghdad early in the tenth century, studied and taught. In addition to religious centers, other prominent cities in pre-Islamic times also maintained a tradition of some Greek learning; an example would be al-Ḥīra close to the Euphrates in southern ʿIrāq, the capital of the Laḫmids [*EI* III,462], which, despite the waning of its fortunes after the rise of Islam, could still be the home town of the famous Ḥunayn ibn-Isḥāq [*EI* III,578–81]. To these should be added at least two other major centers of Greek learning at the antipodes of each other and, in a way, embracing the Hellenized world that was to be the birthplace of the ʿAbbāsid Graeco-Arabic translation movement, Ḥarrān (Carrhae) in northern Mesopotamia just south of Edessa [*EI* III,227–30] and Marw in northeasternmost Persia at the gates of Central Asia [*EI* VI,618–21]. The former remained obstinately pagan well into the tenth century and kept alive numerous Greek ideas, beliefs, and practices that seem to have been extinguished in most other areas, while the latter combined a vigorous Hellenism, as exhibited in its brand of Zoroastrianism that was to play a significant role in early ʿAbbāsid times (see chapter 2.5), with an equally Hellenized Nestorianism.

3 See the fundamental studies by S. Brock, "From Antagonism to Assimilation: Syriac Attitudes to Greek Learning," in N. Garsoian, T. Mathews, and R. Thompson (eds), *East of Byzantium: Syria and Armenia in the Formative Period*, Washington, DC, Dumbarton Oaks, 1980, pp. 17–34; and "Syriac Culture in the Seventh Century," *Aram*, 1989, vol. 1, pp. 268–80.

We have little direct information on the kind of instruction and study of secular Greek learning that went on in these centers, but we can get some idea about school practice during the time of Ḥunayn ibn-Isḥāq from his own pen, who compares as follows curricular procedures in Alexandria in late antiquity with those of his day:

> [The members of the medical school in Alexandria] would gather every day to read and study one leading text among those [books by Galen], just as our contemporary Christian colleagues gather every day in places of teaching known as *skholē* (σχολή) for [the study of] a leading text by the ancients. As for the rest of the books, they used to read them individually – each one on his own, after having first practiced with those books which I mentioned – just as our colleagues today read the commentaries of the books by the ancients.[4]

Ḥunayn's passage refers specifically to medical instruction, and one is not sure whether the description given here can be assumed to apply in general to other fields as well; logic in the form of the first three or four books of Aristotle's *Organon* almost certainly was included in the formal training. Ptolemaic astronomy and astrology may also have been studied, though these subjects seem to have been particularly cultivated by Persian scholars who were also in contact, for developments in these fields, with their Indian counterparts.

With the advent of Islam, all these centers were united politically and administratively, and, most important, scholars from all of them could pursue their studies and interact with each other without the need to pay heed to any official version of "orthodoxy," whatever the religion. We thus see throughout the region and throughout the seventh and the eighth centuries numerous "international" scholars active in their respective fields and working with different languages. As examples of such scholars we may mention, for the seventh century, Severus of Nisibis (d. 666/7), who was equally conversant with Persian as he was with Greek and Syriac, and his student Jacob of Edessa (d. 708), the major representative of "Christian

4 G. Bergsträsser, *Ḥunain ibn Isḥāq über die syrischen und arabischen Galen-Übersetzungen* [Abhandlungen für die Kunde des Morgenlandes XVII,2], Leipzig, 1925, pp. 18.19–19.1, on the basis of the corrections to the text given in G. Bergsträsser, *Neue Materialien zu Ḥunain ibn Isḥāq's Galen-Bibliographie* [Abhandlungen für die Kunde des Morgenlandes XIX,2], Leipzig, 1932, p. 17.

Hellenism."[5] Less well known but just as important for the transmission of astrology are two scholars of the following century, Theophilus of Edessa (d. 785) and Stephanus the Philosopher (d. after 800), both widely familiar with Greek, Syriac, Pahlavi and (through Pahlavi) Indian sources. Theophilus was the ʿAbbāsid al-Mahdī's court astrologer and military advisor as well as the author, among other things, of a book on military astrology, while Stephanus, possibly his student or associate, worked in Mesopotamia and visited Constantinople in the 790s where he wrote a treatise in praise of astrology that appears to have re-introduced mathematical sciences in Byzantium (see chapter 7.4).[6] Māšā'allāh and Nawbaḫt, their equally international contemporaries and colleagues, are better known through the Arabic sources. The former a Jew from Baṣra apparently of Persian origin and the latter a Persian, they drew up the horoscope which determined for the ʿAbbāsid al-Manṣūr the day (30 July 762) on which construction of the city of Baghdad was to begin.[7]

What is significant to notice about these scholars under the new conditions generated by the Arab conquests and the lifting of the political and religious barriers is that they were representatives of living scientific traditions and experts in their respective fields; they were multilingual and hence could draw on the scientific literature written in languages other than Greek; they were in contact with each other either personally through travel or through correspondence; and, finally and most importantly, because of their multilingualism, they were responsible for the transmission of knowledge without translation. This would explain the appearance, almost overnight, it would seem, of numerous experts in the court of the ʿAbbāsids once they made the political decision to focus the efforts of the available scientists and sponsor the translation of written sources.

5 So called by A. Baumstark, *Geschichte der syrischen Literatur*, Bonn, Marcus und Webers, 1922, pp. 248–56. For Severus see pp. 246–7. Cf. Brock, "From Antagonism to Assimilation," pp. 23–4, and *GAS* VI,111–12, 114–15.

6 See the studies by D. Pingree, "The Greek Influence on Early Islamic Mathematical Astronomy," *Journal of the American Oriental Society*, 1973, vol. 93, p. 35, and "Classical and Byzantine Astrology in Sassanian Persia," *Dumbarton Oaks Papers*, 1989, vol. 43, pp. 236–9; cf. *GAS* VII,48–50.

7 See D. Pingree, "The Fragments of the Works of al-Fazārī," *Journal of Near Eastern Studies*, 1970, vol. 29, p. 104; cf. *GAS* VII,100–1, 102–8.

2. THE ʿABBĀSID REVOLUTION AND THE DEMOGRAPHY OF BAGHDAD

The coming to power of the ʿAbbāsid dynasty and the subsequent transferral of the seat of the caliphate from Damascus to Baghdad had far-reaching consequences for providing a demographic background conducive to the translation movement. The base of power of the ousted dynasty, the Umayyads, was in Syro-Palestine, and their capital was Damascus. After the Arab conquests and throughout the Umayyad period (661–750), and possibly even beyond the mid-eighth century, Greek was widely current in Syria and Palestine as the native language of significant portions of the local population, as the lingua franca of commerce and business, and as the language of learning of Christian clerics, especially the Melkites. As a matter of fact, far from going into disuse, it was employed in a variety of new themes and literary styles in the rapidly changing social, political, and theological environment.[8] The Umayyad central administration in Damascus followed Byzantine practices by and large, while the language of administration, until the reforms of ʿAbd-al-Malik (r. 65/685–86/705), was Greek. Numerous high functionaries and secretaries were Greek-speaking, either Greeks themselves or Greek-educated Arabs; the sources have preserved the names of a number of them, most notable among whom is Sarǧūn ibn-Manṣūr ar-Rūmī (the Byzantine, i.e., in this context, Melkite), who served the first Umayyad caliphs from Muʿāwiya to ʿAbd-al-Malik as the head of the administration and finance (*dīwān*).[9] The Umayyads naturally employed in these positions members of Arab tribes from Syro-Palestine who had had long experience with and involvement in Byzantine affairs: descendants of the Salīḥids, Byzantine *foederati* in the fifth century, and of the Ġassānids, their successors in the sixth and early seventh, figure among the secretaries in the Umayyad administration.

8 See the summary and programmatic article by A. Cameron, "New Themes and Styles in Greek Literature: Seventh–Eighth Centuries," in A. Cameron and L.I. Conrad (eds), *The Byzantine and Early Islamic Near East* [Studies in Late Antiquity and Early Islam 1], Princeton, Darwin Press, 1992, pp. 81–105, and the references to recent work on the subject on p. 87 and note 17; see further Cameron and Conrad's references in the Introduction to the volume, p. 11 and note 13.

9 *Fihrist* 242.25–30; see especially Ṣ.A. al-ʿAlī, "Muwaẓẓafū bilād aš-Šām fi l-ʿahd al-Umawī," *al-Abḥāṯ*, 1966, vol. 19, pp. 60–1; cf. *EI* IV,755a, VII,268a. The *Fihrist* also records that ʿAbd-al-Malik asked Sarǧūn to translate the *dīwān* into Arabic; Sarǧūn, however, procrastinated and ʿAbd-al-Malik, annoyed, had it translated by Sulaymān ibn-Saʿd.

John of Damascus, finally, is perhaps the most famous of Greek-speaking Arabs in Umayyad circles.[10]

What was the cultural orientation of all these Greek-speaking groups surrounding the Umayyads who continued Byzantine practices? More specifically, what was their attitude toward ethnic, i.e., classical Greek learning? It is clear that the social and religious situation in the seventh and eighth centuries in the Eastern Mediterranean is extremely complicated and does not lend itself easily to generalizations – Cameron even speaks of a crisis of identity among the local peoples in the area, including the Greek-speaking communities[11] – while historical investigation is just now in the process of formulating the proper questions to be asked. Nevertheless, for the purposes of the present discussion it is relatively clear that the prevailing high culture, especially among those Greek-speaking groups with whom the Umayyads were in direct contact, was the Greek Orthodox Christianity espoused in imperial Constantinople. The Damascene Byzantine bureaucracy could not but have followed and reflected cultural patterns established in Constantinople, and John of Damascus would be representative, at the level of theology, of such trends among Orthodox Arabs. By the seventh century this Byzantine high culture was inimically indifferent to pagan Greek learning, having left behind the stage of confrontation characterizing the previous age of the church fathers. Hellenism was the defeated enemy, to be treated with contemptuous indifference because it was irrelevant: Greek Christianity, as promulgated by Constantinople, had now turned in upon itself, or upon what it perceived as internal enemies, and tried, in a series of councils that lasted throughout the seventh and eighth centuries, to define with ever-greater precision its own understanding of orthodoxy.[12] This disparaging attitude toward Hellenism would have been shared, among Greek-speaking Christians under the Umayyads, even by groups who may not have been Chalcedonian Christians, such as the Ġassānids who were Mono-

10 The Salīḥids, the Byzantine *foederati* of the fifth century, were Orthodox Christians who were subsequently employed by the Umayyads. Usāma ibn-Zayd, who served a number of Umayyad caliphs, is particularly notable; see I. Shahid, *Byzantium and the Arabs in the Fifth Century*, Washington, D.C., Dumbarton Oaks, 1989, pp. 304–6 and 411, and al-ʿAlī, "Muwaẓẓafū bilād aš-Šām fī l-ʿahd al-Umawī," p. 63. For Ġassānid secretaries see the lists in al-ʿAlī pp. 52–3, 60, 62. It would be desirable and informative to do a complete prosopographical study of all these functionaries.

11 Cameron, "New Themes and Styles in Greek Literature," p. 86.

12 Cameron, "New Themes and Styles in Greek Literature," pp. 88, 93.

physites in pre-Islamic times. This complete turnabout in cultural orientation by Greek-speaking Christians would also explain the desuetude of the old Greek literary themes and styles and the introduction of novel genres of writing, reflecting the new preoccupations and concerns of a Christian society: the homily, the disputation, *quaestiones*, florilegia, miracle stories, and hagiography.[13]

In this intellectual climate, it is impossible to conceive of a translation movement, supported by Greek-speaking Christians, of *secular* Greek works into Arabic; it could have happened only under aggressive promotion by the Umayyads, and this was lacking. In other words, had the ʿAbbāsid dynasty not come into power and moved the capital to Baghdad, there would have been no Graeco-Arabic translation movement in Damascus.

With the ʿAbbāsid revolution, the foundation of Baghdad, and the transfer of the seat of the caliphate to ʿIrāq, the situation of the Arab empire with regard to its cultural orientations changed drastically. Away from Byzantine influence in Damascus, there developed a new multicultural society in Baghdad based on the completely different demographic mix of population in ʿIrāq. This consisted of (a) Aramaic-speakers, Christians, and Jews, who formed the majority of the settled population; (b) Persian-speakers, concentrated primarily in the cities; and (c) Arabs, partly sedentarized and Christian, like those at al-Ḥīra on the Euphrates, and partly nomadic, in the grazing grounds of northern ʿIrāq. The Arab Muslims – other, of course, than those in the new capital – were concentrated, to the north, in the trading center of Mosul (Mawṣil) and in the Sawād to the south, in the original garrison cities founded by them, Kūfa, Baṣra, and Wāsiṭ, the first two of which provided, from the second/eighth century onwards, one of the most significant influences in the formation of the new melting-pot culture. There were, of course, other ethnic groups at the time in ʿIrāq and beyond, especially in Iran (e.g., the Kurds in northern ʿIrāq and in the Zagros mountains, the Baluchis in southeast Iran, etc.), but we have no record of their playing a role in shaping the outcome of the particular issue we are investigating. All of these groups participated, in one capacity or another, in the social, political, and cultural life of the new capital, and what is called classical Islamic civilization is the result of the fermentation of all the divergent ingredients which their various backgrounds, beliefs, practices, and values provided.

Much as the Umayyads had to rely on the local Byzantines and

13 Cameron, "New Themes and Styles in Greek Literature," pp. 94–105.

Christian Arabs in Damascus for their administration, so also did the early ʿAbbāsids have to rely on the local Persians, Christian Arabs, and Arameans for theirs. The culture of these people in the employ of the ʿAbbāsids, in contradistinction to the Christians of Damascus, was Hellenized without the animosity against the ethnic Greek learning evident in Orthodox Christian Byzantine circles. Hence the transfer of the caliphate from Damascus to central ʿIrāq – i.e., from a Greek-speaking to a non-Greek-speaking area – had the paradoxical consequence of allowing the preservation of the classical Greek heritage which the Byzantines had all but extirpated.

3. PRE-ʿABBĀSID TRANSLATION ACTIVITIES

Translation in the Near East had been going on ever since the second millennium BC and the translation of Sumerian documents into Akkadian. Like all manifestations of cultural life, however, such generalizations cannot and should not be given an explanatory function beyond their descriptive one. More specifically for the subject under discussion, the fact that translation of Greek secular works into languages of the Near East, including Arabic, had been going on before the advent of the ʿAbbāsids should not be seen, by itself, as explaining the ʿAbbāsid translation movement, which cannot be interpreted as the continuation of existing practices. All translation activities have their specific reasons and goals, which have to be investigated and analyzed in each particular instance, and accordingly discriminations have to be made. The following sections do not intend to review the terrain once more,[14] but to survey the various pre-ʿAbbāsid translation activities into Arabic and discuss the ways in which they differed from but also paved the way for the ʿAbbāsid translation movement.

The Syriac Translations

The point to be made about the Graeco-Syriac translations is the direction they took and the state they were at by the time the ʿAbbāsids came to power and the Graeco-Arabic translation movement was initiated. Leaving aside the Graeco-Syriac translations

14 See the detailed treatment with comprehensive bibliography by Endress, *GAP* II,407–16, 418–20.

of Christian literature – which, though providing the necessary technical background for the translation of secular works, were responding to a different set of social and ideological needs and demands of the Aramaic-speaking Christians – sophisticated Hellenism made its appearance in Syriac with the work of Sergius of Rēšʿaynā (d. 536), priest, physician, and translator. Sergius was educated in Alexandria at the school of Ammonius. In a work addressed to a student and fellow cleric, Theodorus, bishop of Karḫ Ǧuddān on the Tigris, he outlined his intention to write about all the parts of Aristotle's philosophy in a number of books, starting with logic, the indispensable instrument and foundation of all science. In this connection, Hugonnard-Roche drew the very apt comparison with Boethius who, working at the same time in the Latin-speaking world, conceived of an even more ambitious project of translating into Latin and commenting on all of the works of Plato and Aristotle.[15] As it turned out, neither of these projects materialized. Sergius and his successors restricted themselves, in the translation of Aristotelian philosophy, to the first few books of the *Organon* only, while Boethius did not even have any immediate successors.

There is a widespread misconception in the majority of works dealing with the transmission of Greek knowledge into Arabic that this was effected on the basis of pre-existing Syriac translations, in the sense that the truly significant job of studying, selecting, and translating the Greek classics into a Semitic language had already been accomplished in the Syriac schools and that all that was needed to be done, for the Arabic versions, was merely the mechanical task of rendering the Syriac translations into a cognate Semitic language under the patronage only of an Arab elite.[16] This is very far from the

15 For Sergius of Rēšʿaynā see now the fundamental researches of Henri Hugonnard-Roche, especially his "Aux origines de l'exégèse orientale de la logique d'Aristote: Sergius de Rešʿaina (†536), médecin et philosophe," *Journal Asiatique*, 1989, vol. 277, pp. 1–17, where he draws the comparison with Boethius on p. 12, and his "Note sur Sergius de Rešʿainā, traducteur du grec en syriaque et commentateur d'Aristote," in G. Endress and R. Kruk (eds), *The Ancient Tradition in Christian and Islamic Hellenism*, Leiden, Research School CNWS, 1997, pp. 121–43; he identifies correctly the addressee of Sergius's works on p. 124, note 13 (where the reference to Ḥunayn's *Risāla*, which provides the original identification, should be to p. 80, not 81, of the Arabic text). On the cultural context and significance of Sergius's work see also Brock, "From Antagonism to Assimilation," p. 21.

16 So, for example, P. Kunitzsch, "Zur Problematik und Interpretation der arabischen Übersetzungen antiker Texte," *Oriens*, 1976, vol. 25–26, pp. 119 and 122, on the basis of earlier studies by M. Meyerhof and R. Walzer. This misconception naturally percolated to non-specialists such as Paul Lemerle in his *Le premier humanisme byzantin. Notes et*

truth. Before the ʿAbbāsids, relatively few secular Greek works had been translated into Syriac: other than the eisagogic and logical literature (Porphyry's *Eisagoge* and the first three books of the *Organon*), there were essentially medicine and some astronomy, astrology, and popular philosophy; the bulk of the Greek scientific and philosophical works were translated into Syriac as part of the ʿAbbāsid translation movement during the ninth century.[17]

It is instructive in this regard to consider the outcome of the projects conceived by both Sergius of Rēšʿaynā and Boethius, as mentioned, and compare their relative failure with the similar project undertaken by Arabic philosophers and its brilliant success. The difference here is surely due to the fact that the former, unlike the Arabic scientists and philosophers of the early ʿAbbāsid period, worked without a supporting social, political, and scientific context that would demand such a task. The Syriac-speaking Christians contributed much of the indispensable technical skill for the Graeco-Arabic translation movement, but the initiative, scientific direction, and management of the movement were provided by such a context created by early ʿAbbāsid society.

remarques sur enseignement et culture à Byzance des origines au Xe siècle, Paris, Presses Universitaires de France, 1971; revised translation by H. Lindsay and A. Moffatt, *Byzantine Humanism. The First Phase* [Byzantina Australensia 3], Canberra, Australian Association for Byzantine Studies, 1986. As late as the revised translation of 1986 Lemerle maintained that "Islam knew and retained essentially those parts of Hellenism which the Syrians [meaning, I presume, Syriac-speaking Christians throughout the Near East and not just the inhabitants of historical Syria] had known and retained" (p. 27, note 17 of the English translation). Such a misreading of history had serious consequences for the analysis of his main subject, as discussed below in chapter 7.4.

17 A sense of perspective in this regard is provided by the statement of Brock, "From Antagonism to Assimilation," p. 25: "less Greek secular literature was translated into Syriac than, say, into Armenian." For details on the translated works see R. Duval, *La littérature syriaque*, Paris, J. Gabalda, 1907, pp. 246–58 for the eisagogic and logical literature, pp. 258–67 for popular philosophy, and pp. 269–84 for the scientific literature; cf. the corresponding entries in Baumstark, *Geschichte der syrischen Literatur*. See further the collection of articles by S. Brock, *Syriac Perspectives on Late Antiquity*, London, Variorum, 1984; the articles by H. Hugonnard-Roche, referred to in his study "Note sur Sergius de Rešʿainā;" A.O. Whipple, "Role of the Nestorians as the Connecting Link between Greek and Arabic Medicine," *Annals of Medical History*, 1936, N.S. vol. 8, pp. 313–23; G. Klinge, "Die Bedeutung der syrischen Theologen als Vermittler der griechischen Philosophie an den Islam," *Zeitschrift für Kirchengeschichte*, 1939, vol. 58, pp. 346–86; G. Troupeau, "Le rôle des syriaques dans la transmission et l'exploitation du patrimoine philosophique et scientifique grec," *Arabica*, 1991, vol. 38, pp. 1–10.

Translation from Greek into Arabic

After the initial Arab conquests in Syria, Palestine, and Egypt, the move of Arab rulers and tribesmen into Greek-speaking areas made translation from Greek into Arabic inevitable both in government circles and in everyday life throughout the Umayyad period. Necessity dictated that, for reasons of continuity, the early Umayyads keep both the Greek-speaking functionaries and the Greek language in their imperial administration in Damascus. It was only during the reign of ʿAbd-al-Malik or his son, Hišām (r. 685–705 and 724–43 respectively), as Ibn-an-Nadīm mentions [*F* 242.25–30], that the administrative apparatus (*dīwān*) was translated into Arabic by some of the Umayyad bureaucrats, among whom Sarǧūn ibn-Manṣūr ar-Rūmī (mentioned above in section 2), and his son, Manṣūr, are mentioned. Also related to the needs of the ruling elite in Umayyad times was the translation, sponsored by Hišām's secretary Sālim Abū-l-ʿAlāʾ, of the Greek mirror for princes literature in the form of correspondence between Aristotle and Alexander the Great.[18]

In private life, social and commercial intercourse in Syro-Palestine and Egypt, heavily Greek-speaking until well after the end of the Umayyads, made translation a quotidian reality. Bilingual Greek and Arabic papyri of deeds and contracts attest to this fact for seventh and eighth century Egypt; the practice was doubtless ubiquitous. Due also to the existence of numerous Greek speakers in these areas, translation from the Greek must have been easily available on an individual basis to everybody, scholar or otherwise. Even as late as the fourth/tenth century, the historian Ḥamza al-Iṣfahānī (d. after 350/961) relates that when "he needed information on Graeco-Roman history, he asked an old Greek, who had been captured and served as a valet, to translate for him a Greek historical work orally. This was accomplished with the help of the Greek's son, Yumn, who knew Arabic well."[19] This report establishes that oral translation by native speakers of whatever language within the Islamic domain did occur and that, as might have been expected, it must have been widely practiced.

Translation of scientific texts, however, appears not to have taken place during Umayyad times. It is possible that obvious needs may

18 See M. Grignaschi, "Le roman épistolaire classique conservé dans la version arabe de Sālim Abū-l-ʿAlāʾ," *Le Muséon*, 1967, vol. 80, p. 223, following the *Fihrist* 117.30.

19 Cited by F. Rosenthal, *A History of Muslim Historiography*, Leiden, E.J. Brill, 2nd edn, 1968, p. 74, note 1.

have occasioned the translation of the medical compendium (*kunnāš*) of Ahrun [*EI*, Supplement, p. 52] by Māsarğawayh [*EI* VI, 640–1], allegedly for Marwān I (r. 64/684–65/685) or ʿUmar II (r. 99/717–101/720), though the sources in this regard cannot be implicitly relied upon. In any case, the only other major instance of a pre-ʿAbbāsid translation of scientific material, the report that the Umayyad prince Ḫālid ibn-Yazīd (d. after 85/704) had had Greek books on alchemy, astrology, and other sciences translated into Arabic, has been demonstrated to be a later fabrication.[20]

All these activities of Graeco-Arabic translation during the Umayyad period are instances of random and *ad hoc* accommodation to the needs of the times, generated by Arab rule over non-Arab peoples. The bulk of the material that was translated – administrative, bureaucratic, political, and mercantile documents – was translated for reasons of expediency and the need for communication between the new rulers and the allophonous subject peoples. Even materials that can be considered as cultural, like Alexander's alleged correspondence with Aristotle, had an immediately military or administrative purpose and thus represented individual and uncoordinated translation *activities*. Deliberate and planned scholarly interest in the translation of Greek works (and Syriac works inspired by Greek) into Arabic appears not to have been present in Umayyad times. Only with the earliest ʿAbbāsid caliphs was there set into motion a deliberate translation movement that had profound historical, social, and cultural consequences.

Sanskrit Sources

Indian scientific material in astronomy, astrology, mathematics, and medicine passed into Arabic mainly through Persian (Pahlavi) intermediaries during the ʿAbbāsid period, and as such it is to be seen in the context of the translation movement.[21] Direct translations from Sanskrit appear not to have been made or, if they have, to have been limited mainly to astronomical texts, some of which, according

20 See M. Ullmann, "Ḫālid ibn Yazīd und die Alchemie: Eine Legende," *Der Islam*, 1978, vol. 55, pp. 181–218.

21 See the discussion and references to sources in *GAS* III,187–202; V,191–202; VI,116–21; VII,89–97; Ullmann, *Medizin*, pp. 103–7.

to Pingree, were translated in Sind and Afghanistan in pre-ʿAbbāsid times.[22]

The translations from the Sanskrit were doubtless very important for the development of early ʿAbbāsid astronomy. Beyond, that, however, the pre-ʿAbbāsid translation of some of these astronomical texts into Arabic is significant for establishing the existence of a sufficient number of international scholars, as I called them above (chapter 1.1), whose talents could be drawn upon to serve the translation movement set into motion by the early ʿAbbāsids.[23]

Persian Translations

Translations from Greek into Pahlavi, i.e., the Middle Persian of the Sasanians, and from Pahlavi into Arabic constitute a very significant and often underrated factor in the development not only of the ʿAbbāsid Graeco-Arabic translation movement but also of Arabic literature and culture in general. These translations have various aspects and owe their existence to different historical circumstances and motivations; they cannot all be classed together.[24] It is necessary to differentiate among them and single out those whose characteristics are most relevant to our subject.

There are first the pre-Islamic translations into Pahlavi of Greek scientific and possibly philosophical works. The Sasanian interest in Greek learning was partly also motivated by a Zoroastrian imperial ideology that would see all learning ultimately derived from the Avesta, the Zoroastrian canonical scriptures, and it is perhaps in this context that the Graeco-Persian translation acitivites which culminated during the reign of Chosroes I Anūširwān (r. 531–78) are best understood (see chapter 2.3). The story of Anūširwān's reception of the Greek philosophers fleeing from the effects of Justinian's fanaticism is too well known to be repeated here, while the historian of Justinian's reign, Agathias, also mentions the translations

22 See D. Pingree, "Astronomy and Astrology in India and Iran," *Isis*, 1963, vol. 54, pp. 229–46, and especially 242–3; "The Greek Influence on Early Islamic Mathematical Astronomy," p. 37.

23 Cf. Endress, *GAP* II,415: "Die Muslime mit ihrem Vordringen nach Osten Kontakte mit einer Wissenschaftstradition fanden, die weit stärker als die Schulen der sassanidischen Hauptstädte vom Austausch mit Indien geprägt war."

24 A quick survey of these translations and of lexical borrowings from Pahlavi into Arabic was made by P. Kunitzsch, "Über das Frühstadium der arabischen Aneignung antiken Gutes," *Saeculum*, 1975, vol. 26, pp. 273–82, who also emphasized their significance.

commissioned by Anūširwān.[25] Modern research has corroborated these claims in certain fields such as astrology [*GAS* VII,68–88] and agriculture [*GAS* IV,317–18], while the degree to which Pahlavi material in other fields is also dependent on Greek sources has yet to be determined.[26] With regard to philosophy, we know that logical works were dedicated to Chosroes I Anūširwān by Paul the Persian,[27] while one of the Greek philosophers who visited Anūširwān, Priscianus Lydus, wrote a book in response to his philosophical questions on a number of subjects in Aristotelian physics, theory of the soul, meteorology, and biology.[28] The same interest in Aristotelian physics and related subjects is also evident in the Zoroastrian book the *Dēnkard* which was compiled during his reign (see the text cited below, chapter 2.3), though we do not know whether the Greek texts were actually translated into Pahlavi. The significance of these Pahlavi translations lies not so much in the intermediacy they provided between the Greek originals and the eventual Arabic translations as in the fact that they were the result of a certain culture of translation which survived into early ʿAbbāsid times, as will be discussed in chapter 2.

After the Arab conquest of Persia, it is natural to expect translations from Persian into Arabic, as is the case with Greek. As a matter of fact, some of the earliest translations from Pahlavi share the same administrative purpose as those from the Greek. Just as the state functionaries in Syria and Palestine during the Umayyad period translated the administrative apparatus from Greek into Arabic, their counterparts in the eastern regions of the Islamic empire did the same for Pahlavi.[29]

25 Agathias, *Historiae* B 28,1, R. Keydell (ed.), Berlin, W. de Gruyter, 1967, p. 77. See J.-F. Duneau, "Quelques aspects de la pénétration de l'hellénisme dans l'empire perse sassanide (IVe-VIIe siècles)," in P. Gallais and Y.-J. Riou (eds), *Mélanges offerts à René Crozet*, Poitiers, Société d'Études Médiévales, 1966, vol. 1, pp. 13–22.

26 See the pioneering article by C.A. Nallino, "Tracce di opere Greche giunte agli Arabi per trafila pehlevica," in T.W. Arnold and R.A. Nicholson (eds), *A Volume of Oriental Studies Presented to E.G. Browne*, Cambridge, Cambridge University Press, 1922, pp. 345–63, reprinted in his *Raccolta di Scritti*, Rome, 1948, vol. 6, pp. 285–303. For Pahlavi sources in other fields see for astronomy *GAS* VI,115, for mathematics *GAS* V,203–14, and for medicine *GAS* IV,172–86.

27 D. Gutas, "Paul the Persian on the Classification of the Parts of Aristotle's Philosophy: A Milestone between Alexandria and Baġdād," *Der Islam*, 1983, vol. 60, pp. 238–9.

28 See Duneau, "Pénétration de l'hellénisme dans l'empire perse sassanide," p. 20.

29 Ibn-an-Nadīm [*F* 242,12ff.] informs us about these translations just as he does about the Greek. This subject was studied in great detail by M. Sprengling, "From Persian to Arabic," *The American Journal of Semitic Languages and Literatures*, 1939, vol. 56, pp. 175–224, 325–36, and 1940, vol. 57, pp. 302–5.

Other pre-ʿAbbāsid translations from Pahlavi have a literary or historical character, and have received most of the scholarly attention.[30] The increasing Arabization of the empire and the Islamization of the Persian-speaking population also generated demand for Arabic translations of Pahlavi literary and historical sources. The precise motivations for this activity among the different classes have yet to be investigated, though we hear of such interest among the highest Muslim patrons, in whose service men like Ibn-al-Muqaffaʿ worked. Al-Masʿūdī, for example, reports about a history of the Sasanian emperors and their policies that was translated into Arabic for the Umayyad caliph Hišām ibn-ʿAbd-al-Malik in 113/731.[31]

A third set of texts translated from Pahlavi into Arabic, different from the first two, concerns us immediately. They are different because they were sponsored by Persian groups or individuals with a social and ideological agenda precisely during the time of the ʿAbbāsid revolution (ca. 720–54), and thus stand in contrast to the other Perso-Arabic translations which were due to cultural interests or administrative exigencies. These texts, which can be considered as carriers of Zoroastrian Sasanian ideology, and as such belong to the same category as those translated from Greek into Pahlavi in Sasanian times, were primarily of an astrological nature, dealing specifically with political astrology or astrological history. Their translation was addressed both to Arabized Persians, among whom knowledge of Pahlavi quickly dwindled after the early Islamic conquests of Persia in mid-seventh century, and to Persianized Arabs. The translations would appear to be related to the incipient ʿAbbāsid cause (*daʿwā*) and to have played a significant role in the ideological campaigns of those groups aspiring to a return to the Sasanian past. Their influence is most visible during the reign of al-Manṣūr, which is the subject of the next chapter.

30 See, for a brief but far from comprehensive review of the subject, C.E. Bosworth, "The Persian Impact on Arabic Literature," in A.F.L. Beeston *et al.* (eds), *Arabic Literature to the End of the Umayyad Period*, Cambridge, Cambridge University Press, 1983, pp. 483–96. For proper appreciation of the depth and pervasiveness of the translations from Pahlavi, as well as of the extent of the effacement of their traces in Arabic literature, see the study of a major representative of these translations by M. Zakeri, "ʿAlī ibn ʿUbaida ar-Raiḥānī. A Forgotten Belletrist (*adīb*) and Pahlavi Translator," *Oriens*, 1994, vol. 34, pp. 76–102, and especially pp. 89ff.

31 Al-Masʿūdī, *at-Tanbīh wa-l-išrāf*, M.J. de Goeje (ed.), Leiden, E.J. Brill, 1894, p. 106.

2

AL-MANṢŪR

Early ʿAbbāsid Imperial Ideology and the Translation Movement

1. INTRODUCTION

The policies of the early ʿAbbāsid caliphs, and especially of al-Manṣūr (r. 754–75) and his son al-Mahdī (r. 775–85), are of paramount importance in the search for the origins of the Graeco-Arabic translation movement. It was they who initiated it as such; under the Umayyads before them, as mentioned in chapter 1.3, the various translation activities did not have the socially significant role played by the movement set into motion by the ʿAbbāsids. In the attempt to understand their motives, it is necessary to investigate the role played by the imperial ideology of the early ʿAbbāsid administration or, more specifically, the role played by the Zoroastrian Sasanian element in the formation of this ideology.

At the outset it must be remembered that the ʿAbbāsid dynasty came into power as a result of a civil war between rival factions of the house of the Prophet Muḥammad, what has been customarily referred to as the ʿAbbāsid revolution. The task that faced the early ʿAbbāsid rulers, and that was energetically addressed by al-Manṣūr, was, understandably, the reconciliation not only of former rivals, but also of the different interest groups that participated in the revolution, each for its own purposes, on behalf of the ʿAbbāsid cause. This reconciliation had to be effected both on the political and on the ideological level. The considerable historical research that has been conducted on the ʿAbbāsid revolution has sufficiently demonstrated that the success which al-Manṣūr and his successors had in keeping unified the newly formed state depended on their great abilities to form political coalitions with the different major factions, to convince them that their interests lay in the preservation of the ʿAbbāsid state, and to render politically irrelevant as well as to discredit ideologically those elements that they portrayed either as fringe or extremist.[1] Alongside with this political accommodation, however, al-Manṣūr and his successors also had to legitimize, after a civil war, the ʿAbbāsid dynasty in the eyes of the various factions and therefore had to be mindful of their ideological appeasement. In this regard, the faction that needed to be satisfied the most was the coalition that was the most instrumental in bringing the ʿAbbāsids to power, the so-called "Persian" faction. This included primarily the Arab tribes that had moved to Ḫurāsān with the early conquests and who subsequently identified with the local populations, Persianized Arabs and Arameans who had lived before the rise of Islam under the Sasanian empire, Persians who had converted to Islam, and also Zoroastrian Persians – at the time of al-Manṣūr still the majority of the Persians – who eventually were forced to accept that the Arab conquests were irreversible.

It is now becoming increasingly apparent that the way in which the early ʿAbbāsid caliphs tried to legitimize the rule of their dynasty in the eyes of all the factions in their empire was by expanding their imperial ideology to include the concerns of the "Persian" contingent. This was done by promulgating the view that the ʿAbbāsid dynasty, in addition to being the descendants of the Prophet and hence satisfying the demands of both Sunnī and Shīʿī Muslims, was at the same time the successor of the ancient imperial dynasties in ʿIrāq and Iran, from the Babylonians through the Sasanians, their immediate predecessors. In this way they were able to incorporate Sasanian culture, which was still the dominant culture of large masses of the population east of ʿIrāq, into mainstream ʿAbbāsid culture. Al-Manṣūr was the architect of this policy.

2. AL-MANṢŪR AND THE ORIGINS OF THE GRAECO-ARABIC TRANSLATION MOVEMENT

Al-Manṣūr, the builder of Baghdad, the second ʿAbbāsid caliph and real founder of the ʿAbbāsid state and its policies that ensured it such remarkable longevity, is generally credited by Arabic authors with initiating and promoting the translation movement. This fact is not

1 For an understanding of these developments after the ʿAbbāsid revolution see Hugh Kennedy, *The Early Abbasid Caliphate*, London, Croom Helm, 1981, and in particular pp. 73ff.

widely acknowledged in secondary literature (al-Ma'mūn normally occupies center stage in this respect), but it is indisputable.

To begin with, we have the express testimony of two independent historians who are among our primary sources for early ʿAbbāsid culture. The first is the historian al-Masʿūdī (d. 956), who quotes a conversation between a descendant of al-Manṣūr, the caliph al-Qāhir (r. 932–4), and a certain historian, or reporter of traditions (*aḫbārī*), named Muḥammad ibn-ʿAlī al-ʿAbdī al-Ḫurāsānī al-Aḫbārī. The whole conversation is prefaced by al-Qāhir's request for a candid report about his predecessors, and by his promise not to be offended, and especially not to exact punishment, should al-Aḫbārī relate indelicate or damning incidents about the previous ʿAbbāsid caliphs.[2] Al-Aḫbārī then goes on to say the following about al-Manṣūr:

> He was the first caliph to favor astrologers and to act on the basis of astrological prognostications. He had in his retinue the astrologer Nawbaḫt the Zoroastrian, who converted to Islam upon his instigation and who is the progenitor of this family of the Nawbaḫts. Also in his retinue were the astrologer Ibrāhīm al-Fazārī, the author of an ode to the stars and other astrological and astronomical works,[3] and the astrologer ʿAlī ibn-ʿĪsā the Astrolabist.[4]
>
> He was the first caliph to have books translated from foreign languages into Arabic, among them *Kalīla wa-Dimna* and *Sindhind*.[5] There were also translated for him books by Aristotle on logic and other subjects, the *Almagest* by Ptolemy, the *Arithmetic* [by Nicomachus of Gerasa],[6] the book by Euclid [on geometry], and other ancient books from classical Greek, Byzantine Greek, Pahlavi [Middle Persian], Neopersian, and Syriac. These [translated books] were published among the

2 For al-Aḫbārī see Rosenthal, *Historiography*, pp. 58–9; he was alive in 333/945, according to al-Masʿūdī, *Murūǧ aḏ-ḏahab*, C. Pellat (ed.), Beirut, Université Libanaise, 1965–79, §3458. The preface is in §3444.

3 *GAS* VI,122–4. The extant fragments were collected and translated into English by Pingree, "The Fragments of the Works of al-Fazārī."

4 *GAS* VI,143–4. See also F. Rosenthal, "Al-Asṭurlābī and as-Samaw'al on Scientific Progress," *Osiris*, 1950, vol. 9, p. 563.

5 Translated, respectively, by Ibn-al-Muqaffaʿ (d. 139/757) and al-Fazārī.

6 This would be the old translation from the Syriac by Ḥabīb ibn-Bihrīz for Ṭāhir ibn-al-Ḥusayn Ḏū-l-Yamīnayn (d. 207/822); see *GAS* V,164–6.

> people, who examined them and devoted themselves to knowing them.[7]

The second report is by the Andalusian historian Ṣāʿid (d. 1070) who, after mentioning the accomplishments of ancient nations in various sciences, reports the following about their development among the Arabs:

> In the beginning of Islam, the Arabs cultivated no science other than their language and a knowledge of the regulations of their religious law, with the exception of medicine. It existed in certain individuals among them and was not unknown among the masses on account of the need which people as a whole have for it. [Ṣāʿid then lists some of the earliest Arab physicians, in particular Ibn-Abğar al-Kinānī, to whom the Umayyad caliph ʿUmar Ibn-ʿAbd-al-ʿAzīz used to send his urine when he was sick, and makes special mention of the Umayyad prince Ḫālid ibn-Yazīd as a specialist in medicine and alchemy.]
>
> This was the situation of the Arabs during the Umayyad dynasty. But when God Almighty put an end to this dynasty by means of that of the Hāšimites [i.e., the ʿAbbāsids] and directed the rule to the latter, people's ambitions revived from their indifference and their minds awoke from their sleep. The first among the Arabs who cultivated the sciences was the second caliph, Abū-Ǧaʿfar al-Manṣūr. He was – God have mercy on him – deeply attached to them and to their practitioners, being himself proficient in religious knowledge and playing a pioneering role in [promoting] philosophical knowledge and especially astrology.[8]

In addition to these sources, there are also numerous other incidental references to al-Manṣūr's sponsorship of translations. Ibn-Abī-Uṣaybiʿa reports that he commissioned many translations of Greek works from his physician, Ǧūrǧīs ibn-Buḫtīšūʿ [IAU I,123–7], and Ibn-an-Nadīm says that he had "some ancient books" (*ašyāʾ min al-kutub al-qadīma*) translated by al-Biṭrīq.[9] Centuries later,

7 Al-Masʿūdī, *Murūǧ aḏ-ḏahab*, §3446 Pellat.

8 Ṣāʿid al-Andalusī, *Ṭabaqāt al-umam*, L. Cheikho (ed.), Beirut, Imprimerie Catholique, 1912, pp. 47–8.

9 *F* 244.3 = IAU I,205.9; cf. D.M. Dunlop, "The Translations of al-Biṭrīq and Yaḥyā (Yuḥannā) b. al-Biṭrīq," *Journal of the Royal Asiatic Society*, 1959, p. 140.

Ibn-Ḫaldūn (d. 1406) repeated al-Manṣūr's particular sponsorship of the translation of Euclid's *Elements*:

> The Muslims developed a sedentary culture. . . . Then, they desired to study the philosophical disciplines. They had heard some mention of them by the bishops and priests among (their) Christian subjects, and man's ability to think has (in any case) aspirations in the direction of the intellectual sciences. Abū Jaʿfar al-Manṣūr, therefore, sent to the Byzantine Emperor and asked him to send him translations of mathematical works. The Emperor sent him Euclid's book and some works on physics. . . .
>
> The Greek work on this discipline which has been translated (into Arabic) is the book of Euclid. . . . It was the first Greek work to be translated in Islam in the days of Abū Jaʿfar al-Manṣūr.[10]

Even if the specific details in some of these reports may be questionable, enough are independently verifiable; and this, together with the striking unanimity of the sources in crediting al-Manṣūr with the initiation of the translation movement, make it a reliable historical report that deserves serious consideration.

Now al-Manṣūr's sagacity and political acumen are universally recognized by modern scholars; M.A. Shaban, for example, states that "Abū Jaʿfar [al-Manṣūr] certainly had a genius for long term planning which characterized most of his actions," while Hugh Kennedy ends his authoritative article on him in the second edition of the *Encyclopaedia of Islam* by saying that "he was a politician of genius who pursued his aims with a single-minded but prudent determination." Al-Manṣūr is described in the sources and in secondary literature as taking personal charge in all aspects of his rule, be they administrative, military, economic, or, as in the case of the building of Baghdad, topographical and architectural. On the other hand, though naturally intelligent, keenly interested in culture, and a master orator, al-Manṣūr was no scholar in the conventional

10 Ibn Khaldûn, *The Muqaddimah*, translated by F. Rosenthal, Princeton, Bollingen, 2nd edn, 1967, vol. 3, pp. 115, 130.

sense.[11] Such being the case, his sponsorship of a translation movement, of great moment for the cultural and ideological directions of the empire, could hardly have been accidental or arbitrary. The question then is why al-Manṣūr adopted such a policy and what his motives were.

In these accounts of al-Manṣūr's initiative in promoting the sciences and translations one is struck by the prominence accorded to his interest and belief in astrology. This fact is independently corroborated by other sources; here it is sufficient to mention some well-known incidents. Al-Manṣūr picked 30 July 762, as the day to lay the foundations of Baghdad on the recommendation of his court astrologer Nawbaḫt and his colleagues (Māšā'allāh, al-Fazārī, and ʿUmar aṭ-Ṭabarī); he was advised about the revolt against him of his relative, the ʿAlid Ibrāhīm ibn-ʿAbdallāh (145/762–3), by the same Nawbaḫt; and on his last pilgrimage to Mecca (158/775) he was accompanied, in addition to his court physician, by Abū-Sahl the son of Nawbaḫt, who succeeded his father as court astrologer.[12] Now astrology made its gradual appearance in the public life of Arab rulers as a result of the infiltration of Sasanian cultural patterns. There is no indication of a pre-Islamic or early Islamic astrology in Arab society; and although there are some indications that astrology was already present in the court of caliphs in late Umayyad times, it appears that it became dominant only during al-Manṣūr's reign. By contradistinction, astrology was pervasive in the last century of

11 M.A. Shaban, *Islamic History 2*, Cambridge, Cambridge University Press, 1976, p. 8; H. Kennedy in *EI* VI,428b, drawing on his earlier history, *The Early Abbasid Caliphate*. Neither of these historians mentions al-Manṣūr's role in initiating the translation movement. The most integrated portrait of al-Manṣūr that we possess is still that by Theodor Nöldeke, "Der Chalif Mansur," which first appeared in German in 1892 (in his *Orientalische Skizzen*, Berlin, pp. 111–51); an English translation by J.S. Blake, with revisions by the author, also appeared in 1892 ("Caliph Mansúr," in T. Nöldeke, *Sketches from Eastern History*, London, pp. 107–45) and was reprinted by Khayats in Beirut in 1963. Nöldeke says that "the whole system of his [al-Manṣūr's] government . . . was, as far as possible, personal," and does mention, though only in a sentence, that "he it was . . . who first caused Greek scientific works to be translated into Arabic," pp. 131 and 135 of the English translation. Recently, Sezgin expressly recognized al-Manṣūr's importance for the inauguration of a translation movement, though admittedly in the context of discussing astrology: "Mit der Regierungszeit al-Manṣūr's (136/754–158/775) begann die eigentliche Übersetzungswelle," *GAS* VII,10.

12 For references to the sources about these stories see Pingree, "The Fragments of the Works of al-Fazārī," p. 104 and D. Pingree, "Abū Sahl b. Nawbak̲t," *EIr.* I,369; for Ibrāhīm's revolt see L. Veccia Vaglieri, "Ibrāhīm b. ʿAbd Allāh," *EI* III,983–5 and Kennedy, *The Early Abbasid Caliphate*, pp. 66–70.

Sasanian rule and among the descendants of the last Sasanians in Islamic societies; not only was the practice of astrology intensely cultivated in these circles in both its scientific and popular forms, but it informed their entire world-view.[13]

Indispensable for the ʿAbbāsid victory over the Umayyads in 750 were people from Persia and especially from Ḫurāsān (northeastern Iran and Central Asia). These included, as already stated, Muslim Arabs who had lived in the area for at least two generations and had become "Persianized" either through marriage or cultural assimilation, Arabized Persians who had converted to Islam, Persians who remained Zoroastrians, and people of other backgrounds, like the Aramaic-speaking Christians and Jews, who were natives of territories formerly occupied by the Sasanian empire. To a larger or lesser extent, strong elements of Sasanian culture ranging from the religious to the secular survived among these peoples and their elite occupied prominent positions in the ʿAbbāsid administration – a situation best symbolized by the pre-eminence in early ʿAbbāsid affairs of the Barmakid family in politics (750–803) and the Buḫtīšūʿ family in medicine. The Sasanian culture carried by these elite had two components that proved of immense significance to al-Manṣūr in helping him to consolidate the ʿAbbāsid cause: Zoroastrian imperial ideology and political astrology. Fused together, they formed the cornerstone of al-Manṣūr's ʿAbbāsid dynastic ideology.

3. THE CONTINUITY OF THE ZOROASTRIAN IMPERIAL IDEOLOGY OF THE SASANIANS

The transfer of the seat of the caliphate to ʿIrāq, and eventually to Baghdad, after the accession of the ʿAbbāsids to power, placed ʿAbbāsid life in the center of a Persian-speaking population. The history and culture of this population thus inevitably played a crucial role in defining the new ʿAbbāsid culture that was in the process of being formed. It is important to determine the attitude of this population to classical Greek learning.

The Sasanian empire of Persia (226–642), with its state religion of Zoroastrianism, saw itself as the heir of the Achaemenid empire, of

13 See the discussion about early Arabic astrology in Ullmann, *Geheimwissenschaften*, pp. 272–7 and especially pp. 296–7 for the significance of Sasanian astrology, with references; cf. *GAS* VII,7–14.

hoary antiquity and matchless civilization, and developed an ideology and culture to reflect and promote this self-view. An imposing succession of Sasanian emperors actively engaged in collecting, recording, and editing the historical and religious record of this civilization. The empire fell to the Muslim Arabs barely half a century after the death of one of its most celebrated emperors, Chosroes I (Anūšīrwān, r. 531–78), who was, by all accounts, responsible for the edition of the latest version of this self-image that has come down to us. This treasure-house of Zoroastrianism and Persian civilization also contained an account of the transmission of learning and the sciences in Persia, from the earliest times until the reign of Chosroes I.

This account is extant both in what can be taken to be its original formulation in Pahlavi (Middle Persian) and in a variety of versions in Arabic, in wide circulation ever since the ʿAbbāsid revolution. I am citing below in chronological sequence the three versions that have immediate bearing on our subject. The first is the original version, compiled during the reign of Anūšīrwān himself and recorded in Pahlavi in the Zoroastrian book, the *Dēnkard*, while the other two are in all probability the earliest Arabic versions that we possess from the second half of the eighth century. The passage from *Dēnkard*, Book IV, runs as follows (for easy reference, paragraphs treating the same subject in all three versions carry the same number):[14]

14 Quoted in the translation by M. Shaki, "The Dēnkard Account of the History of the Zoroastrian Scriptures," *Archív Orientální*, 1981, vol. 49, pp. 114–25, based on R.C. Zaehner, *The Dawn and Twilight of Zoroastrianism*, New York, G.B. Putnam's Sons, 1961, pp. 175–7 (which is a slight revision of his earlier translation in *Zurvan. A Zoroastrian Dilemma*, Oxford, Clarendon, 1955, pp. 7–9) and incorporating corrections by M. Boyce and H.S. Nyberg. I have only changed the spelling of the proper names of the Persian emperors to that in the Arabic sources for purposes of consistency and identification. Explanatory additions have been provided in square brackets. The *Dēnkard* itself, in the form that we have it, dates from the ninth century, although the passage cited here is contemporaneous with Chosroes I Anūšīrwān (§8). Informed opinion has it that this is in essence correct, although certain details of the account in the *Dēnkard* may be later interpolations. See the extensive analysis of the development of the report on the transmission of the Zoroastrian religious tradition by H.W. Bailey, *Zoroastrian Problems in the Ninth-Century Books*, Oxford, Clarendon, 1943, chapter V ("Patvand"), pp. 149–76, especially pp. 155ff. Anūšīrwān's borrowing of cultural elements from Greek, however, is independently attested by other texts, such as his *Kārnāmag*, preserved in Arabic in Miskawayh's *Taǧārib al-umam*, facsimile ed. by L. Caetani [Gibb Memorial Series VII], Leiden, Brill, and London, Luzac, 1909–17, I,187–207.

A. From the Zoroastrian *Dēnkard*, Book IV.

[1] Dārā, son of Dārā [Darius III Codomannus, r. 336–31 BC], commanded that two written copies of all Avesta [Zoroastrian sacred texts in Avestan] and Zand [Pahlavi translation and commentary of the Avesta], even as Zoroaster had received them from Ohrmazd [the Spirit of Good], be preserved; one in the Royal Treasury, and one in the Fortress of Archives.

[2] Vologases [I(?), r. ca. 51–ca. 80], the Arsacid,[15] commanded that a memorandum be sent to the provinces [instructing them] to preserve, in the state in which they had come down in [each] province, whatever had survived in purity of the Avesta and Zand as well as every teaching deriving from it which, scattered throughout the kingdom of Iran by the havoc and disruption of Alexander [the Great], and by the pillage and plundering of the Macedonians, had remained authoritative, whether written or in oral transmission.

[6] His Majesty Ardašīr [I, r. 226–41], the king of kings, son of Bābak, acting on the just judgment of Tansar, demanded that all those scattered teachings to be brought to the court. . . .

[7] Sābūr [I, r. 241–71], the king of kings, son of Ardašīr, further collected the non-religious writings on medicine, astronomy, movement, time, space, substance, accident, becoming, decay, transformation, logic and other crafts and skills which were dispersed throughout India, the Byzantine Empire and other lands, and collated them with the Avesta, and commanded that a copy be made of all those [writings] which were flawless and be deposited in the Royal Treasury. And he put forward for deliberation the annexation of all those pure [teachings] to the Mazdean religion. . . .

[8] His present Majesty, Kisrā [Chosroes I Anūširwān, r. 531–78], the king of kings . . . declared: "We have recognized the truth of the Mazdean Religion; and the wise can with confidence establish it in the world by discussion. . . . The realm of Iran took to the course indicated by the teachings of the Mazdean Religion, that is, a synthesis of the accumulated wisdom of our forerunners. . . . We decree that all mōbeds [clergy] should zealously and ever afresh examine the Avesta and Zand, and thereby worthily enrich the wisdom of the people of the realm with the results of their attainments. . . .

15 See M. Boyce in *EIr.* II,541b, and the article there on "Arsacids".

> And since the root of all knowledge is the teaching of the Religion . . . should he, who speaks wisely, present [his knowledge] to men all over the world . . . his utterance, then, ought to be considered an exposition of the Avesta, even though he has not had it from any revelation of the Avesta."

The second version, in all likelihood the first to be recorded in Arabic, is offered in the introduction to an Arabic translation of a Pahlavi work purporting to contain a five-part astrological work by Zoroaster, *The Book of Nativities* (*Kitāb al-Mawālīd*). The political and cultural context of this translation, which was done around 750, is briefly discussed below (see section 5). The text itself reads as follows:[16]

> B. From *The Book of Nativities*, ascribed to Zoroaster.
>
> This is a book which Māhānkard translated.
>
> He who translated the astronomical books of Zoroaster [i.e., Sa'īd ibn-Khurāsān-khurreh, mentioned below] in the days of Abū Muslim [al-Ḫurāsānī, 129/746–137/755] the possessor of rule.
>
> [2] He said [i.e., Māhānkard]:[17] "I translated this book from among the books of Zoroaster . . . and I did not come across any . . . containing the philosophical sciences. . . . For when Alexander conquered the kingdom of Dārā [Darius] the King, he had them all translated into the Greek language. Then he burnt the original copies which were kept in the treasure-houses of Dārā, and killed everyone whom he thought might be keeping away any of them. Except that some books were saved through the protection of those who safeguarded them. And he who could escaped from Alexander by running away

16 The text, which is ascribed to Zoroaster, bears various titles; see the description of its contents and the extant manuscripts in *GAS* VII,85–6. It draws heavily on the astrological work of Dorotheus of Sidon; see Pingree, "Māshā'allāh: Some Sasanian and Syriac Sources," in G.F. Hourani (ed.), *Essays on Islamic Philosophy and Science*, Albany, State University of New York Press, 1975, p. 7. The text is quoted below from the English translation, of part of the introduction from the Istanbul manuscript Nuruosmaniye 2800, by S.M. Afnan, *Philosophical Terminology in Arabic and Persian*, Leiden, E.J. Brill, 1964, pp. 77–8. Afnan's translation is far from satisfactory and there appear to be some inconsistencies, but I have not seen the manuscript and hence cannot control the translation. I have provided the paragraph breaks.

17 It is not clear from Afnan's syntax whether Māhānkard or Sa'īd is meant, though the context makes it obvious that it is the former. For these individuals see Sezgin's discussion in *GAS* VII,83 and 100.

> to the islands of the seas and the mountain tops. Then when they returned to their homes after the death of Alexander they put into writing those parts that they had memorized. What they wrote down from memory was fragmentary. Much of it had passed away and little had remained.
>
> So Māhānkard translated what still survived by his time – when the rule of the Persians fell to the Arabs. And the translations which he made from these was from the language in the Avestan script[18] to the language of [New] Persian *darī.*
>
> Then later Saʿīd ibn-Khurāsān-khurreh translated them into the Arabic language in order that this science should not fall into desuetude and its outlines [i.e., traces] should not be wiped away. . . .
>
> Māhānkard translated it for Māhūyeh ibn-Māhānāhīd the Marzban. . . . When Sunbāḏ the Ispahbud saw that the language of the Persians had lost its usage and the language of the Arabs had outstripped other languages . . . he wished that this mystery [i.e., of astronomy] should be exposed in the Arabic language in order that its knowledge may be rendered more easy . . . and these two [?] books used to be handled by the treasure-keepers and read in the *dīn-nāmeh* [Book of Religion].

The third version comes from the pen of Abū-Sahl ibn-Nawbaḫt whom we have seen earlier, the son of al-Manṣūr's astrologer and successor to that office, and who accompanied al-Manṣūr in his last pilgrimage. He includes the version of the Zoroastrian history of the transmission of the sciences in his *Book of Nahmuṭān on the Nativities*, a book on astrological history. Abū-Sahl's passage appears to be translated from a Pahlavi source that is parallel to the *Dēnkard*; the Arabic style, which is cramped, follows literally the syntax of the original:[19]

18 *Dīn-dabīre*, i.e., 'religious script' used for the Avesta. See Bailey, *Zoroastrian Problems*, p. 153 and note 3, and now the article by A. Tafażżolī, "Dabīre," *EIr.* VI,540a–b. For a discussion of the term *darī* that follows see the article by G. Lazard in *EIr.* VII,34.

19 For Abū-Sahl's name, life, and works see D. Pingree, "Abū Sahl b. Nawbaḵt," *EIr.* I,369. The quotation below is cited by Ibn-an-Nadīm (*F* 238.9–239.23); paragraphs §§6–8 are also translated into Italian by Nallino, "Tracce di opere Greche," p. 363. There is a summary of the entire passage by D. Pingree, *The Thousands of Abū Maʿshar*, London, The Warburg Institute, 1968, pp. 9–10, who discusses it in the context of Sasanian astrological histories. The strange word in Abū-Sahl's title remains unidentified, despite the efforts of a number of scholars; see the remarks by Nallino on p. 362, note 1.

C. From Abū-Sahl ibn-Nawbaḫt's *Kitāb an-Nahmuṭān.*

[2] Alexander, king of the Greeks, set out from a city of the Byzantines called Macedonia to invade Persia. . . . He killed the king Dārā the son of Dārā, occupied his kingdom . . . and destroyed the different kinds of knowledge inscribed on the stones and the wood of various buildings by razing them to the ground, burning them, and scattering whatever was kept together in them.

[3] He had, however, copies made of whatever was collected in the archives and treasuries of Iṣṭaḫr [Persepolis] and translated into Byzantine [Greek] and Coptic. After he was finished with copying whatever he needed from that [material], he burned what was written in Persian [in a regular hand] and in the [ornate and formal] hand called *kaštaǧ.* He took whatever he needed of the sciences of astronomy, medicine, and the [astrological] properties [of the heavenly bodies].[20] These books, along with the rest of the sciences, property, treasures, and learned men that he came upon, he sent to Egypt.

[4] In the confines of India and China, however, there survived some things [of these books] which the kings of Persia had copied and preserved there when charged to do so by their prophet Zoroaster and Ǧāmāsb the learned. . . .

[5] After that, learning was obliterated in ʿIrāq. . . .

[6] Then Ardašīr ibn-Bābak the Sasanian sent to India and China for the books which were there and also to Byzantium. He had copies made of whatever had reached there and traced the few remains that survived in ʿIrāq. He collected those that were dispersed and brought together those that had been separated.

[7] After him, his son Sābūr did the same until all these books had been copied in Persian in the way in which they had been [compiled by] Hermes the Babylonian who ruled over Egypt, Dorotheus the Syrian [of Sidon], Qaydarūs the Greek from the city of Athens which is famed for its science,[21]

20 I assume that, in this context, this is what is meant by *aṭ-ṭabāʾiʿ* ; cf. the similarly entitled book by Abū-Maʿšar, *GAS* VII,149, no. 28.

21 Ullmann, *Geheimwissenschaften*, p. 156 identifies him with the Phaedrus of the Platonic dialogue, under whose name there exists an alchemical treatise in Arabic; however, the other names in whose company Qaydarūs appears are of astrologers. Sezgin (*GAS* VII,31) suggests Antiochus of Athens, an astrologer, but the skeleton of the name *(q/fydrws)* could hardly be read as Antiochus.

> Ptolemy the Alexandrian, and Farmāsb the Indian. They commented upon them and taught them to the people in the same way in which they had learned from all those books which originated in Babylon.
>
> [8] After Ardašīr and Sābūr, Kisrā [Chosroes I] Anūširwān [531–78] collected these books, put them together [in their proper order], and based his acts on them on account of his desire for knowledge and love for it.

The report about the pillage of Alexander and the translation of the Persian books into Greek is derived from the late Sasanian (early seventh century) historical lore, recorded in the various recensions of the Pahlavi *Book of Lords* (*Ḫwadāy-nāmag*/*Ḫudāy-nāma*).[22] One variant is narrated by the Muslim Persian historian Ḥamza al-Iṣfahānī (d. after 350/961) from the Arabic translation or edition of Mūsā ibn-ʿĪsā al-Kisrawī (middle of the eighth century?), according to which the reason for Alexander's burning of the Persian books after their translation into Greek was because "he envied the fact that [the Persians] had gathered together sciences the like of which no other nation had ever gathered."[23]

4. ZOROASTRIAN IMPERIAL IDEOLOGY AND THE CULTURE OF TRANSLATION

The account of the origins and transmission of knowledge and the sciences as depicted in the combined reports is clear. Zoroaster received from Ohrmazd the Good God the texts of the Avesta, which include all knowledge (§1). The destruction wrought upon Persia by Alexander the Great, however, caused these texts to be dispersed throughout the world (§2). The Greeks and the Egyptians derived their knowledge from these Zoroastrian texts which Alexander had translated into Greek and Coptic (§3). Subsequently Sasanian emperors took it upon themselves to collect all these texts *and* the

22 For the composition of the *Ḫwadāy-nāmag* and its translations see Arthur Christensen, *L'Iran sous les sassanides*, Copenhagen, Ejnar Munksgaard, 2nd edn, 1944, pp. 59–62, 71, and Mary Boyce, "Middle Persian Literature," in *Iranistik II, Literatur I* [Handbuch der Orientalistik I,iv,2.1], Leiden, E.J. Brill, 1968, pp. 57–9.

23 Ḥamza al-Iṣfahānī, *Taʾrīḫ sinī mulūk al-arḍ wa-l-anbiyāʾ*, Beirut, Dār Maktabat al-Ḥayāt, 1961, p. 24.

knowledge that was derived from them from the various places where they had been scattered (§§6–7): the sources name India and Byzantium, and Abū-Sahl adds China (§§4, 6). Specifically, the emperor Ardašīr and his vizier, Tansar, are credited with forming the religious canon of Mazdean writings (§6), while Sābūr is said to have collected all non-religious writings that dealt with the subjects listed in (§7), to have established those conformable with the Avesta and to have annexed them to the Mazdean religion. Abū-Sahl adds that these books were translated back into Persian (Pahlavi) and provides specific names of authors whose texts were recovered (§7). Then Chosroes I Anūširwān promulgated all these texts, which collectively form the Zoroastrian religion, and decreed that they be studied and discussed for the benefit of mankind (§8). The introduction to the ps.-Zoroastrian astrological *Book of Nativities* (passage B above), finally, adds the very important details of two further stages of translation: from Pahlavi to New Persian at the time of the Muslim conquests (middle of the seventh century), and then from New Persian into Arabic a century later, during the ʿAbbāsid revolution.

The thrust of the accounts naturally differs to a certain extent, given the varied authorship and audience of the texts. The *Dēnkard* is an official text of the Zoroastrian religion, the astrological work attributed to Zoroaster is interested in establishing in its introduction the authenticity of this attribution, while Abū-Sahl's text is a document by the hand of a Zoroastrian convert to Islam in his official capacity as court astrologer to the ʿAbbāsid caliphs from al-Manṣūr to Hārūn ar-Rašīd.[24] The *Dēnkard* views all essential knowledge as being contained in the Avesta and regards "secular" knowledge – the subjects enumerated in §7 – as being derivative from it.[25] The Muslim Abū-Sahl cannot claim the same for Zoroastrianism; he thus puts the origins of all the sciences in Babylon and seems to establish ʿIrāq as their geographical focus. He then traces their dispersal after Alexander and credits the Sasanians, just like the *Dēnkard*, for their retrieval and return to ʿIrāq.

24 It is fruitless to speculate the depth of his commitment to Islam as a religion; he was certainly committed to the ʿAbbāsid cause. The fact remains, however, that he was born a Zoroastrian and had an insider's knowledge of the old religion and its language. See his biography by D. Pingree in *EIr*, above, note 19.

25 "As all beneficial knowledge was considered by the Mazdeans to have been originated from the Good Religion . . . its adoption, therefore, was regarded as a contribution to the Mazdean wisdom"; Shaki, "*Dēnkard*," p. 125.

The main point made by the accounts as a whole is that *all* the sciences derive originally from the Avesta, i.e., the Zoroastrian canon, and that their preservation, collection, and promulgation are due to the Sasanians and most prominently to Ardašīr I, Sābūr I, and Chosroes I Anūširwān. This view, which was widespread in the first ʿAbbāsid century and can be witnessed in a number of related works,[26] also found expression, at what may be considered a popular level, in the belief that Zoroaster himself was the author of all existing sciences and that he wrote them in all the languages of the world. The great translator and scholar Qusṭā ibn-Lūqā (d. 912), in a correspondence with his Muslim patron and friend Abū-ʿĪsā ibn-al-Munaǧǧim, says the following:

> The Zoroastrians claim that Zoroaster composed a book in twelve thousand volumes, bound in water-buffalo skin and written in gold ink, which contains all the sciences and all the languages. . . . For example, when writing "*bi-smi llāhi r-raḥmāni r-raḥīm*" [the Islamic formula "In the Name of God, the Merciful, the Compassionate"], he would say "*bi-smi*" in Persian, "*Allāh*" in Sanskrit, "*ar-Raḥmān*" in Slavic, "*ar-Raḥīm*" in Syriac, and so on in the rest of his text until he went through all the languages. Then he would start all over again until he filled the twelve thousand volumes bound in water-buffalo skin. These volumes exist to this day among them, either completely or in part. I was informed about this by someone known as Ibn-Zubayda, Adūyā al-Mu'ayyad, al-Muqallad ibn-Ayyūb, and a few other Persians.[27]

This ideological reconstruction of history would appeal to a number of population groups (or "constituencies," as we would call them today) in early ʿAbbāsid ʿIrāq. Zoroastrian Persians living under the ʿAbbāsids would naturally consider it their religious duty to study, in addition to the Avesta, all the other sciences deriving

26 The legend of the "re"-collection of books in Iran from India and Rome also appears in an astrological work by the great Māšā'allāh, preserved only in Latin and recently identified as his; see D. Pingree and C. Burnett, *The* Liber Aristotilis *of Hugo of Santalla*, London, The Warburg Institute, 1997, pp. 6–7.

27 K. Samir and P. Nwyia, *Une correspondance islamo-chrétienne entre Ibn al-Munaǧǧim, Ḥunayn ibn Isḥāq et Qusṭā ibn Lūqā* [Patrologia Orientalis, vol. 40, fascicle 4, no. 185], Turnhout, Brepols, 1981, p. 610 (text), p. 611 (French translation). As Samir and Nwyia remark, Qusṭā's informants remain unidentified.

from it and mentioned in the *Dēnkard*; they had Anūširwān's express decree to that effect (§8). Persian converts to Islam under the early ʿAbbāsids could identify the study of all the sciences as part of their heritage. The majority of non-Persians living in ʿIrāq at the time were Aramaic speakers, both those recently converted to Islam and Christians or Jews. For these people, for whose benefit the report by Abū-Sahl would appear to have been written, the ideological message would have a special significance. Despite their philhellenism, Aramaic speaking natives of Mesopotamia appear to have been conscious of the fact that they were the descendants of the ancient Babylonians. Severus of Nisibis, the foremost Syriac scholar of the seventh century (see chapter 1.1), says as much explicitly: "Nobody I think will dispute that the Babylonians are Syrians" [i.e., Aramaic speakers].[28] The adoption of such a view by the ʿAbbāsid rulers could only have won the support of the Arameans, who would have welcomed it, especially after centuries of persecution, literal and cultural, by the Chalcedonian Byzantines. As for the Arab Muslims, finally, the matter would have been of little consequence at the time since they had no ethnic or historical stake in it; by all accounts it appears that they viewed the study of all the sciences as a continuation of the indigenous tradition as well as of the policies of glorious emperors of previous ages, something inherently commendable.

What all three versions agree in conveying, moreover, is that *any* Greek book is by definition part of the Zoroastrian canon since it was Alexander's pillage of Iran that caused these books to be known among the Greeks; and hence its translation and study would mean recovering the ancient Persian knowledge. This comes through most clearly in account C. This account eventually gained ascendancy and became accepted wisdom. It appears, centuries later, in Ibn-Ḫaldūn's exposition of the development of the sciences:

> Among the Persians [in antiquity], the intellectual sciences played a large and important role, since the Persian dynasties were powerful and ruled without interruption. The intellectual sciences are said to have come to the Greeks from the Persians, (at the time) when Alexander killed Darius and gained control

28 F. Nau, "Le traité sur les 'Constellations' écrit en 661 par Sévère Sebokht, évêque de Qennesrin," *Revue de l'Orient Chrétien*, 1929–30, vol. 27, p. 332, quoted by S. Brock "From Antagonism to Assimilation," pp. 23–4.

of the Achaemenid empire. At that time, he appropriated the books and sciences of the Persians.[29]

The list of subjects given in §3 leaves no doubt about the nature of these books and their provenance; as stated correctly in the text itself, they come from Byzantine (i.e., Greek) and Indian sources. The Indian component, though significant, is relatively minor and not our immediate concern. The Byzantine provenance, however, is of prime significance, for the subjects listed belong to the canon of Greek sciences studied in late antiquity and eventually translated into Arabic under the ʿAbbāsids. Specifically, the canon indicated here is the following:[30] medicine; astronomy – the *Dēnkard* mentions elsewhere Ptolemy's *Almagest* – which would also include astrology; the next five words – movement, time, space, substance, and accident – refer directly to Aristotle's *Physics*, which deals specifically with these subjects. The next three words – becoming, decay, transformation – refer to Aristotle's *On Coming to Be and Passing Away* (*De generatione et corruptione*) even by its very title, along with a subject treated in it. Logic obviously refers to the Aristotelian *Organon*, while in the "other crafts and skills" there may be a hidden reference to alchemy.[31] There are scattered references to some of these other arts throughout the *Dēnkard*; Bailey mentions logic and dialectics and geometry.[32] Some of these books reached the Persians doubtless through Syriac, as Arameans were subjects of the Sasanian empire throughout its existence. That Syriac was an intermediary in at least part of this transmission from Greek into Pahlavi is indicated by the form of certain Greek words which also appear in Pahlavi, e.g. "philosopher" and "sophist."[33]

What plays a crucial role in this Zoroastrian Sasanian imperial ideology – indeed the indispensable element that lends it credibility and coherence – is the culture of translation that it assumes and promotes. Unless translation is assumed not only to exist but also to be a cultural good, the ideological claim of the Avesta as the source and origin of all science and philosophy for all nations cannot be

29 Ibn Khaldûn, *The Muqaddimah*, trans. F. Rosenthal, vol. 3, pp. 113–14.

30 This passage was commented upon in great detail by Bailey, *Zoroastrian Problems*, pp. 81–7.

31 As suggested by Bailey, *Zoroastrian Problems*, p. 228, addendum 33.

32 Bailey, *Zoroastrian Problems*, p. 86.

33 See the etymological discussion by Bailey, *Zoroastrian Problems*, p. 85, note 3 and p. 86, note 1; also p. 157.

reconciled with the historical facts of, first, the incontrovertible supremacy of Greek letters in the post-Hellenistic world in the Near East and, second, translations actually made from Greek (and from Sanskrit) into Pahlavi during the Sasanian empire (the list actually provided by Abū-Sahl in §7). In order to be effective, the Zoroastrian ideology thus rests completely on translation: on the alleged translations, occasioned by Alexander's conquests, from Avestan into Greek and other languages, and on the historical translations from Greek and other languages into Pahlavi during the Sasanian period. The astrological text of "Zoroaster" provides us with yet a further stage in the culture of translation, this time occasioned by the Arab conquests: from Pahlavi to Neo-Persian at the time of the conquests themselves, and from Persian into Arabic a century later. With the collapse of the Sasanian empire and the elimination of a centralized Zoroastrian authority to promote the Avesta in the old language, translation of the Avestan texts to the current language (Neo-Persian) was a matter of survival for these texts. The causes of the further translation from Persian into Arabic are given by the text itself and they do not seem to be far off the mark: Zoroastrian revivalism in Arabic, as advocated by Sunbāḏ, to be discussed in the next section.

Zoroastrian imperial ideology thus provided both a corpus of works as the foundation of civilization – in essence, all extant works from antiquity in all languages, since they had been allegedly either translated from the Avesta or derived from it – and a cultural outlook that made their acquisition both possible and desirable, the virtues of translation. Al-Manṣūr's adoption, for the reasons suggested in the following section, of the Sasanian imperial ideology thus also entailed the comcomitant adoption of the culture of translation.

5. ASTROLOGICAL HISTORY AS POLITICAL IDEOLOGY

Astrological history is the account of dynastic history in terms of cyclical periods of varying lengths of time governed by the stars and the planets. Abū-Sahl's *Kitāb an-Naḫmuṭān*, from which the citation above (passage C) was taken, is precisely an astrological history and one of the first, if not the very first book of its kind in Arabic. After giving the history of the transmission of the sciences, Abū-Sahl ends his account by stating the moral of the story explicitly. He says, after §8 above, the following:

> The people of every age and era acquire fresh experiences and have knowledge renewed for them in accordance with the decree of the stars and the signs of the zodiac, a decree which is in charge of governing time by the command of God Almighty.

The message to the ʿAbbāsid rulers is clear: by God's command, the stars have decreed – and that is the purpose of Abū-Sahl's astrological history – that it is now the ʿAbbāsids' turn to renew the sciences, just as it was that of the Sasanians previously. The decree to spread knowledge, originally issued by Chosroes I Anūširwān and stated in the *Dēnkard*, is now repeated by Abū-Sahl with consummate skill as having been issued by the stars and ultimately by God. In other words, what was originally a Zoroastrian decree is now objectified and "Islamized" by Abū-Sahl.

The motive behind Abū-Sahl's astrological history is thus political ideology. Astrological history, or, political astrology, was important for the early ʿAbbāsids because it performed two vital functions: a *political* one in that it presented the dominion of the ʿAbbāsid state, whose cycle was just beginning, as ordained by the stars and ultimately by God, with the implied message to all potential opponents of the ʿAbbāsid regime that political activity against them would be futile; and an *ideological* one in that it inculcated the view of the ʿAbbāsid state as the legitimate and only successor, in the grand scheme of things governed by the stars, of the ancient empires in Mesopotamia and Iran, and most immediately of the Sasanians.[34]

Al-Manṣūr had good reasons to adopt a policy that would send the political message that the dynastic rule of the ʿAbbāsids is unassailable, and the ideological message that the newly founded dynasty is in fact the heir to the Sasanians, for he had to fight against opposition to ʿAbbāsid rule in the form of revivalist Persian and Zoroastrian movements.

During the long gestation period of the ʿAbbāsid revolution in

34 For political astrology see D. Pingree, "Ḳirān," *EI* V,130–1. Astrological history thus makes its entrance in Arabic Islamic historiography for clearly political reasons and influences its earliest stages; al-Yaʿqūbī's entries on the caliphs are preceded by their horoscopes drawn from Māšāʾallāh's *Nativities*. This is a significant area that needs to be investigated further. See Rosenthal, *Historiography*, pp. 110–13 and p. 134, note 3. Astrology was not merely one of the subjects *covered* by historians, but also, as is clearly the case with Abū-Sahl ibn-Nawbaḫt and Ḥamza al-Iṣfahānī, the motive *behind* the writing of this kind of history.

Iran and Ḫurāsān among a predominantly Persian population, the two parts of the principal message that was being spread by the ʿAbbāsid cause (*daʿwā*) were that the Umayyad dynasty was about to fall and that it would be replaced by a leader from the family of the Prophet acceptable to all (*ar-riḍā*). To numerous groups among the non-converted population, the two parts did not necessarily have the same impact. There were many who were very much interested in ousting the Arab rule of the Umayyads, just like the ʿAbbāsids, but had different ideas about their replacement. In other words, the propaganda of the ʿAbbāsid revolution raised expectations about the fall of Arab rule and hence the prospects of a new politico-religious order which, however, was not uniformly identified by all involved as Islamic and ʿAbbāsid. Various revivalist groups of Persian national religions were putting forward simultaneously their agenda and ideology, also expressed in religious terms in response to those of the Muslims.

The first source of opposition was constituted by most elements or classes of the local population, other than the big landowners, whose interests were harmed by direct Muslim control of Ḫurāsān and which can be loosely termed as separatist or secessionist movements. The revolts they staged against al-Manṣūr's reign aimed to overthrow Arab rule and restore varying forms of Persian national religions, or a religious syncretism of motifs from Zoroastrianism and Mazdakism.[35] The revolts were connected with the name of Abū-Muslim al-Ḫurāsānī, the leader of the ʿAbbāsid revolutionary armies in Ḫurāsān [*EI* I,141]. His singularly significant role in the successful outcome of the revolution and his broad base of support in the area, centered in Marw, eventually made his execution inevitable (137/755). The first insurrection occasioned by this event was that led by the army chief (*ispahbaḏ*) Sunbāḏ (d. 137–8/755), a general of Abū-Muslim's army, the sponsor of the translation in account B above. Sunbāḏ's rebellion was followed by those of Barāz (142/759) and of Isḥāq the Turk (142/759).

35 For these movements see in general G.H. Sadighi, *Les mouvements religieux iraniens au IIe et au IIIe siècle de l'hégire*, Paris, Les Presses Modernes, 1938, pp. 111ff. The social, economic, and religious constitution of these movements is described in detail by B. Scarcia Amoretti, "Sects and Heresies," in R.N. Frye (ed.), *The Cambridge History of Iran*, vol. 4, Cambridge, Cambridge University Press, 1975, pp. 481–519. W. Madelung, "Mazdakism and the Khurramiyya," in his *Religious Trends in Early Islamic Iran*, Albany, Bibliotheca Persica, 1988, pp. 1–12, concentrates more on the religious aspects; see also the more brief treatment by W. Madelung, "Khurramiyya," *EI* V,63–5.

A second type of opposition to ʿAbbāsid policies came from the local landed aristocracy, the *dehqāns*. At the end of the Sasanian empire, this class had gained significant power vis-à-vis the Sasanian emperor and ruled the local population in their respective areas like virtual governors. Under Arab rule, which for the most part they accepted by signing treaties of capitulation, they kept their privileges. Umayyad policy in their regard was to allow them to continue to function as local rulers over the non-Muslim population from whom they were bound to collect taxes; Muslims – both Arabs and converted Persians – would of course not fall under their jurisdiction, but this was hardly a problem during Umayyad times due to the small number of conversions involved. With the ʿAbbāsids, however, and their call for an egalitarian Muslim society, the power of the *dehqāns* gradually diminished because of growing Islamization. Hence their opposition to the ʿAbbāsid cause, as evidenced not only by the very few aristocratic families participating in the revolution but by the actual rebellion against al-Manṣūr by one of their rank, Ustād̲sīs, in 150/767.[36]

The ideology of all these opposition groups was, to different degrees and with varying emphases, revivalist Zoroastrian. During the entire course of the ʿAbbāsid revolution and its aftermath, translation came to play a prominent role in their attempts to reach the population, gain recruits, and spread propaganda. The reasons appear to be the need to reach those elements of the Persian population who by then had become more fluent in Arabic than the Pahlavi of many Zoroastrian religious texts, as well as to preserve in the ascendant language of the Arabs the religious texts of the Zoroastrian community which, since the destruction a century earlier of the Sasanian state and religious structure, were in danger of being lost for lack of official curators. Translations of traditional Zoroastrian material into Arabic was an important propaganda tool to convince those Arabized Persians who would not have known Pahlavi of the inevitability of the Umayyad downfall and of the validity of the Zoroastrian tradition whose revival was envisaged.

36 For the rebellions of Sunbād̲ and Ustād̲sīs and the latter's *dehqān* base, see Kennedy, *Early Abbasid Caliphate*, pp. 63–5, 44, 90–2, 183–4, and the references cited there. See also, most concisely, A.K.S. Lambton, "Iran," *EI* IV,16, and the corresponding articles in R. Frye (ed.), *Cambridge History of Iran*, vol. 4, for further references. For the *dehqāns* under Arab rule in the early Islamic period see M.A. Shaban, *The ʿAbbāsid Revolution*, Cambridge, Cambridge University Press, 1970, pp. 95–9, and A. Tafażżolī, "Dehqān," *EIr.* VII,223–5.

This is clearly evident from the activities of Sunbād who, in addition to his political claims, also had clear ideological and cultural agendas. His revolt may have broken out openly only after Abū-Muslim's execution, but it clearly was many years in the making. He had commissioned the translation from New Persian into Arabic of the Zoroastrian astrological text cited in account B above (section 3), and thus by happy coincidence we have textual attestation for his policies to revive Sasanian imperial ideology. As we read in the introduction of that account, Sunbād had ordered the translation because he felt that the rapid spread of Arabic was making the traditional Zoroastrian books in Pahlavi obsolete. An analogous reason was adduced by a certain Māhānkard who, the introduction continues, had translated the book from Pahlavi into New Persian about a century before, when the Sasanian empire fell (ca. 650).[37] That the work selected for translation was one on astrology, including political astrology, indicates its significance for the ideology of the movements in opposition to the ʿAbbāsids.

These rebellions varied in the degree to which they posed serious threat to the survival of the ʿAbbāsid state; al-Manṣūr, however, not only dealt decisively with all of them but also adopted a policy of ideological cooptation, that is, he appropriated as ʿAbbāsid the Zoroastrian ideology espoused by the pro-Abū-Muslim movements in order to pre-empt its appeal and significance. The reason behind al-Manṣūr's pragmatic decision in favor of political suppression *together with* ideological cooptation of anti-ʿAbbāsid movements is the obvious fact in any revolt that though those who actually take up arms may be relatively few, their sympathizers are many. Al-Manṣūr must have been aware that this was particularly relevant in the case of Ḫurāsān, a vast province of the highest economic significance, with a predominantly Persian Zoroastrian population. The survival and vigor of Zoroastrian religious ideology and its Sasanian imperial background are best exemplified by the traditions of the population of the ʿAbbāsid capital of Ḫurāsān, Marw. Always a stronghold of Persian culture, Marw was the city which the ʿAbbāsid Muḥammad ibn-ʿAlī picked as the center of the revolutionary activities of his family and over which Abū-Muslim gained control in 130/748.[38]

37 See Pingree, "Māshā'allāh," p. 7.

38 The centrality of Marw in the ʿAbbāsid revolution is discussed in detail by Shaban, *ʿAbbāsid Revolution*, pp. 149–63; see also C.E. Bosworth, "Marw al-Shāhidjān," *EI*, VI,620b, with reference to the work of Shaban.

Again our Zoroastrian astrological text comes to corroborate political history; it calls Abū-Muslim "the possessor of rule," obviously in Marw, the center of the ʿAbbāsid revolution; Marw is thus also identified as the locus of the translation activity from Pahlavi or New Persian into Arabic.

Persian cultural activity continued in Marw for a number of centuries after Abū-Muslim. Toward the end of the eighth century, al-Manṣūr's great grandson and future caliph, al-Ma'mūn (whose mother was Persian and – according to some accounts – the granddaughter of the rebel *dehqān* Ustā̱dsīs mentioned earlier), studied there astrology and modeled his behavior on that of the Sasanians, according to al-Aḫbārī's report in al-Masʿūdī (cited in chapter 4.1). Al-Ma'mūn also made Marw his headquarters during the civil war against his brother al-Amīn, and it was only after the consolidation of his power in Baghdad that he went to al-Manṣūr's city. Marw was famous for its libraries until the fall of the ʿAbbāsids, and there are reports of scholars studying and copying Persian books there.[39]

This very brief sketch, which could be expanded at will, delineates the social and cultural background that kept Zoroastrian ideology alive centuries after the Arab conquest. Al-Manṣūr was fully cognizant of this and was particularly wary of Marw itself as the center of such ideologies; just to make sure that things were under control, he appointed his own son and successor, al-Mahdī, as viceroy of Ḫurāsān in Marw between 759 and 769. Al-Manṣūr also knew, however, that relatively easy though it might have been to eliminate the foolhardy, it was neither possible nor indeed desirable to eradicate entire cultural backgrounds. In this context, al-Manṣūr's decision to coopt Zoroastrian ideology and transfer it to Baghdad appears not even particularly wise, just pragmatic and sensible.

Once Zoroastrian Sasanian cultural attitudes became acceptable in Baghdad right after its foundation, the translation of secular knowledge into Arabic became part of the process. This would explain to a large extent the motives behind the support given to the translation movement by the early ʿAbbāsid caliphs. This interpretation is corroborated by the facts: the earliest translations of Greek works that we have are *indeed* made not directly from the Greek but

39 Like, for example, the theologian al-ʿAttābī (d. ca. 220/835), as reported by Ṭayfūr, *Kitāb Baġdād*, H. Keller (ed.), Leipzig, Harrassowitz, 1908, p. 87; cf. further van Ess, *Theologie und Gesellschaft*, III,100–2.

through Pahlavi intermediaries, and the texts translated are overwhelmingly astrological in nature (cf. chapter 5.2).

Al-Manṣūr's attention to every detail of his rule in all political and administrative matters is well known and freely acknowledged, and it clearly also extended to ideology. His policy of military elimination of his rivals and of cooptation of their ideology can be seen in other areas as well. Most significant appears to be his assumption of the honorific title "al-Manṣūr," i.e., "he who is granted victory [by God]," or, as put by M.A. Shaban, "the one destined to win." The messianic implications of this title are obvious, and it would seem that it was adopted to counteract the claims of the Shīʿites to divine favor after al-Manṣūr's final victory, by the end of 145/March 763, over the Shīʿite pretenders to the caliphate, as mentioned by the historian al-Masʿūdī. This appears all the more plausible if one also considers that it was al-Manṣūr himself who selected the honorific title of his son and successor, al-Mahdī, "the messiah," a Shīʿite title par excellence.[40]

More difficult to evaluate with certainty, though certainly indicative of a distinctive imperial ideology that al-Manṣūr wished to project, were the shape, size, and splendor of the city he built, Baghdad.[41] There has been some controversy concerning the significance and origin of the round shape of the city, and opinions have ranged widely. Some claim a cosmic and astral significance while others see nothing more than prosaic expedient; one author even changed his mind in two successive publications and went from one extreme to the other. Ideological concerns in historical personalities are of course the most difficult to ascertain, especially when the sources available hardly provide any information. In light of the preceding discussion, however, there is sufficient anecdotal information in the sources to allow us to discern similar and familiar ideological concerns at work also in the construction of Baghdad, namely al-Manṣūr's dual approach of asserting firmly his control

40 Al-Masʿūdi mentions al-Manṣūr's adoption of the title in his *at-Tanbīh wa-l-išrāf*, p. 341.13 de Goeje. Shaban, *History 2*, p. 8, who does not mention al-Masʿūdī, favors the time right after Abū-Muslim's execution in 137/755. For the honorific titles adopted by the ʿAbbāsids see C.E. Bosworth, "The Heritage of Rulership in Early Islamic Iran and the Search for Dynastic Connections with the Past," *Iran*, 1973, vol. 11, pp. 51ff. and references; see also Shaban, *ʿAbbāsid Revolution*, pp. 166–7.

41 For a succinct account of all the other reasons – political, economic, and administrative – that led al-Manṣūr to the choice of the site see Kennedy, *Early Abbasid Caliphate*, pp. 86–7, where I count no fewer than nine such factors.

while coopting ideological elements of the various constituent peoples and traditions of the ʿAbbāsid empire.

To begin with, the round shape of the city, with the caliph's palace situated in the center, is symbolical of centralized rule and vividly asserts that al-Manṣūr is in control. However, the sources tell us that al-Manṣūr selected this form because, when situated at the center of the circle, he would be equidistant from all sections of the city. This appears to be an application to city planning of Euclid's definition of the circle (*Elements* Book I, definition 15). At the outset of this chapter I recorded the repeated claims by historians of science that al-Manṣūr was interested in the translation of Euclid; apparently he did read, or had others read and tell him about, what he had commissioned. The significance of this, however, for those elements in the society who knew about Euclid, is that the caliph was applying this ancient knowledge. Hence the injunction in the *Dēnkard*, restated by Abū-Sahl in Islamic terms, to seek and use the ancient knowledge, whatever its origin, is here fulfilled by al-Manṣūr. Furthermore, the mere site of Baghdad, in such close proximity to Ctesiphon, the Sasanian capital, could not but symbolize, again in the eyes of those who would so see it, that the new dynasty was indeed the successor to the Persian empires of old. Al-Manṣūr was, also in this regard, continuing the Sasanian imperial tradition.

The sources also tell us about the doors of the Round City, some of which had reportedly been used by the biblical Solomon in a city he had built near Wāsiṭ and had again been used by al-Ḥaǧǧāǧ in Wāsiṭ itself; another door, which came from Syria, had allegedly been made for the pharaohs. The constituencies represented by these legends are again not arbitrary. If the proximity to Ctesiphon and the round shape itself were meaningful to people imbued with Sasanian culture, then the alleged origins of the doors were significant for the People of the Book, Jews and Christians, to Egyptians, and to the Umayyads. Thus al-Manṣūr presented Baghdad not merely as a symbol of his indisputable rule but also of the ʿAbbāsid dynasty as the heir to the rich past of the Near East with its mosaic of various peoples, religions, and traditions.[42]

42 The foundation of Baghdad and the earliest ʿAbbāsid policies were discussed extensively by J. Lassner, first in *The Topography of Baghdad in the Early Middle Ages*, Detroit, Wayne State University Press, 1970, and then in *The Shaping of ʿAbbāsid Rule*, Princeton, Princeton University Press, 1980, where he gives extensive references on the subject. Lassner touched upon the ideological significance of the site and shape of Baghdad in *Topography*, pp. 128–37 where he argued that al-Manṣūr attempted "to promote himself as an heir to

6. THE TRANSLATION MOVEMENT AND THE QUESTION OF THE *BAYT AL-ḤIKMA*

Al-Manṣūr's adoption of salient aspects of Sasanian imperial ideology is also reflected in his choice of top administrative personnel. It is obvious that for a number of reasons, some of which I briefly traced above though most of them fall outside the scope of our subject, he made the calculation that Persians steeped in Sasanian culture, regardless of their record of conversion and attachment to Islam, would be faithful servants of his caliphate and the ʿAbbāsid dynasty in general. His immediate successors concurred in this estimate (if anything, the power of Persians in the caliphal court was enhanced under al-Mahdī), and thus we see the highest levels of ʿAbbāsid administration and court life firmly in the hands of such families, the Barmakids and the Nawbaḫts among them being perhaps the most widely known. This situation continued effectively until the assassination in 202/818 of al-Ma'mūn's mentor and vizier, al-Faḍl ibn-Sahl, who had been a Barmakid protégé, though it had been attenuated by the fall of the Barmakids in 187/803 and the instability during the civil war between al-Amīn and al-Ma'mūn.[43]

the defunct Sassanian Empire, and as such, could claim the allegiance of those subjects who dwelled on its former territories, the followers of Abū Muslim notwithstanding" (p. 131). In his subsequent *ʿAbbāsid Rule*, however, he repudiated his former view along with those of others who tended to see cosmic significance in the site and shape of Baghdad. Oleg Grabar, in his *The Formation of Islamic Art*, New Haven, Yale University Press, 2nd edn, 1987, pp. 43–71, who approached the question from an art historian's point of view, tended to agree with Lassner's initial position: "Baghdad must be seen not merely as a symbol of contemporary universal rule but also as an attempt once again to relate the Muslim world to the rich past of the Near East" (p. 67). Even if some of the more exuberant interpretations of art historians are to be discounted, the fact remains that the site and shape of Baghdad, whatever pragmatic considerations went into their choice, must have also been consistent with al-Manṣūr's overall ideological tendencies. In this regard, Lassner's parsimonious arguments against his former position fail to convince; cf. van Ess, *Theologie und Gesellschaft*, III,4.

43 This subject has been discussed at length in secondary literature. For the historical record, see Kennedy, *Early Abbasid Caliphate*, especially the chapter on al-Mahdī and al-Hādī. D. Sourdel, *Le Vizirat ʿAbbāside de 749 à 936 (132 à 324 de l'Hégire)*, Damascus, Institut Français de Damas, 1959, vol. 1, pp. 127–81, provides the standard treatment of the administrative functions of the Barmakids. For a general overview of the "Barmakids" see the article by I. Abbas in *EIr.* III,806–9; for the Nawbaḫts the standard treatment is still ʿA. Eqbāl, *Ḫāndān-e Nawbaḫtī*, Tehran, 2nd edn, 1345 Š/1966, a summary of which is given by A. Labarta, *Mūsà ibn Nawbajt, al-Kitāb al-kāmil*, Madrid, Instituto Hispano-árabe de Cultura, 1982, pp. 15–21; see also "Abū Sahl b. Nawbaḵt" and "Abū Sahl Esmāʿīl Nawbaḵtī" by D. Pingree and W. Madelung, respectively, in *EIr.* I,369 and I,372–3.

The significance of this policy of the earliest ʿAbbāsid caliphs for the translation movement can hardly be exaggerated. The Zoroastrian Sasanian ideology adopted by al-Manṣūr included the concept of "recovery" through translation of ancient works into Pahlavi; in the century between the downfall of the Sasanian dynasty and the coming of the ʿAbbāsids, this activity of recovery was re-directed to translating Pahlavi works into Arabic; with the early ʿAbbāsids, major carriers of precisely this translation culture came into the highest posts of the administration and received institutional backing and financial support to carry out this activity.

It is in this light that the very scanty reliable reports about the *bayt al-ḥikma* should be evaluated. Much ink has been used unnecessarily on descriptions of the *bayt al-ḥikma*, mostly in fanciful and sometimes wishful projections of modern institutions and research projects back into the eighth century. The fact is that we have *exceedingly little historical* information about the *bayt al-ḥikma*. This in itself would indicate that it was not something grandiose or significant, and hence a minimalist interpretation would fit the historical record better.[44]

In the first place, *bayt al-ḥikma*, as a term, is the translation of the Sasanian designation for a library. This much is clear from the statement of Ḥamza al-Iṣfahānī (d. after 350/961), one of the most knowledgeable authors on pre-Islamic Persia [*EI* III,156]. In the introduction to his collection of poetic proverbs (*al-Amṯāl aṣ-ṣādira ʿan buyūt aš-šiʿr*), he says that in pre-Islamic Sasanian Iran, books which contained Persian historical lore, reports about wars, and various pieces of information about famous pairs of lovers, and which were originally composed in prose, were recast into poetry for the Sasanian kings. These poems were written down in books and deposited in storehouses (*ḫazāʾin*) which were the "houses of wisdom" (*buyūt al-ḥikma*). The report clearly implies that these were

44 The maximalist position is offered by Y. Eche, *Les bibliothèques arabes publiques et semi-publiques en Mésopotamie, Syrie, Egypte au Moyen Age*, Damascus, Institut Français de Damas, 1967, pp. 9–57, i.e., forty-nine pages of imaginary reconstruction on the basis of barely a dozen one-line references in the sources. The recent re-examination of the problem by M.-G. Balty-Guesdon, "Le *Bayt al-ḥikma* de Baghdad," *Arabica*, 1992, vol. 39, pp. 131–50, offers a reasoned and methodical discussion without, however, avoiding making excessive claims; moreover, it overlooks entirely the Sasanian background and its implications, to be mentioned below. Eche and Balty-Guesdon contain full references to earlier literature. Balty-Guesdon's study is marred by inaccuracies in the references and especially by the use of the least standard edition of the *Fihrist*, the undated Beirut edition.

royal libraries, or at least somehow affiliated with state administration, since the historical poems were for the benefit of the kings. Also from the context it would appear that this was the function, and hence the appellation, of these "houses of wisdom": they were supposed to store books, poetry especially, that *had to do with the Iranian past* – in other words, books that contained a poetic record of Sasanian (and, according to Zoroastrian Sasanian ideology, Achaemenid) glory.[45] This designation for a palace library is further corroborated in another work inspired by Sasanian models, on royal deportment (*Ādāb al-mulūk*), ascribed to as-Saraḫsī. In its sixth chapter it contains a discussion of the king's study of royal history and provides information on the role of the palace library (*bayt al-ḥikma*) in this connection.[46]

Now in secondary literature there is frequent discussion about the "founding" or "establishment" of the *bayt al-ḥikma* in the ʿAbbāsid court, with al-Ma'mūn and Hārūn ar-Rašīd presented as the caliphs responsible. In reality we have absolutely no mention in our most reliable sources of any such "founding."[47] As far as I can ascertain, there are only *two* source passages that mention ar-Rašīd's name in association with *bayt al-ḥikma*, both in the *Fihrist* by Ibn-an-Nadīm: (a) He says (274.8–9) that Abū-Sahl ibn-Nawbaḫt, the author of the astrological history I cited above (section 3), "was at the *ḫizānat al-ḥikma* [storehouse of wisdom] for Hārūn ar-Rašīd; he translated from Persian into Arabic and relied in his scholarship on the books of Iran." The meaning of being "at" the *ḫizānat al-ḥikma* is presumably that he was employed there "for" ar-Rašīd, i.e., during his caliphate. Ibn-al-Qifṭī (Q 255.4–7), who repeats the information from the *Fihrist*, adds that "ar-Rašīd appointed him to be in charge of the

45 Ḥamza's book remains unpublished. I am citing from the summary information about the contents of the Berlin manuscript or. quart. 1215 given by Gregor Schoeler, *Arabische Handschriften*, Teil II, Stuttgart, F. Steiner, 1990, p. 308. I owe the reference to van Ess, *Theologie und Gesellschaft*, III,200, note 5.

46 See F. Rosenthal, "From Arabic Books and Manuscripts, XVI: As-Sarakhsī(?) on the Appropriate Behavior for Kings," *Journal of the American Oriental Society*, 1995, vol. 115, p. 109a.

47 M. Rekaya, in his article "al-Mamūn" in *EI* VI,338a, goes so far as even to have a date for this alleged event, without mentioning his source: "al-Ma'mūn did not neglect cultural matters (foundation of the *Bayt al-Ḥikma* in 217/832)." Al-Ma'mūn, of course, died the following year, in 833; if the date of "foundation" is correct, it means that he managed to employ and reap the scholarly benefits of everybody who is known to have worked there – the algebraist al-Ḫwārizmī, the astronomer Yaḥyā ibn-Abī-Manṣūr, and the Banū Mūsā (see below, chapter 6.1d) – all within that year!

storehouse of books on wisdom (*ḫizānat kutub al-ḥikma*)," apparently an arbitrary variation on the usual appellation of the library due to Ibn-al-Qifṭī or some scribe. I do not know where the additional information of the appointment comes from; it could be Ibn-al-Qifṭī's own conjecture. (b) He mentions (105.24) that ʿAllān aš-Šuʿūbī "would copy manuscripts at the *bayt al-ḥikma* for ar-Rašīd, al-Ma'mūn, and the Barmakids." This information is repeated by Yāqūt in his dictionary of learned men, copied from the *Fihrist.*[48]

This is just about the only information we have on the nature of the early ʿAbbāsid *bayt al-ḥikma.* On this basis, we are justified in assuming only that it was a library and, as an institution, part of the Sasanian administrative and bureaucratic state apparatus that was adopted under the early ʿAbbāsids. As such, it has no independent date or specific purpose of "founding"; by all appearances it was just another "bureau" that was created as the early ʿAbbāsid administration was physically taking shape on the basis of Sasanian models and under the direction of bureaucrats steeped in Sasanian culture. We have no information on whether it was part of the original state apparatus put together at the very beginning of the ʿAbbāsid administration; the earliest *reference* to it that we have dates from the time of Hārūn, though it may have already been in existence under al-Manṣūr and al-Mahdī.

In Sasanian times, the *bayt al-ḥikma*, or palace library, functioned as an idealized national archive: as the place where poetic accounts

48 Yāqūt, *Iršād al-arīb*, D.S. Margoliouth (ed.), London, Luzac, 1907–26, V,66.10–11. One possible source for the confusion about the alleged "founding" of the *bayt al-ḥikma* may be a misunderstanding of the Arabic preposition *li-* used with the name of a caliph or patron after the *bayt al-ḥikma. Li-* in this context indicates not possession as such but rather relation. The *bayt al-ḥikma* thus is not "of" ar-Rašīd or al-Ma'mūn in the sense that it belonged to them or especially that it had been founded by them, but rather in the sense that the people who are mentioned worked there "during" the caliphate and "in the service of" ar-Rašīd and al-Ma'mūn. This is obvious in the second citation where ʿAllān is said to have worked as copyist *li-*, for or during the time of, ar-Rašīd, al-Ma'mūn, and the Barmakids. The library eventually came to be designated by subsequent authors as "al-Ma'mūn's library" in a different grammatical construction, as in the *Fihrist* 5.29 and 19.15: *ḫizānat al-Ma'mūn* ("al-Ma'mūn's [book-]storehouse"), not *ḫizānat al-ḥikma li-l-Ma'mūn* ("al-Ma'mūn's storehouse of wisdom"). This is, as Eche, *Bibliothèques*, p. 37 and p. 57, suggests, possibly due to the fact that after his time it ceased to function (in publicly perceptible ways?) and thus al-Ma'mūn was the last caliph to whom the library in its original form could be attributed. B. Dodge, *The Fihrist of al-Nadim*, New York, Columbia University Press, 1970, pp. 651 and 230, respectively, gets both quotations from the *Fihrist* wrong.

of Iranian history, warfare, and romance were transcibed and preserved – at least this is the part of its function that we know about. We have no reason to doubt that in the early ʿAbbāsid administration it retained this function since its adoption was effected by individuals who were carriers of Sasanian culture and under the mandates of a caliphal policy to project Sasanian imperial ideology. Its function, in other words, was to transcribe and preserve books on *Iranian* national history, warfare, and romance. The two references to its function that we have actually support this conclusion; in the only two passages in the *Fihrist* where a translation activity is mentioned in association with the *bayt al-ḥikma*, it concerns translation from Persian, not Greek, into Arabic: in the report cited above about Abū-Sahl Ibn-Nawbaḫt, who was manifestly employed in the *bayt al-ḥikma* precisely in order to translate Persian books, and in the brief sentence about "Salm, the director of the *bayt al-ḥikma* with Sahl ibn-Hārūn, who translated from the Persian into Arabic" (120.17).[49]

Second, as far as the contents of this palace library are concerned, the very few references that we posses would also appear to support the assumption that the *bayt al-ḥikma* was, indeed, an antiquarian library, though the evidence is inconclusive. Ibn-an-Nadīm says that he copied the Ḥimyarite and Ethiopian alphabets from books he believed to have originally been in "al-Ma'mūn's library" [*F* 5.29 and 19.15], and he further mentions that "there was in the library of al-Ma'mūn a parchment manuscript written in the hand of ʿAbd-al-Muṭṭalib ibn-Hāšim" [*F* 5.18], the Prophet's grandfather. All this is very uncertain; even if one were to assume that "al-Ma'mūn's library" is identical with the *bayt al-ḥikma*, it easy to see that, a century and a half after al-Ma'mūn, when his library had assumed legendary qualities at the time of Ibn-an-Nadīm, every rare and ancient book, or books in strange alphabets, would be ascribed to it; Ibn-an-Nadīm almost says as much himself: "I came across a very old manuscript *which appears to be* from al-Ma'mūn's library" (*kitāb waqaʿa ilayya qadīm an-nasḫ yušbihu an yakūna min ḫizānat al-Ma'mūn* [*F* 21.26]; emphasis added). Other than Ibn-an-Nadīm's testimony, we have an extremely dubious report – though also of

49 It is also perhaps not fortuitous that the reports about al-Manṣūr's patronage activity that we have indicate that he asked for works on the same subjects as those treated in Sasanian poetic accounts: he commissioned from Muḥammad ibn-Isḥāq (d. 150/767) a book on world and Arab history (*GAS* I,287–8) and from ʿAbd-al-Ǧabbār ibn-ʿAdī a book on warfare (*F* 314.27).

antiquarian interest – in the Nestorian Chronicle of Seert about an apocryphal copy of the treaty between Muḥammad and the Christians of Nağrān which allegedly came from the *bayt al-ḥikma,*[50] and two references to books on royal qualities and conduct, which would be in accord with Sasanian practices.[51]

Finally, the only reports about the *bayt al-ḥikma* during the reign of al-Ma'mūn state that Muḥammad ibn-Mūsā al-Ḫwārizmī the algebraist and astronomer "was employed full-time in it in the service of al-Ma'mūn" (*wa-kāna munqaṭiʿan ilā ḫizānat al-ḥikma li-l-Ma'mūn* [*F* 274.24]), and that Yaḥyā ibn-Abī-Manṣūr, also an astronomer, had a position in it along with the three young Banū-Mūsā [Q 441–2]. This is the first indication in our scanty sources that persons engaged in pursuits other than the study and translation of the Sasanian heritage were employed or affiliated with the *bayt al-ḥikma.* At the same time, however, it should be noted that al-Ma'mūn's director of the library was Sahl ibn-Hārūn, the great Persian nationalist (*šuʿūbī*) and Pahlavi expert [*F* 120.3–4, 125.24; *EI* VIII,838–40].

This is all the substantive and reliable evidence that we have and it allows only the following reconstruction of the nature and function of the *bayt al-ḥikma:* It was a library, most likely established as a "bureau" under al-Manṣūr, part of the ʿAbbāsid administration modeled on that of the Sasanians. Its primary function was to house both the activity and the results of translations from Persian into Arabic of Sasanian history and culture. As such there were hired translators capable to perform this function as well as book binders for the preservation of books [*F* 10.2]. This was its function in Sasanian times, and it retained it throughout the time of Hārūn ar-Rašīd, i.e. the time of the Barmakids. Under al-Ma'mūn it appears to have gained an additional function related to astronomical and mathematical activities; at least this is what the names associated with the *bayt al-ḥikma* during that period would imply. We have, however, no specific information about what those activities actually were; one would guess research and study only, since none of the people mentioned was himself actually a translator. Al-Ma'mūn's new rationalist ideological orientations, discussed in chapter 4, would explain the additional functions of the library during his reign.

50 *Chronique de Séert,* A. Scher and R. Griveau (eds) [Patrologia Orientalis XIII,4], Paris, Firmin-Didot, 1919, p. 601, cited by Balty-Guesdon, "Le *Bayt al-ḥikma,*" p. 144.

51 See the references in Balty-Guesdon, "Le *Bayt al-ḥikma,*" p. 132, note 12.

This then is all we can safely say about the *bayt al-ḥikma*. We have absolutely no evidence for any other sort of activity. It was certainly not a center for the translation of Greek works into Arabic; the Graeco-Arabic translation movement was completely unrelated to any of the activities of the *bayt al-ḥikma*. Among the dozens of reports about the translation of Greek works into Arabic that we have, there is not even a *single* one that mentions the *bayt al-ḥikma*. This is to be contrasted with the references to translations from the Persian: we have fewer such references and yet two of them, both in the *Fihrist* as cited above, do mention the *bayt al-ḥikma*. Most amazingly, the first-hand report about the translation movement by the great Ḥunayn himself does not mention it. By the same token, the library was not one which stored, as part of its mission, *Greek* manuscripts. Ḥunayn mentions the efforts he expended in search of Greek manuscripts and again he never mentions that he looked for them right under his nose in the *bayt al-ḥikma* in Baghdad (cf. chapter 7.4). Ibn-an-Nadīm, who claims that his Ḥimyarite and Ethiopian manuscripts came from al-Ma'mūn's library, says nothing of the sort when he describes the different kinds of Greek writing.

The *bayt al-ḥikma* was certainly also not an "academy" for teaching the "ancient" sciences as they were being translated; such a preposterous idea did not even occur to the authors of the spurious reports about the transmission of the teaching of these sciences that we do have (discussed in chapter 4.2). Finally, it was not a "conference" center for the meetings of scholars even under al-Ma'mūn's sponsorship. Al-Ma'mūn, of course (and all the early ʿAbbāsid caliphs), did host scholarly conferences or rather gatherings, but not in the library; such gauche social behavior on the part of the caliph would have been inconceivable. Sessions (*maǧālis*) were held in the residences of the caliphs, when the caliphs were present, or in private residences otherwise, as the numerous descriptions of them that we have indicate (for one hosted by al-Ma'mūn see chapter 4.3).[52]

What the *bayt al-ḥikma* did do for the Graeco-Arabic translation movement, however, is to foster a climate in which it could be both demanded and then conducted successfully. If indeed the *bayt al-ḥikma* was an ʿAbbāsid administrative bureau, then it *institutionalized* the Pahlavi into Arabic translation culture. This

52 The theological discussion that allegedly took place in the *bayt al-ḥikma*, as reported in ʿAbd-al-ʿAzīz al-Kinānī's *Kitāb al-Ḥayda*, is hardly to be taken seriously (see Balty-Guesdon, "Le *Bayt al-ḥikma*," p. 138). This is an apocryphal apologetic book written against al-Ma'mūn's *miḥna* policies; see van Ess, *Theologie und Gesellschaft*, III,504–8.

means that all the activities implied or suggested by this culture – the Zoroastrian ideology of the recovery of ancient Avestan texts through the (re-)translation of Greek works and all that that implied – could be conducted as semi-official activities, or at least as condoned by official policy. The numerous translations from the Greek which were commissioned by the Barmakids, for example, should be seen in this light. The example set by the caliphs and the highest administrators was naturally followed by others of lesser rank, both civil servants and private individuals. Once the existence of this additional official – though indirectly so – sanction for Graeco-Arabic translations is realized, the origins and rapid spread of the movement in early ʿAbbāsid times is better understood.

3

AL-MAHDĪ AND HIS SONS

Social and Religious Discourse and the Translation Movement

1. THE EXIGENCIES OF INTER-FAITH DISCOURSE: ARISTOTLE'S *TOPICS* AND MUSLIM–CHRISTIAN DIALOGUE

It is reported on quite unimpeachable authority that the caliph al-Mahdī (d. 785), al-Manṣūr's son and successor, commissioned the translation into Arabic of Aristotle's *Topics*. The translation was done, on the basis of a Syriac intermediary but also after consultation of the Greek, around 782 AD by the Nestorian patriarch Timothy I with the help of Abū-Nūḥ, the Christian secretary of the governor of Mosul. This translation of the *Topics* was not to be the only one; about a century later the book was translated again, this time directly from the Greek, by Abū-ʿUṯmān ad-Dimašqī, and approximately fifty years later yet again by Yaḥyā ibn-ʿAdī (d. 974) from Isḥāq ibn-Ḥunayn's previous Syriac version.[1]

1 The evidence for the first Arabic translation comes from the pen of Timothy I himself, in his letters; see the text and related bibliography in Fiey, *Chrétiens syriaques sous les Abbassides*, p. 38, and H. Putman, *L'église et l'Islam sous Timothée I (780–823)*, Beirut, Dar el-Machreq, 1975, p. 106. Timothy does not refer to the caliph by name, but there are good reasons, to which is to be added the discussion in this section, that al-Mahdī is meant; see Fiey and Putman, just mentioned, and cf. van Ess, *Theologie und Gesellschaft*, III,23 and note 8. P. Kraus, "Zu Ibn al-Muqaffaʿ," *Rivista degli Studi Orientali*, 1934, vol. 14, p. 12 and note 3, who was not concentrating on this issue, had suggested incidentally that the caliph was "probably" (wahrscheinlich) Hārūn. Kraus's essay was translated into Arabic by ʿA. Badawī (*at-Turāṯ al-yūnānī fī l-ḥaḍāra al-islāmiyya*, Cairo, 1946, pp. 101–20), where he correctly reproduced Kraus's doubt with "*laʿallahu*." The Arabic translation of Kraus was read by A.F. El-Ahwānī who reproduced this tentative identification as if it were certain fact in his introduction to the edition of the *Topics* part of Avicenna's *aš-Šifāʾ* (*al-Manṭiq, al-Ǧadal*, Cairo, 1965, p. 11 of the Arabic introduction). El-Ahwānī's mistake is reproduced by Elamrani-Jamal in *DPA* 525–6, which summarizes the relevant information about the Arabic translations of the *Topics*, with further bibliographical references.

At first appearance, this is astounding. The *Topics* is hardly light reading, so the question why it attracted such attention at the initial stages of the translation movement is significant. Even more important is the seemingly incredible fact that a Muslim caliph would wish to have a translation of this particular book by Aristotle. There can be little doubt that the selection of the book was because of its contents and their relevance to the needs generated within Islamic society that al-Mahdī felt had to be addressed. Al-Mahdī was certainly not interested in the book because of its place, rather insignificant, in the Graeco-Syriac logical curriculum of late antiquity: as far as we know there were no Syriac commentaries on it. There was, however, an earlier Syriac translation, by Athanasius of Balad (d. 686),[2] which would imply that it was known also to those unable to read Greek; it was therefore somehow brought to al-Mahdī's attention.

Now the *Topics* teaches one dialectic, *ǧadal*, the art of argumentation on a systematic basis. Its stated aim is to develop a method that would enable one to debate for or against a thesis on the basis of commonly held beliefs; accordingly, it provides rules of engagement concerning the question and answer process between two antagonists, the interrogator and his respondent, and it lists at great length test cases – about three hundred of them – that provide approaches to arguments, or their topics (the *topoi*).[3] The question is what the need for such a discipline was in the time of al-Mahdī.

In the preceding chapter I discussed how al-Manṣūr fashioned an imperial ideology with universalist claims on the basis that the ʿAbbāsid state was pre-ordained, by the stars and ultimately by God, to be the successor to the world empires that preceded it in the area. The obverse of this ideology, and the one which preceded it, was the ʿAbbāsid claim to create a commonwealth of Muslim citizens with equal rights and privileges. The Islamic component of this ideology, first conceived by the Umayyad ʿUmar II (r. 717–20) as a way to halt the breakdown of the Umayyad empire due to Arab exclusivist

2 For the state of the *Topics* in Syriac see S. Brock, "The Syriac Commentary Tradition," in C. Burnett (ed.), *Glosses and Commentaries on Aristotelian Logical Texts*, London, The Warburg Institute, 1993, pp. 3–15.

3 A fine summary of the purpose and philosophical and historical significance of dialectic in Aristotle and in subsequent Peripatetic doctrine as initiated by Theophrastus is offered by H. Baltussen, *Theophrastus on Theories of Perception*, Utrecht, University of Utrecht, 1993, pp. 10–51; on pp. 278–84 there is also a very useful specialized bibliography of secondary works on Aristotelian dialectic.

rule, became eventually the rallying point of ʿAbbāsid propaganda and was the main element of the cause (*daʿwā*) that brought the ʿAbbāsids to power. The effects of this policy were twofold. On the one hand, it meant that "assimilated" Arabs, or Persianized Arabs who had lost touch with their Arab tribal connections, and non-Arabs who had converted to Islam – the mainstays of the ʿAbbāsid revolution in both ʿIrāq and Ḫurāsān – had access to positions of power and prestige.[4] That this in fact did happen is evidenced by the rise to power from the very beginning of non-Arab personnel in the highest echelons of the ʿAbbāsid administration and military; and this is precisely what Arabs in subsequent times complained about, regardless whether they had pro-Umayyad leanings or not. It is stated in no uncertain terms as a major characteristic of al-Manṣūr's reign in the report by al-Aḫbārī to al-Qāhir, right after the passage cited in chapter 2.2:

> He was the first caliph to employ his [non-Arab] clients and freedmen (*mawāliyahu wa-ġilmānahu*) as provincial governors or tax collectors (*aʿmāl*) and delegate to them authority, preferring them over Arabs; subsequent caliphs in his line followed this example. The commanding position of the Arabs was thus abolished, their leadership came to an end, and their high rank vanished.[5]

The second consequence of this policy is that it necessarily made of Islam, both directly and indirectly, something which it was not under the Umayyads: a proselytizing religion; directly, in that a dynasty that came to power on the universalist and egalitarian claims of Islam had to ensure, in order to realize the claims, that there *was* a mass following of the new religion; and indirectly, in that these very claims, to say nothing of the concomitant reduction in taxes for converts, when realized, were a strong incentive to the non-Arab populations for conversion. Hence we see a significant rise in the rate of conversion with the accession to power of the ʿAbbāsids; this is dramatically demonstrated in the case of Iran where an accelerated

4 The course and ideology of the ʿAbbāsid revolution are analyzed in detail in the eponymous book by Shaban; for the significance of the Umayyad ʿUmar II's policies see pp. 89–92. There is a succinct review of the revolution by Kennedy, *Early Abbasid Caliphate*, pp. 35–45.

5 Al-Masʿūdī, *Murūǧ aḏ-ḏahab*, §3446 Pellat.

rate of conversion can be discerned already at the time when the ʿAbbāsid cause first started being promulgated in Ḫurāsān soon after 100/719, only to increase at a frenetic pace after 126/743, the date when the revolutionary council in Marw decided to support the cause of the ʿAbbāsid family. The correlation is too precise to leave any doubts about the centrality of the Islamist claims of the ʿAbbāsids for the victory of their cause and its significance for the course of conversion subsequently.[6] The implications of the ʿAbbāsid revolution for proselytism had also dramatic consequences for the translation movement initiated by al-Manṣūr.

Proselytism, by definition, implies that *one* religion, and within that religion, *one* version of it, is true; this is the foundation of its appeal. As such, any currents of proselytism in a society generate opposition from two general quarters: within the religion, from those who feel excluded because they have adhered, for whatever reasons, to different versions; outside the religion, from the adherents of other religions, who resist not only because they naturally defy the implication that *their* religion is not true, but also because they would necessarily be supplying the converts and hence lose power. Right after al-Manṣūr consolidated ʿAbbāsid power and established firm political control, therefore, the stage was set for confrontation between what the ʿAbbāsid establishment defined as Islam and its opponents, as well as between Islam and the other religions in the area from whose adherents the new converts were to be made. The confrontation in this case took predominantly – and necessarily – the form of disputation and debate because of the huge masses of people involved: right after the revolution, the Muslims – and indeed the Muslims who were in agreement with the ʿAbbāsids – were by far

6 The social and political background of the lack of a policy of conversion in Iran under the Umayyads is discussed by Scarcia Amoretti, "Sects and Heresies," pp. 481–7. The rate of conversion to Islam in Iran is analyzed by R.W. Bulliet, *Conversion to Islam in the Medieval Period*, Cambridge, Mass., Harvard University Press, 1979, pp. 16–32; see in particular Graph 2 and Graph 3 on p. 23. For the stages of the development of the ʿAbbāsid movement in Ḫurāsān see M. Sharon, "Ḳaḥṭaba b. Shabīb," *EI*, IV,446a. Anecdotal evidence for proselytism under the early ʿAbbāsids is provided by numerous reports of conversion "at the hands of" (*ʿalā yad*) caliphs or prominent personalities, like Abū-l-Huḏayl al-ʿAllāf (d. after 840), one of the founders of Muʿtazilism, who is reported to have converted three thousand men: Ibn-al-Murtaḍā, *Ṭabaqāt al-Muʿtazila*, S. Siwald-Wilzer (ed.), Beirut, F. Steiner, 1961, p. 44, cited by S. Pines, "An Early Meaning of the Term *Mutakallim*," *Israel Oriental Studies*, 1971, vol. 1, p. 229, reprinted in his *Studies in the History of Arabic Philosophy* [Collected Works III], S. Stroumsa (ed.), Jerusalem, The Magna Press, 1996, p. 67.

the smallest religious minority in the Fertile Crescent and Persia and beyond; persuasion and coercion through the social pressure that state power can apply had to be the only means of subjugation. The translation movement, already set in motion by al-Manṣūr for a different purpose as discussed in the previous chapter, now received further support by the measures which al-Mahdī had to adopt in order to solve the political and social opposition generated by the rising tide of conversion due to proselytism. In order to understand al-Mahdī's role in this process, it is again useful to turn to the report on his reign by al-Masʿūdī's fellow historian and source, Muḥammad al-Ḫurāsānī al-Aḫbārī:

> Al-Mahdī devoted all his efforts to exterminating heretics and apostates. These people appeared in his days and publicly proclaimed their beliefs during his caliphate on account of[7] the wide dissemination of books by Mani, Bardesanes, and Marcion (among those transmitted by Ibn-al-Muqaffaʿ and others), which were translated from Neopersian and Pahlavi into Arabic, and of works on this subject, in support of the doctrines of Manichaeism, Bardesanism, and Marcionism, composed by Ibn-Abī-l-ʿAwǧāʾ, Ḥammād ʿAǧrad, Yaḥyā ibn-Ziyād, and Muṭīʿ ibn-Iyās. In this fashion Manichaeans increased in number and their opinions came out in the open among people. Al-Mahdī was the first caliph to command the theologians who used dialectic disputation (*al-ǧadaliyyīn*) in their research to compose books against the heretics and other infidels we have just mentioned. The theologians then produced demonstrative proofs against the disputers (*muʿānidīn*), eliminated the problems posed by the heretics, and expounded the truth in clear terms to the doubters.[8]

Al-Aḫbārī's report is again accurate in identifying the core of the problem. Right after al-Manṣūr had established the *political* domination of the ʿAbbāsid dynasty, there arose movements which contested the *religious* implications of that domination, as discussed in chapter 2.5. Most vocal and socially most aggressive were the movements

7 Reading *li-mā* for *lammā* in Pellat's edition.

8 Al-Masʿūdī, *Murūǧ ad-ḏahab*, §3447 Pellat. For the Manichaean personalities mentioned in this report see G. Vajda "Les zindîqs en pays d'Islam au debut de la période Abbaside," *Rivista degli Studi Orientali*, 1938, vol. 17, pp. 193–6, 204–6, 210–13, 214.

identified by al-Aẖbārī; if imperial Zoroastrian ideology had been coopted by al-Manṣūr for the furtherance of ʿAbbāsid goals, then Persian opposition reappeared in the guise of "heretics and apostates" who belonged to variants of Persian national religions: the Manichaeans, the Bardesanites and the Marcionites. The first ʿAbbāsid century saw a constant struggle between the state and these groups, a struggle which at times broke out in violent rebellions, like that of Bābak.

Naturally, however, Manichaeism was not the only religion to react to the proselytizing implications of the policy of Islamic universalism followed by the early ʿAbbāsids. Judaism and Christianity also felt the effects of this policy which can perhaps be best observed, in the case of the latter religion, in the developments within the Melkite community. As a result of the new social situation after the ʿAbbāsid revolution, the Melkite church was faced with the decline of the Greek language in the population in Syro-Palestine and eventually was compelled to switch to Arabic even for liturgical purposes.[9] The encroachment of Arabic Islam into the religions in the Near East was felt on many fronts, and indeed in unexpected ways of which non-Muslims had no experience from Umayyad times. Hence the palpable need to explain themselves and to maintain, enlarge, and at times even re-establish their rights and positions. As a result, the first ʿAbbāsid century saw an unprecedented rise in *Arabic* Christian apologetic writings directed against Islam.

A concrete indication of the significance of inter-faith disputation is provided by the disproportionately high number of apologetic and polemic treatises written in Arabic during the period of the translation movement: the complete list of *known* Muslim and Christian polemical works written in Arabic alone, prepared by R. Caspar and his colleagues, runs for twenty-seven pages;[10] if one adds to these the Muslim Arabic works in refutation of other religions and sects, in particular Manichaeism, and the responses to them, the list would grow considerably.

Christians were, of course, no strangers to polemical literature. Disputation was the main form of communication in the seventh century, particularly in the conflict among Chalcedonians, Mono-

9 See S.H. Griffith, "Eutychius of Alexandria on the Emperor Theophilus and Iconoclasm in Byzantium: A Tenth Century Moment in Christian Apologetics in Arabic," *Byzantion*, 1982, vol. 52, p. 161.

10 Published in *Islamochristiana*, 1975, vol. 1, pp. 143–69.

physites, and Nestorians which was exacerbated as a result of the Fifth Ecumenical Council of 553. Formal public debates on matters of religion, in which at times dozens of individuals participated, became regular occurrences from then on. These debates were recorded, as a result of which the dialogue form of disputation became one of the most widely used genres of Christian (Greek and Syriac) literature in the seventh century. When the Christian–Muslim dialogues began on Christian initiative, as discussed above, after the ʿAbbāsid revolution, they "owed a great deal to the long preexisting tradition of using the dialogue form for Christian apologetic and polemic purposes." As a matter of fact, the very first Arabic Christian defense against Islam that we possess dates from the middle of the eighth century and is in dialogue form.[11]

Al-Mahdī was faced with mighty ideological foes. The various Manichaean sects which came out in the open in his time are singled out for mention by al-Aḫbārī on account of the important role the fight against *zandaqa* (Manichaeism, and hence all heresy) acquired in retrospect in Arabic historiography; al-Mahdī took them very seriously because of the Persian revivalist trends they represented and their ideological appeal to many in the ʿAbbāsid administration with Persian background, clearly established by the numerous documented cases of such individuals. The Christians and Jews, though from a legal perspective they had an unambiguous social standing and thus presented no political threat, were nevertheless formidable intellectual opponents with centuries of experience in inter-faith debate. In this context, a handbook in Arabic that would teach the art of argumentation and disputation was clearly needed. Al-Mahdī must have had good advisors; they suggested nothing less than the work that started it all, Aristotle's *Topics.*

Al-Mahdī was a good student; he read the book carefully and even had an opportunity to apply it, for he is the first Muslim to defend Islam in an extant debate with a Christian. The Christian was none other than the Nestorian patriarch Timothy I, the very man from whom he commissioned the translation of the *Topics*. It is interesting

11 Recent research on the history of the Near East in the sixth to the eighth centuries has shed much light on the social and cultural life of all the communities in the area and their interaction. For Greek literary genres in particular and the quotation in this paragraph see the article by one of these scholars, Averil Cameron's "New Themes and Styles in Greek Literature," pp. 97–100 and the literature cited there. A fragment of the anonymous Christian Arabic apologetic treatise is preserved in the Heidelberg papyrus Schott-Reinhart 438; see the references in R. Caspar *et al.*, "Bibliographie," p. 152, no. 12.2.

to note that Timothy, who reports the debate (and inevitably – and ever so politely – leaves no doubt that he was able to discredit all of al-Mahdī's objections to Christianity), mentions at the very beginning that he was surprised that the caliph should have initiated a theological *debate* with him:

> We were granted an audience by our victorious King [al-Mahdī]. In the course of our discussion about the divine nature and its eternity *a parte ante*, the King said to us something which we had never heard from him before; he said, namely, "O Catholicus, it does not befit someone like you, a man of learning and experience, to say about God Almighty that He took Himself a wife and bore from her a son." We responded and said, "O King, friend of God! Who is that person who uttered such blasphemy about Almighty God?" Whereupon the Victorious King said to me, "What, then, do you maintain about Christ? Who is he?"[12]

Al-Mahdī, who apparently had been content until that point to listen to Timothy's discourses about theological subjects, felt confident enough to challenge him to a debate; in a most intelligent manner, he asks a highly provocative – indeed almost insulting – question which, though implied in the Qur'ān, is not a direct quotation from it. In the Qur'ān it says, with obvious reference to Christian dogma, "The Creator of the heavens and the earth – how should He have a son, seeing that He has no consort?"[13] By asking the question in a way that could be safely countered in the presence of the Muslim Caliph – Timothy could hardly have called a direct Qur'ānic quotation a blasphemy – al-Mahdī hinted to Timothy that what he was after was an honest debate, not the formal obsequious platitudes that would have been expected from a Christian subject responding to the Muslim sovereign. Timothy, who obviously knew his Qur'ān (as is also evident from the course of the debate), caught the hint and was pleasantly surprised. The ensuing debate presents an excellent example of the application of the rules of disputation laid down in the *Topics*.[14]

12 Arabic text in Putman, *L'église et l'Islam*, pp. 7–8, §§2–5. For a discussion of the social and religious context of the debate see van Ess, *Theologie und Gesellschaft*, III,22–8.

13 Qur'ān 6.101, cited in A.J. Arberry's translation, *The Koran Interpreted*, London, George Allen & Unwin, 1955.

14 The logical structure of the debate is brought out in the paragraph division and headings supplied by the editor; see Putman, *L'église et l'Islam*, p. xvi.

The *Topics* was therefore manifestly relevant to the inter-faith debates during the first two ʿAbbāsid centuries, hence the many translations. As al-Aẖbārī notes in the passage quoted above, al-Mahdī introduced into the Muslim world, and was the first to champion, both the method and the social attitude of disputation for settling or promoting religio-political debates. This had far-reaching consequences, the most significant of which would appear to be, in subsequent centuries, the rise of law as the dominant social expression of Islam as a religion.

The political struggles in the time of al-Mahdī and the quest of the ʿAbbāsid house for legitimacy rested on religious or theological positions which had to be defended against their opponents. Theologians were already deeply involved in argument, and soon the jurists joined in. It was amply clear to Muslims participating in the debates that excellence in disputation was politically significant, and disputation eventually became the practice *par excellence* in legal studies and methodology. When the jurists established the first Islamic schools in the fourth/tenth century, it was to teach dialectic and jurisprudence (*fiqh*).[15] What this indicates is that during this early ʿAbbāsid period, political activity, and, more significantly, political activism, in Islamic society were expressed through dialectical argumentation of theological questions. Hence al-Mahdī's request for the primary textbook that taught this art, and hence the repeated translations of the same book in order to achieve greater accuracy and a better understanding.

2. THE EXIGENCIES OF INNER-FAITH DISCOURSE: ARISTOTLE'S *PHYSICS* AND EARLY *KALĀM*

The beginnings of Islamic theology (*ʿilm al-kalām*) have been the subject of much debate. For our purposes here it is not so much important to identify these beginnings as to note certain aspects of it that bear directly upon the impulse given to the translation

15 For disputation see now van Ess, *Theologie und Gesellschaft*, IV,725–30, with full bibliography. See the works by G. Makdisi for an exposition of the significance of dialectic and law for the foundation of the *madrasas*, especially his *The Rise of Colleges: Institutions of Learning in Islam and the West*, Edinburgh, Edinburgh University Press, 1981, pp. 71ff.; there is also a brief exposition by him in "The Juridical Theology of Shāfiʿī: Origins and Significance of uṣūl al-fiqh," *Studia Islamica*, 1984, vol. 59, p. 21.

movement. In the first place, it is generally acknowledged that the first discussions among Muslims that might be called "theological" were the result of political and social developments during the first century of Islam, before the beginning of the translation movement. The questions of legitimacy of succession, the relationship of leadership to faith and the concomitant problem of unbelief, when that relationship was not deemed adequate, appear to have been, understandably, at the center of discussion. So also were disputations with non-Muslims. Out of this background there arose a "theology of controversy," as termed by van Ess, which, in essence, constituted part of the political discourse of the nascent Muslim Arab society.[16]

The question is to identify and understand the process by which discussions that were centered around subjects of immediate concern to this society shifted their focus to subjects which forced the opposing debating groups to have recourse to translated sources in search of material for their position and vindication. In other words, why and how these discussions moved on to subjects which eventually necessitated the translation of Greek and other foreign works; or, alternatively put, how the theology of controversy over specific issues stemming directly from Islamic history in the first century was transformed into a "theology" discussing abstract matters *ostensibly* unrelated to historical and political events.

Al-Aḫbārī mentions in his account of the controversies in al-Mahdī's time the Manichaeans, Bardesanites and Marcionites. It is fruitful to start from there. The historical record is clear that these dualist sects played a major role in Islamic society during its second century and indeed right after the ʿAbbāsids came to power. Al-Mahdī took severe measures against them, and although the persecutions had a fluctuating progress until the final demise of these sects by the end of the fourth/tenth century, the fact remains that *zandaqa*, the official term both for Manichaeism and heresy in general (often deliberately confused) influenced enormously the course and development of Islam as a religion and ideology during the early ʿAbbāsid era. The question is, how, precisely. Van Ess has most recently suggested that the phenomenon of *zandaqa* is best explained not so much through the assumption of a Manichaean missionary activity which, presumably, would have threatened Islam, as through the fact that certain Muslim intellectuals found in Manichaeism and related dualistic systems certain things that the Islam of their time could not

16 See van Ess, *Theologie und Gesellschaft*, I,48ff.

offer them. It was therefore a matter of intellectuals coming in contact not with religious sects but with an ambience of intellectualism.[17]

However this might be – and if it was merely a matter of intellectual discussions without a corresponding perceived threat to the ʿAbbāsid state the persecutions and executions could hardly be accounted for – it seems almost certain that it was members of such groups (or, as van Ess also remarks, new converts to Islam from such groups) who injected into the Muslim "theology of controversy" a new subject for discussion, that of cosmology.[18] And indeed the earliest abstract theological discussions we hear about have to do with questions of physical theory – atoms, space, and the void – which, as Dhanani has recently argued, have dualist origins.[19] Although we do not yet know the precise stages through which, and the specific reasons for which, cosmological theories – and atomistic ones at that – should have become one of the main and highly contested foci of Islamic theology (which until that time had been concerned with such issues, understandably significant for the "theology of controversy," like the nature of faith and the right of succession to the caliphate), the fact remains that atomism occupied center stage from the beginning and continued in this vein for centuries to come.

There are other considerations that also point to a preoccupation with cosmological questions among intellectuals under the early ʿAbbāsids. In the preceding chapter we saw Zoroastrian interest in astrology adopted as part of official ʿAbbāsid ideology. This implies the concomitant adoption of an underlying cosmological theory that supports the practice of astrology. The Aristotelian–Ptolemaic picture of the universe readily lends itself to such a purpose, and in one of the works of Māšā'allāh we find precisely such a position presented.[20] Subjects in physics and cosmology also figure prominently in the *Dēnkard*, the canonical book of the Zoroastrians cited in the preceding chapter (2.3, §7), and if bureaucrats who were carriers of this culture became active in state administration under the early ʿAbbāsids, these concerns would naturally emerge in public view. Furthermore, the injunction of Chosroes I Anūširwān in the same

17 Van Ess, *Theologie und Gesellschaft*, I,423–7.

18 Van Ess, *Theologie und Gesellschaft*, I,423–4; 436–43.

19 A. Dhanani, *The Physical Theory of Kalām. Atoms, Space, and Void in Basrian Muʿtazilī Cosmology*, Leiden, E.J. Brill, 1994, pp. 182–6.

20 Pingree, "Māshā'allāh," p. 10, where Pingree calls the physical and cosmological theories presented by Māšā'allāh, "Peripateticism tailored for the astrologer."

document to "establish in the world by discussion" (see chapter 2.3, §8) the tenets of the state religion appears to be, in general terms, a definition of disputational theology, or *kalām*. It seems to have played some role in the energetic defense of Islam undertaken by the theologians (*mutakallimūn*) under the early ʿAbbāsids who appear to have used them as propagandists. S. Pines has argued that Abū-Muslim used individuals called *mutakallimūn* precisely for such purposes.[21] To close the circle with the dualists, finally, mention should also be made of H.A.R. Gibb, who, following Michelangelo Guidi, suggested that the first Muʿtazilī theologians (*mutakallimūn*) "were the militant wing of orthodoxy against the dualist heresies" using dialectic weapons which "they found in Greek logic and dialectic" of the translated works.[22]

It is this constellation of circumstances that contributed to the translation of Greek books on the subject, just as they made the translation of the *Topics* necessary during the caliphate of al-Mahdī. If in the religious debates occasioned by ʿAbbāsid policies the translation of Aristotle's *Topics* was required in order to provide guidance in Arabic for the method of disputation, then the translation of other books was sought after for factual information to be used in these theological debates. In this category belongs Aristotle's *Physics*, which also has a long and complicated history of translation into Arabic.

Its earliest translation is attributed by Ibn-an-Nadīm to a certain Sallām al-Abraš, "one of the earliest translators at the time of the Barmakids" [*F* 244.6], i.e., 750–803, or, strictly speaking, during the reign of Hārūn, 786–803. Ibn-an-Nadīm cites this piece of information directly from ʿĪsā ibn-ʿAlī (914–1001), the son of the "good" vizier ʿAlī ibn-ʿĪsā, who had made a name for himself for his assiduous pursuit of the Greek sciences (cf. chapter 6.1c). Also as a student of Yaḥyā ibn-ʿAdī, the major informant of Ibn-an-Nadīm in matters philosophical, ʿĪsā can be trusted to have had reliable

21 See Pines, "An Early Meaning of the Term *Mutakkallim*," pp. 224ff., but cf. van Ess, *Theologie und Gesellschaft*, I,49–50.

22 H.A.R. Gibb, "The Social Significance of the Shuubiya," in his *Studies on the Civilization of Islam*, S.J. Shaw and W.R. Polk (eds), Boston, Beacon Press, 1962, pp. 70–1; reprinted from *Studia Orientalia Ioanni Pedersen dicata*, Copenhagen, 1953, pp. 105–14. Gibb goes on to suggest that al-Ma'mūn saw "in this work of translation the most propitious means of ridding Islam of the legacies of dualist *zandaqa*" (p. 71), which, though not exactly accurate according to my analyses in this book, is on the right track in trying to find social causes for the translation movement.

information.[23] Sallām al-Abraš's translation was followed by at least three others, and by translations of numerous Greek commentaries on the *Physics* as well as by original compositions on the subject in Arabic.[24]

That the reason behind the demand for the translation of the *Physics* was the cosmological component of the theological debates becomes relatively clear from the role Aristotle seems to have played in them at their very inception. Hišām ibn-al-Ḥakam, one of the influential and controversial theologians who took part in the discussions of the circle of intellectuals in the Barmakid court between 786 and 795 (i.e., an exact contemporary of Sallām al-Abraš) wrote a treatise in refutation of Aristotle on the concept of God. The object of Hišām's attack could only have been *Physics* VIII or *Metaphysics Lambda*, and we have no information about a translation of the *Metaphysics* before the first decades of the ninth century. A generation after Hišām the famous theologian an-Naẓẓām also is reported as having refuted Aristotle on the subject of natural philosophy. Thus the very fact that Hišām and an-Naẓẓām attacked Aristotle in the context of theological polemics indicates that his works – and in both cases doubtless the *Physics* – were in fact used for theological purposes.[25] The antagonism betweem atomism and Aristotelianism that dominated Arabic intellectual history for centuries thus began early and it appears that it was the introduction of dualist, and hence, atomist cosmological doctrines into the debate that occasioned the introduction of Aristotelian physics into Arabic thought. The opponents of atomism could hardly find a mightier weapon for their purposes.

23 See H. Bowen, "'Alī b. 'Īsā," *EI* I,387, and Sourdel, *Vizirat*, pp. 523–4. 'Īsā and his father belonged to the influential Ibn-al-Ǧarrāḥ family of administrators from Dayr Qunnā, about whom see further in chapter 6.1.

24 See the information on the subject from both primary and secondary sources presented by F.E. Peters, *Aristoteles Arabus*, Leiden, E.J. Brill, 1968, pp. 30–4. The *Physics* continued to dominate philosophical discussion also after the period of the translation movement; see the material collected by P. Lettinck, *Aristotle's* Physics *and Its Reception in the Arabic World*, Leiden, E.J. Brill, 1994.

25 For Hišām see the exhaustive treatment by van Ess, *Theologie und Gesellschaft*, I,349ff. His early career is discussed there on pp. 350ff., and his concept of God on pp. 358–9. His work against Aristotle, *K. ar-Radd 'alā Arisṭālīs fī t-tawḥīd*, is listed in his catalogue of works given by van Ess, V,70, no. 8. For an-Naẓẓām see most conveniently the article by van Ess in *EI* VII,1057–8; also his "Ḍirār b. 'Amr und die 'Cahmīya'. Biographie einer vergessenen Schule," *Der Islam*, 1967, vol. 43, p. 256, and the corresponding passages in his *Theologie und Gesellschaft*, III,296ff.

Finally, with regard to translations during the time of al-Mahdī, one more point is worth making in order to emphasize the complexity of the subject. In the discussion of the causes of the translation movement, emphasis so far has been laid on factors of historical relevance rather than on those due to individual whim. However, it must also be pointed out that the individual propensities of the caliphs, though not essential for the translation movement as a whole, nevertheless had something to do with the nature of the material translated. It has been shown that al-Mahdī, who liked falconry, had an experienced falconer, al-Ġassānī, compile a book for him on the subject using not only Arab but foreign sources as well. The result was a book which became archetypical in subsequent Arabic literature on the subject.[26] Had al-Mahdī not enjoyed falconry we might not have had this book; on the other hand, had there not been in place a translation culture, which fostered the attitude of looking outside of Arab tradition for information on all subjects, al-Ġassānī's book may have given us just Arab lore on falconry and nothing more.

26 See the exhaustive study on the subject by D. Möller, *Studien zur mittelalterlichen arabischen Falknereiliteratur*, Berlin, W. de Gruyter, 1965.

4

AL-MA'MŪN

Domestic and Foreign Policies and the Translation Movement

1. THE TRANSLATION MOVEMENT IN THE SERVICE OF CENTRALIZED AUTHORITY

Al-Ma'mūn came into power in the wake of a fratricidal civil war that shook the ʿAbbāsid state to its foundations. Briefly to review the events in order better to appreciate the enormity of the tumult: his father, Hārūn ar-Rašīd, died in 193/809. Of the two brothers, al-Amīn succeeded as caliph in Baghdad, while al-Ma'mūn was stationed in Marw as governor of Ḫurāsān. The conflict between the two brothers started almost immediately and lasted until al-Amīn's defeat and execution upon orders of al-Ma'mūn's victorious general, Ṭāhir (198/813). After the fall of Baghdad and al-Amīn's death, al-Ma'mūn remained in Marw from where he intended to rule, and this decision caused the civil war to be protracted for another six years. When al-Ma'mūn finally emerged victorious from the second phase of the civil war and decided to return to Baghdad in 204/819, the instability in al-Manṣūr's city had lasted for over ten years.

Civil wars have lasting consequences, and this one was no exception; an argument could be made that the disintegration of the effective power of the ʿAbbāsids that came with the advent of the Būyids in 945 began with this civil war. Al-Ma'mūn was faced with numerous problems, the most significant of which would appear to have been a crisis in legitimacy, more intractable by far than that faced by his great-grandfather, al-Manṣūr. Al-Manṣūr was able to counter this, largely successfully because he was operating from a position of strength, by following a policy of inclusion and accommodation, appropriating ideologies of the factions to be appeased in order to maintain their support; hence his adoption of a Zoroastrian imperial ideology, as discussed in chapter 2.

Al-Ma'mūn could not be so lucky; the situation was dramatically different than it had been seventy years before. In the first place, the legitimacy crisis cut deeper. Al-Amīn's execution, in addition to being the first regicide in ʿAbbāsid history, was apparently also gratuitous. The amount of damage it did to al-Ma'mūn's image can be gauged from the inordinate efforts al-Ma'mūn and his propagandists expended in order to revise historiography in justification of the act. Second, the policies of the early ʿAbbāsids, al-Ma'mūn's predecessors, in promotion of their cause eventually generated their own antitheses which, precipitated as they were by the civil war, it devolved upon al-Ma'mūn to resolve.

The policies of inclusion and ideological accommodation initiated by al-Manṣūr and followed by his successors had the effect of allowing the unchecked development of a variety of ideas, ideologies, and disciplines. As we saw, the translation movement was a direct beneficiary of these policies; by the same token, however, there also developed and were in the process of being recorded in written form other approaches to Islam which did not stem from those classes in Baghdad which promoted the translation movement. In particular, codification of legal theory and practice would appear to have been the most significant development. The famous legal scholar aš-Šāfiʿī, whose essay on legal method was destined to champion the cause of law on the basis of texts purporting to convey the Prophet's precedent (*sunna*), died in 204/820. His essay, as pointedly noted by El-Hibri, was the result of such tendencies in the community rather than the cause.[1] To this one should also add the encouragement provided to such developments by another policy of the early ʿAbbāsids, that of proselytism. There thus developed in the major cities of Islam during the first seventy years of ʿAbbāsid rule groups of scholars or intellectuals, primarily preoccupied with law, who were by and large independent of central caliphal policies.

The drive to centralization and firm control by the caliph was already apparent in the time of al-Manṣūr – the city plan of Baghdad with the caliph at the center being the most conspicuous symbol of this – though even al-Manṣūr knew that he had to be flexible in order to maintain the largest amount of support. Nothing can illustrate this fact better than the reported incident between him and Mālik ibn-Anas, the founder of the Mālikī school of law. Al-Manṣūr asked him

1 T. El-Hibri, *The Reign of the Abbasid Caliph al-Ma'mūn (811–833): The Quest for Power and the Crisis of Legitimacy*, unpublished Ph.D. dissertation, Columbia University, 1992, p. 306.

to have his, Mālik's, book *al-Muwaṭṭa'* adopted as the standard book on (acceptable) *ḥadīṯs* by the Prophet, but Mālik declined. This story indicates two things; first, that al-Manṣūr attempted to create a canonical legal text that would be used uniformly and hence provide the caliph a measure of control, and, second, that Mālik expressly desired to remain independent of caliphal authority on the grounds, indeed, of the variety of Muslim practice in the different cities.

Al-Ma'mūn's response to these challenges resulted in his adoption of policies that have been at the center of discussion, both partisan and scholarly, ever since his time. These policies are best represented by his imposition of the *miḥna*, or inquisition, the official institution of the doctrine of the created Qur'ān, punishable by flogging or imprisonment for those who failed to profess their support of the doctrine in the course of legal proceedings. The question concerning the translation movement in this context is twofold: the role that it historically played in al-Ma'mūn's overall policies, and the reasons for the by and large distorted picture of that role given by mainstream historiography. I say distorted because al-Ma'mūn is almost universally credited in subsequent Arabic historiography and the modern studies that depend on it for having initiated, either actually or effectively, the translation movement. This of course is not true, as already discussed, but the question why there developed a perception that he did is worthy of comment.

In the preceding chapters, I found useful the exposition of early ʿAbbāsid policies by al-Aḫbārī, as reported by al-Masʿūdī. Here again he provides a unique perspective with which it is profitable to start. He says about al-Ma'mūn:

> At the beginning of his reign, when he was under the influence of al-Faḍl ibn-Sahl and others, he used to spend time investigating astrological rulings and prognostications, to follow what the stars prescribed, and to model his conduct on that of the past Sasanian emperors like Ardašīr ibn-Bābak and others. He worked hard at reading ancient books; he was keen on their study and assiduous in their reading to the point that he became skilled in their understanding and proficient in their comprehension.
>
> When, however, after the well-known fate befell al-Faḍl ibn-Sahl, al-Ma'mūn arrived in ʿIrāq, he turned his back on all that and promulgated the doctrine of Unity and the Promise of Reward and Threat of Punishment. He held sessions with

> theologians and admitted to his company scholars who had distinguished themselves in dialectic disputation and debate, people like Abū-l-Hudayl and an-Naẓẓām as well as their partisans and adversaries. He had jurists and the learned among men of general culture attend his sessions; he had such men brought from various cities and stipends for them allocated. As a result, people developed an interest in conducting theoretical investigations and learned how to do research and use dialectic; each group among them wrote books in which it championed its cause and through which it supported its doctrines.[2]

Al-Ma'mūn was the product of the policies of his forefathers described in the preceding chapters; al-Aḫbārī's report on him is significant in corroborating this. His mother was Persian (possibly the granddaughter of the rebel Ustāḏsīs against al-Manṣūr), and no doubt this fact weighed heavily in Hārūn's decision to make him governor of Ḫurāsān, but it was his education, which was imbued with the Zoroastrian Sasanian imperial ideology first applied to the Islamic empire by al-Manṣūr, that lent him an outlook wholly consistent with that ideology; hence his reliance on astrology and hence his deep study of the "ancient books," precisely along the lines described in chapter 2. His support during the years he spent in Marw, both before and after al-Amīn's death, came from the provincial elite of Ḫurāsān who in all probability entertained notions of the revival of the Sasanian empire. The incident about al-Ma'mūn's initial adoption of green, the color of the Sasanians, as state color, only to be exchanged for the black of the Muslim ʿAbbāsids upon his return to Baghdad, would seem to be indicative of such tendencies.[3]

Al-Faḍl ibn-Sahl, al-Ma'mūn's mentor, advisor, and vizier, was the representative of the interests of that class. Whatever reason it was that made al-Ma'mūn's father, Hārūn ar-Rašīd, turn against and remove the Barmakids from power in Baghdad in 187/803, it must have been related to al-Ma'mūn's decision to eliminate al-Faḍl, the erstwhile protégé of the Barmakids, once he had decided to return to Baghdad. Judging by these two incidents alone, it is obvious that the old "Sasanian" faction and its policies were no longer relevant to

2 Al-Masʿūdī, *Murūǧ aḏ-ḏahab*, §3453 Pellat.

3 For the significance of the color change see El-Hibri, *al-Ma'mūn*, p. 207.

the situation the ʿAbbāsid dynasty found itself in at the beginning of the ninth century. The historical situation had changed.

For one thing, the old Sasanian ideology could no longer have had the same function as it did sixty years before. Not only did the intervening years see a rapid conversion to Islam among the Persian population, but their elite, who had supported al-Ma'mūn during his years in Marw, were in no position to do the same for him as caliph of the entire Islamic empire; besides, their irrevocable support had already been won by al-Ma'mūn and there was no need for further gestures. Second, the Zoroastrian ideology and its astrological history as interpreted for al-Manṣūr viewed the ʿAbbāsid dynasty as the inheritors of the past empires in the area. After the civil war, however, and especially after al-Ma'mūn's decision to name the ʿAlid ar-Riḍā as his heir while he was still in Marw, the political power and prestige of the ʿAbbāsid family had much waned. In this context, al-Ma'mūn must have clearly realized that staying in Marw and continuing with this ideology would have made of him a provincial governor, not the caliph of a world empire. He had no choice but to return to Baghdad.

Abandoning Marw also entailed abandoning the Zoroastrian ideology and replacing it with something else. The choice was obvious; al-Ma'mūn would be the Islamic emperor, "God's caliph," as the title that he newly adopted in 201/816–17 implied.[4] Al-Ma'mūn's choice in a way was forced upon him by the ascendancy of Islam as a religion throughout the empire, the legacy of his predecessors' policies of proselytism. However, the manner in which al-Ma'mūn decided to apply Islamist ideology was his own decision, a decision that resulted in the *miḥna*, "inquisition."

Al-Ma'mūn's new policy was based on an absolutist interpretation of Islam, with the caliph as the ultimate arbiter of dogma. This was largely unprecedented in Islamic history and completely against the current of decentralization of religious authority that had been gaining momentum until al-Ma'mūn's time. This decision must be evaluated in the context of other policy efforts of al-Ma'mūn that have one common theme and concern, the overarching policy to centralize *all power* in the hands of the caliph and those immediately

4 For the significance of the adoption of this title by al-Ma'mūn see the discussion in El-Hibri, *al-Ma'mūn*, pp. 114–23, in which he differentiates it, against Crone and Hinds, from the use made of it by previous caliphs: P. Crone and M. Hinds, *God's Caliph: Religious Authority in the First Centuries of Islam*, Cambridge, Cambridge University Press, 1986.

and absolutely under his control. On a broad political level, al-Ma'mūn sought to re-establish, especially after the negative impact of the civil war, the centralized authority of his office. On the military level, he adopted policies that centralized the army. On an administrative level, given the considerable trouble he had with some of his judges, he paid special attention to the judicial system and tried to gain firmer control over it.[5] On the fiscal level, he instituted a far-reaching coinage reform that produced uniformity in, and granted the capital control over, provincial mint outputs.[6] On an ideological level, the centralizing tendencies of al-Ma'mūn's policies were in a way a reaction to developments within Islam: the appearance, by his time, of numerous religious scholars who were perceived as the proper interpreters of Islam and as taking power away from the central authorities; al-Ma'mūn was not willing to subordinate caliphal authority to that of anybody else. Finally, on a personal level, al-Ma'mūn's decision was conditioned by his upbringing in the Sasanian ideology, which provides a significant clue for an understanding and interpretation of his overall centralizing policies.

Al-Aḫbārī very perspicaciously mentions that al-Ma'mūn behaved like the Sasanian emperors, especially like Ardašīr ibn-Bābak, i.e., Ardašīr I, the founder of the Sasanian dynasty (r. 224–42). Ardašīr was understandably famous in Sasanian history for his political wisdom, and there is attributed to him a "testament" (*andarz, ʿahd*) in which he offers advice to future Sasanian emperors on how to rule. The document, which in its original Pahlavi form would appear to date from the period just before the Arab conquests, is extant in an early Arabic translation. On the subject of religion and its function in government, "Ardašīr" has the following advice to give:

> Know that royal authority and religion are two brothers in perfect agreement with each other. Neither can subsist without the other, because religion is the foundation of royal authority, and subsequently royal authority becomes the guardian of religion; royal authority cannot do without its foundation, and religion cannot do without its guardian, because whatever has

5 For al-Ma'mūn's military and administrative centralization policies see Kennedy, *Early Abbasid Caliphate*, pp. 164–74; El-Hibri's *al-Ma'mūn* provides much of the documentation and argument on this issue.

6 T. El-Hibri, "Coinage Reform under the ʿAbbāsid Caliph al-Ma'mūn," *Journal of the Economic and Social History of the Orient*, 1993, vol. 36, pp. 72–7.

no guardian gets lost and whatever has no foundation is demolished. The very first thing which I fear for you is that people of low social standing will surpass you in the study of religion, its interpretation, and in learning it and that your confidence in the power of royal authority will lead you to underestimate them; there will thus come about in the domain of religion concealed leaderships among those from the subject lower classes and the riffraff commoners whom you had at one time wronged, treated harshly, dispossessed, intimidated, and humiliated.

Know that there can never come together in a single state a concealed religious leader and a declared political leader without the religious leader usurping the power from the political leader, because religion is the foundation and royal authority the pillar, and he who controls the foundation is in better control of the entire edifice than he who controls the pillar. . . .

Know that your rule extends only over the bodies of your subjects, and that kings have no rule over hearts. Know that even if you subdue the power of people you shall not subdue their minds. Know that the dispossessed person who is intelligent will unsheath against you his tongue, which is sharper than his sword, and that he can inflict upon you the most severe harm with it [the tongue] when he wends its contrivances toward religion; for it is in terms of religion that he will argue, for the sake of religion that he will pretend to get angry, and on account of religion that he will cry and religion that he will invoke. . . .

The king ought not to concede to worshippers, ascetics, and the pious that they are worthier of the religion, more fond of it, and more angry on its account than himself.[7]

As Fritz Steppat pointed out, the wording in the translation of this document is very similar to that selected by al-Ma'mūn in his edict

7 For the text I follow the readings in al-Ābī's *Naṯr ad-durr*, Munīr M. al-Madanī (ed.), Cairo, 1990, vol. 7, pp. 87, 89, rather than the edition of I. 'Abbās, *'Ahd Ardašīr*, Beirut, Dar Sader, 1967, pp. 53–4, 56, 57. There is also an edition by M. Grignaschi, "Quelques spécimens de la littérature sassanide conservés dans les bibliothèques d'Istanbul," *Journal Asiatique*, 1966, vol. 254, pp. 46–67, with a following French translation; for the relevant passages see pp. 70–2. On testamentary literature in Pahlavi see S. Shaked, "Andarz," *EIr.* II,11–16.

ordering the *miḥna.*[8] Following Ardašīr's advice, al-Ma'mūn clearly perceived that the pluralism implied in religious authority vested in a number of religious scholars was inimical to the interests of the state. The *miḥna* was his attempt to wrest control back for the central government and avoid the dangers against which Ardašīr's text warned.

In order to succeed in his efforts to re-establish the centralized authority of the caliph and even expand its extent in his person, al-Ma'mūn engaged in an intensive propaganda campaign that rested on two pillars: that he was indeed the champion of Islam, the foundation of the state, and that he was the final arbiter about the true interpretation of Islam, all others being secondary. In order to achieve the first objective, al-Ma'mūn initiated an imperialist war against the infidels, the Byzantines – imperialist in the sense that it was qualitatively different from the seasonal raids engaged in by his ʿAbbāsid predecessors.[9] Al-Ma'mūn's campaigns had the purpose of wresting territory from the Byzantines and settling it with Muslims in order to expand the domain of *Dār al-Islam.*

The second objective could be achieved only by divesting the criteria for religious authority from the religious scholars who had reigned supreme until his day and by concentrating them in the person of the caliph who would be supported by an organic intellectual elite; this in turn could be effected only by making the caliph's personal judgment in interpreting the religious texts, based on reason, the ultimate criterion. The caliph could arrive at a judgment, and convince others that it was the proper one, by means of debate and dialectic argumentation; these would be the tools in deciding religious questions and forming a judgment about them, and not the dogmatic statements of religious leaders based on transmitted authority. Hence al-Ma'mūn's policies of encouraging debate and the popularity of dialectic, as al-Aḫbārī informs us.

It is perhaps siginificant to register a distinction. Al-Ma'mūn did not so much desire to have the final say in religion on personal grounds, though of course this was a beneficial by-product, as not to concede to "people of low social standing," as the Testament of Ardašīr puts it, the upper hand in matters of religion; he did not want

8 F. Steppat, "From *ʿAhd Ardašīr* to al-Ma'mūn: A Persian Element in the Policy of the *miḥna,*" in W. al-Qāḍī (ed.), *Studia Arabica & Islamica* [Festschrift for Iḥsān ʿAbbās], Beirut, American University of Beirut, 1981, pp. 451–4.

9 See the detailed analysis of al-Ma'mūn's Byzantine campaigns by El-Hibri, *al-Ma'mūn,* chapter 8, pp. 253–89.

to abdicate the right of the ruler to be the ultimate arbiter of religious orthodoxy and belief. Hence he wanted to create a class *from above* who would be, together with him, in charge of religion, and not the masses *from below* who, with their "hidden leaderships," would be in control. This was apparently a new orientation in Islamic society; it seems that al-Ma'mūn was consciously trying to create a religious aristocracy to go along with the political one.

In both these policies, al-Ma'mūn built upon and modified those of his predecessors. He adopted the Zoroastrian imperial ideology of centralized government and merely substituted Islam for Zoroastrianism; and he adopted the policy of proselytism to Islam on the basis of dialectic argumentation, with the proviso that his judgment would be final. In both these policies, the translation movement offered him significant support.

2. FOREIGN POLICY AND THE TRANSLATION MOVEMENT: THE IDEOLOGY OF ANTI-BYZANTINISM AS PHILHELLENISM

Al-Ma'mūn was born in 170/786 when the translation movement was well on its way and grew up in the cultural environment impregnated by the attitudes of the Barmakids, arguably its most avid supporters. As a young man he read and studied zealously the books of the ancients, al-Aḫbārī tells us. By the time he became caliph, it is certain not only that he as an individual had internalized values that considered the translation movement and all that it stood for as a cultural good, but also that these values were the dominant ones among intellectuals in his Ḫurāsānī capital of Marw, where he was proclaimed caliph in 196/812, and of course in Baghdad, where he entered as caliph in 204/819. That he would actively further promote the translation movement, therefore, as all his predecessors had done before him, never came then, and it should not come now, into question. The reports that he initiated or that he was the one caliph most responsible for the translations should accordingly be discounted as later and obviously tendentious revisionist versions. Rather the question should be, given that the translation movement was a social fact, and that, assuming even these revisionist reports to contain a kernel of truth insofar as they indicate that he made much of the translation movement, what particular use he made of it.

As the social history of early ʿAbbāsid society becomes better known, it becomes increasingly clear that propagation of caliphal policies through "public relations" campaigns that exploited rhetoric to which the public was most sensitive, or to use a crasser term, through propaganda, was part and parcel of the work of administration. Al-Ma'mūn paid particular attention to this aspect of administration for good reason: not only did he come to power as a result of regicide which had the additional onus of also being fratricide, as already briefly mentioned, but he also initiated, after his return to Baghdad, a vigorous drive for centralization and consolidation of power that was bound to draw fire from numerous quarters. He therefore instituted powerful propaganda campaigns in order to legitimize his accession to power, justify the regicide and fratricide, propagate and advertise his policies, and have them finally accepted. An excellent example of the workings of such campaigns is provided by the way in which al-Ma'mūn (i.e., the circles around him) tried to justify the deposition and murder of al-Amīn by rewriting the Mecca Protocol for succession that had been promulgated in 802 by their father Hārūn ar-Rašīd. Historical record has preserved both the original document, which clearly stated that the succession was going unconditionally first to al-Amīn and then to al-Ma'mūn, and the "revised" version from pro-Ma'mūnid circles that justified the revolt should al-Amīn not adhere to the conditions stipulated.[10]

In foreign affairs, al-Ma'mūn's attempt to present himself as the champion of Islam, according to the dictates of his new ideological drive, resulted in a distinctly aggressive policy against the Byzantines. This policy crystallized after he had secured, militarily and administratively, the western provinces toward the end of his reign, specifically when he started instituting the *miḥna*; it is therefore all the more apparent that the campaigns against the Byzantines and the harsh new domestic policies are related. The total war against the Byzantines that he initiated had an ideological component that was new. The Byzantines were portrayed as deserving of Muslim attacks not only because they were infidels – this was the theme already present in Muḥammad's alleged letter to Heraclius – but because they were also culturally benighted and inferior not only to Muslims but also to their own ancestors, the ancient Greeks. The Muslims, by contradistinction, in addition to being superior because of Islam, were also superior because they appreciated ancient Greek science

10 See T. El-Hibri, "Harun al-Rashid and the Mecca Protocol of 802: A Plan for Division or Succession?" *International Journal of Middle East Studies*, 1992, vol. 24, p. 463.

and wisdom and had translated their books into Arabic. This superiority is even transferred to Islam itself as a religion; the Byzantines turned their back on ancient science because of Christianity, while the Muslims had welcomed it because of Islam. Anti-Byzantinism thus becomes philhellenism. The translation movement was providing the Muslims with ideological tools to fight against the Byzantines; in the process, the translation movement and all that it stood for gained further in valorization within Islamic society.

These anti-Byzantine and anti-Christian aspects of al-Ma'mūn's propaganda campaign can be seen in their initial stages reflected in the works of al-Ǧāḥiẓ (d. 255/868), the propagandist-laureate of al-Ma'mūn and his Muʿtazilī successors.[11] He describes the Byzantines (*Rūm*) as people of great merit and scientific accomplishments, and then asks how it is possible for such people, under the influence of Christianity, to believe in three gods and claim that a mere mortal who urinates and defecates was actually a god:

> The Byzantines possess an architecture different from that of others. They can produce carving and carpentry as nobody else can. Besides, they have a holy book and a religious community. It is unmistakable and undeniable that they possess beauty, are familiar with arithmetic, astrology and calligraphy, and have courage, insight and a variety of great skills. . . .
>
> Despite all this, they believe that there are three gods, two secret and one visible, just as a lamp requires oil, a wick and a container. The same applies [in their opinion] to the substance of the gods. They assume that a creature became creator, a slave became master, a newly created being became an originally uncreated being, but was then crucified and killed with a crown of thorns on the head, and then disappeared, only to bring himself back to life after death. . . .
>
> If we had not seen it with our own eyes and heard it with our own ears, we would not consider it true. We would not believe that a people of religious philosophers [*mutakallimūn*], physicians, astronomers, diplomats, arithmeticians, secretaries

11 Al-Ǧāḥiẓ was first brought to the attention of al-Ma'mūn in 200/817–18 through his writings on the question of the imamate, i.e., the leadership of the Muslim community, which the caliph found much to his liking. Al-Ǧāḥiẓ then moved to Baghdad and spent most of his life there. See, most conveniently, the introduction by C. Pellat, *The Life and Works of Jāḥiẓ*, Berkeley and Los Angeles, University of California Press, 1969, pp. 5–9 and his references there.

> and masters of every discipline could say that a man who, as they themselves have seen, ate, drank, urinated, excreted, suffered hunger and thirst, dressed and undressed, gained and lost [weight], who later, as they assume, was crucified and killed, is Lord and Creator and providential God, eternal and not newly created, who lets the living die and brings the dead back to life and can create at will a great deal more for the world, and that they still take pride in his crucifixion and slaying, as do the Jews.[12]

It is to be noted that the thrust of the argument against the Christian Byzantines is not that Christianity is to be disapproved of simply because Islam superseded it, but because Christian beliefs are inherently *irrational*, a regrettable situation that can befall even an otherwise enlightened people. The allusion to Islamic society in this argument by al-Ǧāḥiẓ is unmistakable: there is a lesson to be learned from the Byzantines, because the Muslims, equally enlightened, run the risk, if they follow the anthropomorphic nonsense of certain Muslims, of lapsing into similar irrationality. This particular bent which al-Ǧāḥiẓ lends to his argument requires that the ancient Greeks and Byzantines be considered as one people, and he thus deliberately blurs the distinction between the ancient Greeks and the Byzantines.[13] However, in another work, on the refutation of Christians, where the argument is based on drawing a distinction between the two, al-Ǧāḥiẓ contrasts the ancient Greeks and the Byzantines who, he claims, have no science but are mere artisans. He introduces that section also by drawing a contrast between Christians and Jews:

> The difference between the Christians and the Jews is that the latter consider that the study of philosophy is a cause of unbelief, that the application of dialectic to the study of religion is a heresy and the very fountainhead of doubt, that the only true learning is that contained in the Pentateuch and the writings of the Prophets, and that the belief in the efficacy of

12 From al-Ǧāḥiẓ's *Kitāb al-Aḫbār*, translation by Rosenthal, *Classical Heritage*, pp. 44–5; a less literal translation also by Pellat, *Jāḥiẓ*, p. 38, discussed by C. Pellat, "Al-Ǧāḥiẓ. Les nations civilisées et les croyances religieuses," *Journal Asiatique*, 1967, vol. 255, p. 86; reprinted in his *Études sur l'histoire socio-culturelle de l'Islam (VIIe-XVe s.)*, London, Variorum, 1976, no. V.

13 This was noted by Pellat, "Nations civilisées," p. 71.

medicine and faith in astrologers' predictions are likewise causes of heresy, leading towards heterodoxy and away from the path trodden by their forefathers and models. They go to such extremes in the matter that they suffer the blood of those who do those things to be spilt with impunity, and silence any who are tempted to follow their example.

Had the common people but known that the Christians and the Byzantines have neither wisdom nor clarity [of mind] nor depth of thought but are simply clever with their hands in wood-turning, carpentry, plastic arts, and weaving of silk brocade, they would have removed them from the ranks of the literati and dropped them from the roster of philosophers and sages because works like the *Organon, On Coming to Be and Passing Away*, and *Meteorology* were written by Aristotle, and he is neither Byzantine nor Christian; the *Almagest* was written by Ptolemy, and he is neither Byzantine nor Christian; the *Elements* was written by Euclid, and he is neither Byzantine nor Christian; medical books were written by Galen, who was neither Byzantine nor Christian; and similarly with the books by Democritus, Hippocrates, Plato, and on and on. All these are individuals of one nation; they have perished but the traces of their minds live on: they are the Greeks. Their religion was different from the religion of the Byzantines, and their culture was different from the culture of the Byzantines. They were scientists, while these people [the Byzantines] are artisans who appropriated the books of the Greeks on account of the geographical proximity. Some of those books they ascribed to themselves while others they converted to their religion, except for those Greek books that were too famous and the philosophical works that were too well known; unable, then, to change the names [of the authors] of these books, they claimed that the Greeks were but one of the Byzantine tribes. They used their religious beliefs to boast superiority over the Jews, to display arrogance toward the Arabs, and to wax haughty over the Indians to the point that they actually claimed that our sages are followers of theirs, and that our philosophers have followed their example. And that is that.[14]

14 Al-Ǧāḥiẓ, *ar-Radd ʿalā n-Naṣārā*, in *Rasāʾil al-Ǧāḥiẓ*, ʿA. M. Hārūn (ed.), Cairo, al-Ḫānǧī, 1979, vol. 3, pp. 314–15. Translation of the first paragraph on the Christians and the Jews by Pellat, *Jāḥiẓ*, p. 87. Cf. further Pellat, "Nations civilisées," p. 71.

Here the identity of the Byzantines with the ancient Greeks, with some of the greatest names listed for rhetorical effect, is presented as a false claim put forth by the Byzantines for self-serving purposes. As Christians, however, they have no philosophers – and neither do Jews – with the unavoidable implication in al-Ǧāḥiẓ's time that Muslims do. The lengthy description of the irrational fanaticism of the Jews which precedes again could have only contemporary resonance for al-Ǧāḥiẓ; if Muslims wish to abandon reason and cling only to tradition, then they would be no better than the Jews.

Al-Ma'mūn's propaganda campaign found fertile ground among intellectuals who sought to capitalize on the implications of such an ideological stand. Apparently among the first to elaborate on such implications for the benefit of the cultivation of the translated sciences in ʿAbbāsid society was the famous philosopher, al-Kindī (d. shortly after 256/870). He devised a genealogy according to which Yūnān, the eponymous ancestor of the ancient Greeks (i.e., the Ionians), was presented as the brother of Qaḥṭān, the ancestor of the Arabs. In this way the sciences of the ancient Greeks could be presented as Arab in origin, and their cultivation in ʿAbbāsid society through the translation movement would be no more than a repatriation of these sciences among their original owners. This schema, as a matter of fact, is exactly parallel to the Zoroastrian Sasanian ideology discussed earlier in chapter 2.3; just as Sābūr and Chosroes I sought to bring together again the ancient Persian wisdom allegedly scattered through Alexander's conquests and retranslate it into a Persian language, so did the ʿAbbāsid Arab intellectuals try to "re-"translate into their language and cultivate the sciences which, though belonging to them genealogically, happened to be written in a different language for historical reasons.[15]

The anti-Byzantine and philhellenic rhetoric among intellectuals continued apace in the following century; it also intensifed, became more specific, and gained in sophistication. At the propaganda level, this would indicate that the promoters of the translation movement found it extremely beneficial to their cause; while at a broader level it is a sign of the wider acceptance of this version as historical fact in ʿAbbāsid culture.

15 Al-Kindī was criticized in a poem by a younger contemporary theologian, an-Nāšiʾ al-Akbar, who drew the negative implications of al-Kindī's attempt at genealogical reconstruction; he said, addressing al-Kindī, "Would you relate heresy to the religion of Muḥammad?" See the texts in al-Masʿūdī, *Murūǧ*, §666 Pellat, and the discussion by J. van Ess, *Frühe Muʿtazilitische Häresiographie*, Beirut/Wiesbaden, F. Steiner, 1971, p. 4.

Al-Mas'ūdī, the cultural historian par excellence of the fourth/tenth century, provides interesting documentation in this regard. For him, the Byzantines are different from the ancient Greeks not merely through hearsay but because of their specific genealogies. The Greeks are descendants of Yāfiṯ, the Byzantines of Sām; they are thus essentially different though the Byzantines imitate the Greeks:

> Both in their spoken and written language the Byzantines follow in the footsteps of the Greeks, though they never reached their level either in the essential purity or absolute eloquence of the language. The language of the Byzantines is inferior in comparison with that of the Greeks and its syntax, in the way in which it is expressed and in the customary manner of address, is weaker.[16]

Regardless, however, whether there is a real or supposed genealogical connection between the ancient Greeks and the Byzantines, the critical event that separates them, the decisive factor that makes them essentially different and renders the Byzantines *inferior*, is the advent of Christianity. Al-Mas'ūdī, again, is quite explicit about this:

> During the time of the ancient Greeks, and for a little while during the Byzantine [i.e., in this case, Roman] empire, the philosophical sciences kept on growing and developing, and scholars and philosophers were respected and honored. They developed their theories on natural science – on the body, the intellect, the soul – and on the quadrivium, i.e., on *arithmētikē*, the science of numbers, on *geōmetrikē*, the science of surfaces and geometry, on *astronomia*, the science of the stars, and on *mūsīkē*, the science of the harmonious composition of melodies. The sciences continued to be in great demand and intensely cultivated until the religion of Christianity appeared among the Byzantines; they then effaced the signs of philosophy, eliminated its traces, destroyed its paths, and they changed and corrupted what the ancient Greeks had set forth in clear expositions.[17]

16 Al-Mas'ūdī, *Murūǧ*, §664 Pellat.

17 Al-Mas'ūdī, *Murūǧ*, §741 Pellat. See the extensive discussion of the Muslim view of the Byzantines during these centuries by A. Miquel, *La géographie humaine du monde musulman jusqu'au milieu du 11e siècle*, Paris/La Haye, Mouton, 1975, vol. 2, pp. 368–70, and chapter 8, in particular pp. 466–70.

The significance of this attitude among Muslim intellectuals and what it indicates should not be misapprehended. Its intention is *not* to extol paganism at the expense of Christianity, an impossible stance for any Muslim; Christianity, after all, is a Book religion acknowledged as such in the Qur'ān, and Jesus a respected prophet, while the paganism and polytheism of the ancient Greeks are anathema. The intended referent is again Islam, or the different versions of it vying for supremacy in the third–fourth/ninth–tenth centuries. This attitude is indicative of the apparently unquestioned assumption that the Greek sciences, as transmitted through the translation movement, are a cultural good, because it is on the basis of this assumption that Christianity can be shown to have been an evil for the Byzantines. The moral is thus there for everybody to draw: were Muslims to reject the Greek sciences they would be no better than the Christian Byzantines; the superiority of Islam over Christianity in this context, therefore, is solely based on the Muslim acceptance of the fruits of the translation movement.

That this attitude was dominant and widespread in the fourth/tenth century, the last century of the translation movement, can be seen from numerous instances of its occurrence; the Byzantines are frequently reported as prohibiting philosophy and the sciences. Ibn-an-Nadīm in his *Fihrist* transmits from someone "trustworthy" that the Byzantines burned fifteen loads of books by Archimedes [*F* 266.19 = *GAS* V,121]. Elsewhere he offers a summary of a sympathetic version of the Julian romance. The Christian Byzantines are portrayed as initially prohibiting philosophy because "it is contrary to prophetic laws"; then Julian, under the influence of Themistius, the commentator of Aristotle's books, restores the study of philosophy which, however, is prohibited once again by the Christians after his death.[18]

This attitude found its widest currency, however, in the notorious but fictitious history of the transmission of Greek philosophy and medicine from Alexandria to Baghdad. This history appears, with significant variations, in a number of important authors, but it was on the basis of the account attributed to al-Fārābī that Meyerhof formulated his famous essay "From Alexandria to Baghdad" over sixty years ago.[19]

18 *F* 241.16–242.6; English translation by Rosenthal, *Classical Heritage*, pp. 45–7.

19 M. Meyerhof, "Von Alexandrien nach Bagdad. Ein Beitrag zur Geschichte des philosophischen und medizinischen Unterrichts bei den Arabern," *Sitzungsberichte der Berliner Akademie der Wissenschaften*, Philologisch-Historische Klasse, 1930, pp. 389–429. English translation of the text by al-Fārābī in Rosenthal, *Classical Heritage*, pp. 50–1. The

The version that can be considered closest to the original, however, is that preserved, independently of each other, by the autodidact Cairene physician, Ibn-Riḍwān (d. 460/1068), and by the personal physician of Saladin, Ibn-Ǧumayʿ (d. 594/1198). This version, in Ibn-Ǧumayʿ's words, runs as follows:

> [The history of medicine begins with a brief account of the development in antiquity from Asclepius to Galen.] After Galen, the community of the Christians emerged from and prevailed over the Greeks. The Christians considered it a fault to study intellectual matters and their kings cast away the care for medicine and failed to take care of its students. So its students ceased to commit themselves to the toilsome study of medicine and found reading Hippocrates' and Galen's works too tedious; thus, it fell into disorder and its condition worsened.
>
> Then came Oribasius, after the Christian kings' lack of interest in the instruction [of medicine] was firmly rooted. He intended to spread instruction among the masses by means of popularization, facilitation, and by limiting the material and the time required for study lest it perish and vanish. He compiled compendia in which he popularized the art for the masses and through which he facilitated its study for them. In that he was followed by Paul [of Aegina] and others after him up to the present time. Thus, books in the art became numerous in the form of compendia, abridgments, summaries, and the like, and Hippocrates' and Galen's works on medicine fell into oblivion.
>
> When none of the kings any longer felt the desire to promote the teaching [of medicine] and the people found Hippocrates' and Galen's works on it too tedious and tended to compendia and abridgments, the most prominent Alexandrian physicians, afraid that the art would vanish altogether, asked those kings to retain the teaching [of medicine] in Alexandria and [to

evidence presented by Meyerhof was analyzed critically by G. Strohmaier, "'Von Alexandrien nach Bagdad' – eine fiktive Schultradition," in J. Wiesner (ed.), *Aristoteles. Werk und Wirkung, Paul Moraux gewidmet*, vol. 2, Berlin, W. de Gruyter, 1987, pp. 380–9. G. Endress objected to the term "fictitious" for which he would substitute "one-sided": "The Defense of Reason: The Plea for Philosophy in the Religious Community," *Zeitschrift für Geschichte der Arabisch-Islamischen Wissenschaften*, 1990, vol. 6, pp. 16–17.

> allow] only twenty books on medicine to be read, sixteen from Galen's and four from Hippocrates' works. They granted that request, and the instruction [of medicine] continued in Alexandria until the days of ʿUmar ibn-ʿAbd-al-ʿAzīz when the supervisor of instruction converted to Islam at his hands and became his companion. This was before ʿUmar had become caliph.
>
> After he had become caliph, instruction was transferred to Antioch, Ḥarrān, and other places, and the teaching stood on shaky ground until al-Ma'mūn ʿAbd-Allāh ibn-Hārūn ar-Rashīd became caliph, who revived and spread it and favored excellent physicians. But for him, medicine and other disciplines of the ancients would have been effaced and obliterated just as medicine is obliterated now from the lands of the Greeks, which had been most distinguished in this field.
>
> As regards the twenty books to whose instruction the most prominent physicians restricted themselves, these are the following [there follows a list of Galen's and Hippocrates' works contained in the *Summaria Alexandrinorum*.][20]

The origin of the core element of this "history" is in all likelihood to be sought in an account of the genesis of the medical curriculum in late antiquity in Alexandria known as the *Summaria Alexandrinorum* (*Ǧawāmiʿ al-Iskandarāniyyīn*). The earliest exemplar of such an account, without the anti-Christian sentiments, is found in the work on medical conduct (*adab aṭ-ṭabīb)* by the ninth-century scholar from Edessa, Isḥāq ibn-ʿAlī ar-Ruhāwī. After mentioning that Galen wrote a separate book for all the principles of nature which a physician must know in order to practice medicine, he adds,

> When the learned physicians of Alexandria, in the course of their assemblies and gatherings of students of medicine, saw that the zeal of most of the young men of their time did not go so far as to induce them to study all of these books – and especially those which Galen composed – and wished to

20 H. Fähndrich (ed.), *Ibn Jumayʿ: Treatise to Ṣalāḥ ad-Dīn on the Revival of the Art of Medicine* [Abhandlungen für die Kunde des Morgenlandes XLVI,3], Wiesbaden, F. Steiner, 1983, pp. 18–19. For Ibn Ǧumayʿ's work in general see M. Meyerhof, "Sultan Saladin's Physician on the Transmission of Greek Medicine to the Arabs," *Bulletin of the History of Medicine*, 1945, vol. 18, pp. 169–78, and especially 177.

> facilitate the study of medicine for the students, they organized the books of Galen as sixteen books, abridged them as compendia in an effort to shorten and summarize them, and taught them in the *skholē* (σχολή), the place where they used to teach. Therefore he who claims to know the nature of the human body and how to treat it in health and illness must be informed about these books. He should know their arrangement and should read them with the aid of a learned professor. [Ar-Ruhāwī then goes on to list the sixteen books.][21]

It would appear that al-Ma'mūn's public relations managers took over such a core account and added the anti-Christian polemic and the final eulogy to him, as in Ibn-Ǧumayʿ's version. As a matter of fact, the version of the account as preserved in Ibn-Riḍwān has an even more elaborate final section in praise of al-Ma'mūn, one that makes precisely the point that the caliph and his partisans wished to convey by means of their anti-Byzantine but philhellenic policies:

> Al-Ma'mūn revived [the teaching of medicine] by favoring the most excellent of men. But for that, all the sciences of the ancients, including medicine, logic, and philosophy, would have been forgotten, <just as they are forgotten> today in the lands in which they were most specifically cultivated, I mean Rome, Athens, the Byzantine provinces, and in many other lands.[22]

This drives home the main point al-Ma'mūn's new anti-Byzantine ideology wishes to promote: the Islamic polity, under the leadership

21 Ar-Ruhāwī, *The Conduct of the Physician* [Facsimile of the unique Edirne ms. Selimiye 1658], Publications of the Institute for the History of Arabic-Islamic Science edited by F. Sezgin, Series C, vol. 18, Frankfurt am Main, 1985, pp. 193–4. To be used with caution is the English translation by M. Levey, *Medical Ethics of Medieval Islam, Transactions of the American Philosophical Society*, 1967, vol. 57, part 3, p. 84a. About the kind of instruction offered in the *skholē* see Ḥunayn's statement cited in chapter 1.1.

22 Ibn Riḍwān, *Al-Kitāb an-nāfiʿ fī kayfiyyat taʿlīm ṣināʿat aṭ-ṭibb*, K. as-Sāmarrā'ī (ed.), Baghdad, Maṭbaʿat Ǧāmiʿat Baġdād, 1986, pp. 107–8. The text at the top of p. 108 is probably to be emended to: *nusiyat <ka-mā nusiyat> al-yawma fī l-buldān*. . . . For the work in general see A.Z. Iskandar, "An Attempted Reconstruction of the Late Alexandrian Medical Curriculum," *Medical History*, 1976, vol. 20, pp. 235–58. Cf. further Ullmann, *Medizin*, p. 159.

of the caliph, is the true heir to ancient Greece and all the human sciences. Byzantium, the main political enemy of the Islamic empire, is culturally defunct; there now only remains to eliminate it politically as well.

It is interesting to note that in promoting such an ideology al-Ma'mūn was not really introducing a completely new direction but merely re-orienting the ideological attitudes espoused by the ʿAbbāsid ruling house since his great-grandfather al-Manṣūr. The latter had appropriated Zoroastrian imperial ideology which also portrayed the ʿAbbāsid caliphate as the heir to the ancient empires and the promoter, indeed, of the very same Greek sciences. The only difference is that the Iranian ideology viewed those sciences as originally Iranian and the Sasanian empire as the vehicle of their transmission, whereas al-Ma'mūn's re-orientation concentrates on ancient Greece and Byzantium. This shift removes from the picture the Iranians insofar as their territorial conquest was complete and ideological and religious cooptation nearly so, and functions to localize attention to the Byzantines and the Christians who are now presented both as the new enemy of and foil to Muslims, and as examples to be avoided of religious irrationality and obscurantism.

Al-Ma'mūn's ideological campaign in this regard proved successful. For example, Ṣāʿid al-Andalusī's perception of the translation movement in relation to the Byzantine empire is precisely what al-Ma'mūn's propaganda had intended to convey:

> The first among the Arabs who cultivated the sciences was the second caliph, Abū-Ǧaʿfar al-Manṣūr. He was – God have mercy on him – deeply attached to them and to their practitioners, being himself proficient in religious knowledge and playing a pioneering role in [promoting] philosophical knowledge and especially astrology.
>
> Then the caliphate devolved upon the seventh ʿAbbāsid caliph, al-Ma'mūn – the son of Hārūn ar-Rašīd, the son of al-Mahdī, the son of al-Manṣūr – who completed what his forefather al-Manṣūr had started. [There follows a long eulogy of the accomplishments of al-Ma'mūn and his promotion of all sciences, Greek and non-Greek alike.] As a result, the ʿAbbāsid state almost rivaled the Byzantine empire in its heyday and period of greatest unity.[23]

23 Ṣāʿid al-Andalusī, *Ṭabaqāt al-umam*, pp. 48–9.

Using the ancient Greeks, during the reign of al-Ma'mūn, to enhance the deficiencies of Byzantium and Christianity could only have been accomplished on the basis of a philhellenic atmosphere created by a pre-existing translation movement. This in turn generated a cultural attitude, in the centuries after al-Ma'mūn, which could easily regard as factual the tendentious "histories" of Greek philosophy and science in which the Christians are portrayed as having prohibited philosophy and medicine (and the sciences) because of their fear of reason, while the Muslims are pictured as champions of the truth. In this complex, al-Fārābī's version narrates the philosophy aspect of this tendentious history, and Ibn-Riḍwān (the Muslim) and Ibn-Ǧumayʿ (the Jew) the medical aspect.

With his policy of anti-Byzantinism as philhellenism al-Ma'mūn accomplished a number of objectives. He successfully managed a campaign against the Byzantines which depicted them as villainous because they were not only Christians but also unworthy – and usurping – successors of the ancient Greeks; he incorporated the translation movement into his policies and used it for new purposes; and he drew attention to reasoned discussion as the basis of religious policy, which, following Ardašīr's Testament, is to be in the hands of an intellectual elite. The last point gained further support from al-Ma'mūn's Aristotelian dream, which I will discuss next.

3. DOMESTIC POLICY AND THE TRANSLATION MOVEMENT: THE ARISTOTELIAN DREAM AND THE IDEOLOGY OF RATIONALISM

The new ideological orientation of al-Ma'mūn after his return to Baghdad involved taking control of the religious discussion in the capital and by extension in the Islamic world and fostering an intellectual elite that would conduct this discussion in acceptable ways. This was necessary both to maintain the image of the caliph as champion of Islam, strengthen his religious and hence political authority, and, as a most important corollary to the preceding, weaken the religious authority of leaders among the masses who might have "concealed leaderships," as the Testament of Ardašīr warned Sasanian emperors (see section 4.1 above). Hence his eventual imposition of the *miḥna* which necessarily promoted the method of disputation as the criterion of authority rather than blind adherence to traditional teachings, the sole claim to authority of those "concealed leaderships."

So much is clear also from al-Aḫbārī's "candid history," which reports the great change in al-Ma'mūn's policies: his turning to the Muʿtazilite doctrines of "Unity [of God] and the Promise of Reward and Threat of Punishment," and his sponsorship of intellectual gatherings and discussions where the dialectic method of argumentation reigned supreme. What al-Aḫbārī does *not* say is what almost everybody else insists on, al-Ma'mūn's sponsorship of the translation movement as the salient characteristic of his reign. Al-Aḫbārī's silence is certainly not to be misconstrued that such sponsorship did not exist but only that it was not salient, i.e., it was a subordinate part of the overall policy just described. Nevertheless, al-Aḫbārī's testimony has to be reconciled with the opposing view that highlights the sponsorship. The opposing view is most seriously put forward by an authority we could hardly impugn, Ibn-an-Nadīm in his *Fihrist*, and it is put forward in connection with a report that has been repeatedly mentioned, *ad satiatem* if not *ad nauseam*, al-Ma'mūn's notorious dream. Ibn-an-Nadīm introduces the section which he entitles, "Why there are so many books to be found on philosophy and the other ancient sciences," with the words, "One reason for this is al-Ma'mūn's dream," goes on to tell the dream, and concludes with the summary statement, "This dream was one of the firmest reasons for the translation of books [into Arabic through the sponsorship of al-Ma'mūn]."

Now we know that, as far as the translations are concerned, this is not true; al-Ma'mūn was simply following a well-established practice in ʿAbbāsid circles, a practice set forth in the preceding pages and documented most incontrovertibly by the numerous details provided, of all places, in the very *Fihrist* itself. We also know, however, that Ibn-an-Nadīm was a reliable and conscientious scholar (even if, perhaps, careless with regard to internal consistency). In his evaluation of the significance of al-Ma'mūn's dream, therefore, he must have been simply following the assessment of his source. In trying to reconcile al-Aḫbārī's realpolitik views of al-Ma'mūn's caliphate and those of Ibn-an-Nadīm's sources we have to look closely and critically at the dream.

Dreams must be taken seriously, and not only in the sense intended by the master oneirocritic, Artemidorus, or his modern-day apprentice, Freud. Their emotive content makes them preferred means for the communication and diffusion of attitudes, ideas, positions – indeed for propaganda – in most societies, and certainly in Greek and Arab. There is no need to elaborate on the point other than to give one relevant example from early ʿAbbāsid history. Al-Manṣūr's mother, Sallāma, is reported as having had the following dream: "When I was pregnant with Abū-Ǧaʿfar [i.e., al-Manṣūr], I saw in my dream a lion coming out in front of me. It sat on its haunches [with its head up] and roared, beating [the ground] with its tail. Lions from all directions began to come out to it, and as each one of them would come up to it, it prostrated itself in front of it." Certainly this is a most appropriate dream for a caliph who had to fight against three pretenders from his own family – the other lions from the house of the Prophet – to maintain his caliphal throne, and its social function and the reasons for its circulation need no special comment.[24] The question is what was behind the circulation of al-Ma'mūn's dream.

The dream is reported in two versions, the comparison of which throws light on the question and somewhat justifies, at some price, the redundance in citing both in full. I have numbered the sentences of the text of the dream for easy reference.

I. Version of ʿAbdallāh ibn-Ṭāhir.[25]

(1) ʿAbdallāh ibn-Ṭāhir relates that (2) al-Ma'mūn said, "I saw in my dream a man (4) seated in the assembly of the philosophers,[26] (6) and said to him, 'Who are you?' He replied, 'Aristotle the philosopher.' (9) I said, 'O philosopher, what is the best speech?' He replied, 'Whatever is correct according to personal judgment.' (10) I said, 'Then what?' He replied, 'Whatever the person who hears it finds to be good.' (11) I said, 'Then what?' He replied, 'That about whose consequences one would have no fears.' (12) I said, 'Then what?' He replied, 'Everything else is the same as a donkey's bray.'" (13) Al-Ma'mūn said, "Had Aristotle been alive, he would not have added anything else to what he said here, since in [this statement] he collected [everything that needed to be said] and refrained [from saying anything superfluous]."

24 Al-Masʿūdī, *Murūǧ*, §2371 Pellat. Nöldeke, who reports the dream, compares the dream of Pericles' mother in Herodotus vi.131: *Sketches from Eastern History*, 1892, reprinted 1963, p. 116.

25 Preserved in Ibn-Nubāta, *Sarḥ al-ʿuyūn fī šarḥ risālat Ibn Zaydūn*, M. Abū-l-Faḍl Ibrāhīm (ed.), Cairo, Dār al-Fikr al-ʿArabī, 1964, p. 213.

26 Reading *al-ḥukamāʾ* for *al-ḥkāʾ* in the text.

II. Version of Yaḥyā b. ʿAdī[27]

(2) Al-Ma'mūn dreamed that he saw a man (3) of reddish-white complexion with a high forehead, bushy eyebrows, bald head, dark blue eyes and handsome features, (4) sitting on his chair. (5) Al-Ma'mūn said: "I saw in my dream that I was standing in front of him, filled with awe. (6) I asked, 'Who are you?' He replied: 'I am Aristotle.' (7) I was delighted to be with him (8) and asked, 'O philosopher, may I ask you [some questions]?' He replied, 'Ask.' (9) I said: 'What is the good?' He replied: 'Whatever is good according to intellect.' (10) I asked: 'Then what?' He replied: 'Whatever is good according to religious law.' (11) I asked: 'Then what?' He replied: 'Whatever is good in the opinion of the masses.'[28] (12) I asked: 'Then what?' And he replied: 'Then there is no more "then".'"

According to another tradition:

(14) "I [i.e., al-Ma'mūn] said, '[Tell] me more.' Aristotle replied, 'He who gives you sincere counsel[29] about gold, consider him to be like gold. It is your duty to declare the oneness of God'."

The dream is transmitted in two traditions independent of each other. The first (I), and apparently original one, goes back to and is reported on the authority of ʿAbdallāh ibn-Ṭāhir, whose father was largely responsible for al-Ma'mūn's victory over his brother al-Amīn during the civil war between the brothers, as well as for the execution of al-Amīn. Ṭāhir had served al-Ma'mūn as governor both in Ḫurāsān and Baghdad, offices in which he was succeeded, in subsequent generations, by his son ʿAbdallāh and his descendants. The family of Ṭāhir, Arabized Persians, played a highly significant role in early ʿAbbāsid history both in furthering and executing the policies of those members of the ʿAbbāsid house who, in historical hindsight, proved victorious, and in creating a cultural and ideological climate that would favor those policies. Their cultural

27 In *F* 243.3–8, copied by Q 29.8–15; translation by Rosenthal, *Classical Heritage*, pp. 48–9, adopted with modifications. For the parallel version in IAU see below, note 33.

28 This section (12) is missing in Q from Lippert's edition, apparently due to a homoeoteleuton in the transmission of the manuscript tradition.

29 The version of Q in Lippert's edition reads *man yaṣḥabka* for *man naṣaḥaka* in *F*.

priorities and activities, well described by Bosworth,[30] should be seen in this light. Thus, ʿAbdallāh ibn-Ṭāhir's account of the dream becomes intelligible in terms of the support it lends to al-Ma'mūn's religious and ideological agenda. The responses that Aristotle gives in ʿAbdallāh's version tally perfectly with al-Ma'mūn's pro-Muʿtazilite stand and his promotion of caliphal authority at the expense of religious law. Aristotle advocates the use of personal judgment (*ra'y*) as the ultimate criterion for what has to be seen, in context, as the official and policy pronouncements of the caliph ("the best speech"). In the legal and religious discourse of the time, the relative position of *ra'y* in regard to the very text of the Qur'ān and Prophetic precedent (*sunna*) in establishing legal authority was at the center of the debate. Conceding the primacy of *ra'y* gave unchecked powers to the person delivering the judgment, i.e., the judge (*qāḍī*) or, in this case, the caliph, while acknowledging the transmitted texts of the Qur'ān and the *sunna* transferred the power to the religious elite who were the keepers and hence the interpreters of the canonical texts. Al-Ma'mūn, whose reign is marked with the attempt to consolidate and centralize power in the person of the caliph, naturally championed the former cause. The *miḥna*, or inquisition, was an extension of this policy.

This policy orientation of al-Ma'mūn provides the reason behind the invention of the dream. The dream itself was in all probability fabricated within circles closest to the caliph, possibly the Ṭāhirids themselves. Another possible source for the dream would have been al-Ma'mūn's inquisition judge, his *qāḍī* during the *miḥna*, Aḥmad ibn-Abī-Du'ād. Al-Bayhaqī reports on his authority another dream of al-Ma'mūn, according to which the caliph, who is initially depicted as not believing in veridical dreams on rational grounds, is forced to concede the point when one of his dreams turns out to be true.[31] As a matter of fact, the dream reported by Ibn-Abī-Du'ād, by establishing the veracity of al-Ma'mūn's dreams through a relatively innocuous – and possibly true – incident, could very well have paved the way for the easier acceptance of the Aristotle dream. Whoever

30 C.E. Bosworth, "The Ṭāhirids and Arabic Culture," *Journal of Semitic Studies*, 1969, vol. 14, pp. 45–79.

31 Al-Bayhaqī, *Al-Maḥāsin wa-l-masāwi'*, F. Schwally (ed.), Giessen, 1902, pp. 343–4; see the translation of the dream by T. Fahd "The Dream in Medieval Islamic Society," in G.E. von Grunebaum and R. Caillois (eds), *The Dream and Human Societies*, Berkeley, University of California Press, 1966, pp. 354–5.

the author of this particular dream may be, however, the fact remains that dreams were used frequently by the circles around al-Ma'mūn for the purposes of propaganda.

In its genesis, therefore, the Aristotle dream was totally unrelated to the translation movement. This is also attested to by the consideration that a policy for which quasi-divine sanction is sought through the public dissemination of a dream must have been in response to a real opposition to the policy. Had the dream been fabricated by the proponents of the translation movement it would imply that in al-Ma'mūn's lifetime there was opposition to this activity; but we hear nothing to this effect in the period concerned. What *was* contested at that time, especially among legal circles, was the relative weight to be granted to elements that were to constitute the pillars of Islam: individual opinion vs. the *sunna* (communal or Prophetic practice) vs. consensus (of the community of scholars).

Seen from this angle, the presence of Aristotle in the dream, or the choice of his person as the authority on whose declaration of principles al-Ma'mūn's policies are to be based, attests to the high regard, if the dream were to have the effect for which it was fabricated, with which he was viewed in intellectual circles in Baghdad at the time of al-Ma'mūn. Thus, rather than providing the incentive for full-scale translation activity from the Greek, as Ibn-an-Nadīm (or his source, Yaḥyā ibn-ʿAdī) and all his followers would have it, the dream signals to the contrary the effect which the translation movement, begun long before al-Ma'mūn's time, had on shaping intellectual attitudes by then. The dream is the social result, not the cause of the translation movement.

This is not to be wondered at, for Aristotle was not the only ancient figure that rose to such prominence and, more significantly, gained such widespread acceptance as an authority figure in the first century of ʿAbbāsid rule. The following report, concerning al-Ma'mūn himself, is indicative of the extent to which ancient personalities had penetrated the discourse of the educated in his circle. In the course of an extensive meal al-Ma'mūn was having in the company of a number of scholars, theologians, and jurists (the very people al-Aḫbārī says al-Ma'mūn patronized), the caliph would remark with precision on the medical and dietary properties of each one of the more than three hundred dishes that were served. When the table was cleared, Yaḥyā ibn-Akṯam (d. 242/856), the judge of Baṣra and later of Baghdad, as well as one of al-Ma'mūn's viziers, addressed the caliph as follows:

> O Commander of the Faithful! If we take up medicine as our subject, you are Galen incarnate in your familiarity with it; if astrology, you are Hermes [Trismegistos] in your calculations; or if religious knowledge, you are ʿAlī ibn-Abī-Ṭālib (God's prayers upon him) in mastering it; or if generosity is mentioned, you are better than Ḥātim in your liberality; or if we mention true speech, you are Abū-Ḏarr in the truth of your tongue; or if nobility, you are Kaʿb ibn-Māma in preferring others over yourself, and if loyalty, you are as-Samaw'al ibn-ʿAdiyā' in your loyalty.[32]

It is a measure of the acceptance of Greek authorities in early ʿAbbāsid society that non-Arab personalities, both historical, such as Galen, and legendary, such as Hermes Trismegistos, should be mentioned in the same breath and at the same level as ʿAlī ibn-Abī-Ṭālib and other Arab heroes and luminaries famous for the qualities enumerated. Al-Ma'mūn's dream simply adds the name of Aristotle to the list, whom the caliph follows in his wisdom. Just as there arose an apologetic and tendentious historiography to justify al-Ma'mūn's revolt against al-Amīn by rewriting Hārūn's Mecca Protocol of 802 for succession (cf. section 4.1 above), so also the original version of al-Ma'mūn's Aristotle dream (version I) was concocted to justify al-Ma'mūn's rationalistic and pro-Muʿtazilī policy.

The second version of the dream (II) is due to Yaḥyā ibn-ʿAdī, the student of al-Fārābī and Abū-Bišr Mattā and head of the Baghdad Aristotelians in the mid-tenth century. It survives in two slightly divergent recensions, one in the *Fihrist*, cited above, and the other in Ibn-Abī-Uṣaybiʿa, who helps us identify both his own and, indirectly, Ibn-an-Nadīm's source: "I am transmitting from [a report in] the hand of al-Ḥasan ibn-al-ʿAbbās, known as aṣ-Ṣanādīqī (God have mercy on him), who said: Abū-Sulaymān [as-Siǧistānī] said: I heard Yaḥyā ibn-ʿAdī say the following . . . [there follows the dream]."[33] Ibn-an-Nadīm, the author of the *Fihrist*, received a

32 Quoted by Ṭayfūr, *Kitāb Baġdād*, H. Keller (ed.), f. 23b. The same report, without the introduction explaining the occasion, is also found in al-Bayhaqī's *al-Maḥāsin wa-l-masāwi'*, p. 413. The last sentence about loyalty is found only in al-Bayhaqī.

33 IAU I,186.28ff., copied in abbreviated fashion by Ibn-Faḍlallāh al-ʿUmarī, *Masālik al-abṣār fī mamālik al-amṣār*, MS Aya Sofya 3422, f. 100v; printed in facsimile, as *Routes toward Insight into the Capital Empires*, F. Sezgin, general ed., Publications of the Institute for the History of Arabic-Islamic Science, Series C, vol. 46,9, Frankfurt am Main, 1988, p. 220. The recension in IAU has slightly different wording than that in *F*, though the crucial section, the questions and answers between al-Ma'mūn and Aristotle, is almost verbatim identical.

significant amount of his information about Greek works in Arabic from Yaḥyā, whom he knew personally and to whose autograph bibliographical notes he had access. The recension of the account about the dream that he provides would appear to be the original one as it is the more detailed; it came in all probability from a note by Yaḥyā, although Ibn-an-Nadīm does not expressly say so. The other recension of Yaḥyā's note is due to a copy made of it by Yaḥyā's student Abū-Sulaymān as-Siǧistānī, whose text was copied by aṣ-Ṣanādīqī, the immediate source of Ibn-Abī-Uṣaybiʿa.

From all the available evidence, it would appear that it was Yaḥyā ibn-ʿAdī who first used the report about al-Ma'mūn's Aristotle dream in order to explain the translation activity. His motivation was at least twofold: to claim caliphal authority for the corpus of translations from the Greek, and to grant primacy, among all ancient thinkers, to Aristotle. The reasons behind the former was the need to provide, also for the translated literature, a narrative of canonization in consonance with the intellectual climate of his time. By the middle of the fourh/tenth century when Yaḥyā was writing, most of the Islamic sciences had come into their own and were beginning to take their canonical form: they each had their founders, tradition, and a corpus of canonical writings. To give but two pertinent examples: the disarray that had reigned in the doctrinally acceptable readings of the Qur'ān (i.e., vocalization and provision of diacritical points in the skeletal text of the words) was finally put in order by the canonization of different sets of readings through the efforts of the Baghdadi scholar Ibn-Muǧāhid (d. 324/936). Ibn-Muǧāhid was assisted in his task by the authorities, who thus continued the process, initiated by al-Ma'mūn himself, of state intervention in the formation of religious doctrine. A similar disarray and unchecked growth in the acceptable traditions of the Prophet were controlled through the compilation of the sound (*ṣaḥīḥ*) collections by al-Buḫārī (d. 256/870) and Muslim (d. 261/875), which led, in the following generation, to the methodological rigor brought to the science of *ḥadīṯ* criticism by the work of Ibn-Abī-Ḥātim ar-Rāzī (d. 327/938).[34]

In this context, al-Ma'mūn's dream lent itself readily to a similar canonization of the translated corpus of ancient sciences. A comparison between the version of al-Ma'mūn's dream as originally told by

34 For a detailed analysis of Ibn-Abī-Ḥātim's methods see E.N. Dickinson, *The Development of Early Muslim* Hadīth *Criticism: The* Taqdima *of Ibn Abī Ḥātim al-Rāzī (d. 327/938)*, unpublished Ph.D. dissertation, Yale University, 1992.

ʿAbdallāh ibn-Ṭāhir (Version I) and its variant formulation by Yaḥyā shows clearly the concerns of the tenth century Baghdadi philosophers. The core of the dream is the exchange of questions and answers between Aristotle and al-Ma'mūn and it is there that the most significant changes take place. In the original version, the caliph's question is a practical one: "What is the best speech?" i.e., the best thing to say in a political and religious sense with regard to policy. Similarly, all the answers are pragmatic and concrete: the first answer establishes, as already discussed, the personal judgment (*ra'y*) of an individual, i.e. of the caliph, as the criterion; the second answer posits as measure the very relative concept of the audience to which the speech is addressed; while the third answer is completely contextual and opportunistic – it is the end, the desired outcome, that determines the 'goodness' of the speech. Yaḥyā's version is exactly the opposite; it is completely non-political and it raises the question and the answers to an abstract philosophical level: the question is not about a specific good thing but about the [absolute] good, while the answers establish universal concepts as the criteria: a human faculty, i.e., the intellect, religious law, and the masses.

The significance of the seemingly innocuous subsitution of *ra'y* (personal judgment) by *ʿaql* (intellect) cannot be overestimated. In one master stroke it establishes the absolute primacy of reason – and hence, of philosophy, the discipline that studies it – in all matters over religious authorities (the law, *šarīʿa)* as well as political considerations (the masses). Just as logic is superior to grammar in that it is universal and supralingual – so Abū-Bišr Mattā's and Yaḥyā's argument in defense of logic ran – so also is philosophy, the use of reason, superior to religion in that it is universal and supranational (since each nation has its own religion). With his version of al-Ma'mūn's dream, therefore, Yaḥyā established the subject matter of philosophy as a field of study, the translated books of the ancients as the canonical books in the field, Aristotle as the most significant predecessor, and caliphal authorization as the sanction for its study.

Aristotle for Yaḥyā had a different signification than he did for al-Ma'mūn or his propagandizer, ʿAbdallāh ibn-Ṭāhir. Whereas to the non-specialist but educated Arabic audience for whom ʿAbdallāh's version of the dream was intended Aristotle simply signified a highly respectable authority in intellectual or philosophical matters of great antiquity – similar to Galen in medicine and Hermes Trismegistos in practical mathematics, as we saw above – to Yaḥyā he signified the founder of the Peripatos and the peripatetic tradition in philosophy, the first ancestor of the school whose head at the very moment Yaḥyā was. By the middle of the tenth century there were various philosophical currents circulating in Baghdad: the Platonizing ideas of the respectable physician ar-Rāzī (Rhazes, d. 925), and the Athenian Neoplatonic tradition of al-Kindī and his successors; associated with the latter was the astral theology, heavily influenced by Hermetism, of the Ṣābi'ans of Ḥarrān represented in Baghdad by the descendants of Ṯābit ibn-Qurra; and at an even lower level was the magical and alchemical thought-world of the writings in the Ǧābirian cycle and their Greek predecessors, representing the earliest stages of the translation activity and its heritage in Arabic. All these had claims to being representatives of the ancient sciences and are to be seen as essentially competing for a position at center stage in the intellectual world of tenth-century Baghdad. Very much like the competing intellectual and political trends vying for acceptance and legitimization through dreams as mentioned above, Yaḥyā could claim the same for his brand of Aristotelianism through the expedient of al-Ma'mūn's dream. As it turned out, the work that he and his predecessor al-Fārābī did, by capturing the imagination (and more significantly, philosophical allegiance) of the great Avicenna, did ensure the survival, and indeed victory, of Aristotelianism in Arabic philosophy. Finally, the claims of Yaḥyā and his school about the intellect were not mere window dressing. They, and all the intellectuals involved with the translation activity, did believe in the primacy of reason. We have significant testimony to this effect from numerous inter-faith philosophical debates and correspondence of the period.[35]

35 For a general survey of the subject see Endress "The Defense of Reason"; for examples see the correspondence among Muslims, Jews, and Christians (including Yaḥyā ibn-ʿAdī) in K. Samir and P. Nwyia, *Une correspondance islamo-chrétienne*, and S. Pines, "A Tenth Century Philosophical Correspondence," *Proceedings of the American Academy for Jewish Research*, 1955, vol. 24, pp. 103–36.

Part II

TRANSLATION AND SOCIETY

5

TRANSLATION IN THE SERVICE OF APPLIED AND THEORETICAL KNOWLEDGE

1. INTRODUCTION

In Part I attention was devoted to analyzing such political and social configurations of early ʿAbbāsid society as found expression in ideologies that made the translation movement a necessary component. Specifically it has been argued that the ʿAbbāsid revolution, the civil war between al-Amīn and al-Maʾmūn, and the religio-political discourse during this initial period of the empire created needs for the ʿAbbāsid dynasty and the ruling elites that could be answered also through the adoption and promotion of a far-flung translation movement. These needs were certainly not only ideological and public relations oriented; they have, however, been given pride of place here because I consider them paramount insofar as they derive from the effort of rulers, any rulers, to stay in power – and the ʿAbbāsids were no exception – and insofar as they imparted the initial impetus for the adoption of translation as imperial policy. It therefore seemed obvious to investigate the extent to which the transformation of pre-ʿAbbāsid translation activities into a translation movement was occasioned by imperial power politics.

This does not mean to say, however, that factors other than ideological were not operative, especially when one considers the remarkable longevity of the translation movement. These factors were related to the demand for applied knowledge in the rapidly evolving social climate of Baghdad and to the demand for theoretical knowledge by the scientific and philosophical tradition in the process of formation. After al-Manṣūr's adoption, dictated by political exigencies, of a Sasanian imperial policy and its attendant culture of translation, such demands proved equally supportive, and for a longer period of time, of an extensive translation movement. Initially, they involved the cultivation of the applied sciences that accompanied Sasanian policies, primarily astrology and its related fields of astronomy and mathematics.[1] Agriculture may also be classed with this group, if we are to judge by the known translations of Greek works from Pahlavi into Arabic. The carriers of the Sasanian translation culture in the early ʿAbbāsid court, foremost among whom were the Barmakids and the Nawbaḫts, were instrumental in expanding the occasional pre-ʿAbbāsid translation activities from Pahlavi into Arabic and directing them into these areas of applied science. Eventually, however, when the scientists working in Baghdad reached a critical mass, they generated for themselves theoretical concerns which, given the continued support of the ruling elite and the intellectual fermentation in the capital, could be addressed by the further expansion of the translation movement to include the philosophical sciences.

2. THE DEMAND FOR ASTROLOGY

By all accounts, astrology was the field for which there was the most practical need, and indeed the one which stood at the center of al-Manṣūr's imperial ideology. Other than the pre-ʿAbbāsid translations noted in chapter 1.3, the advent of the regime saw the manifold increase of translations of astrological treatises. These were initially made from the Pahlavi, but gradually their Greek originals were sought out and translated.

It was not only the practical need for astrological history, as discussed in chapter 2, or horoscopy and the other parts of astrology that made it predominant in the concerns of the first scholars in the ʿAbbāsid court. Alongside – or rather because of – the practical needs served by astrological history and horoscopy, astrology was viewed, in the eyes of scholars, as the "mistress of all sciences."[2] This scholarly attitude toward astrology was adopted by the ruling elite, and astrology saw an unprecedented cultivation during the first ʿAbbāsid century.

1 See Endress, *GAP* II,434, who cites, in support of this point, the Sasanian material preserved in Arabic translation in a work falsely ascribed to al-Ǧāḥiẓ, *Kitāb at-Tāǧ*, A. Zakī (ed.), Cairo, al-Maṭbaʿa al-Amīriyya, 1914, p. 25. In this work, physicians, state secretaries, and astrologers are listed as belonging to the same high rank in the state hierarchy. These professions are discussed below in the different sections of this chapter.

2 Theophilus of Edessa (d. 785) court astrologer of al-Mahdī, called astrology πάσης 'επιστήμης δέσποινα, cited by Ullmann, *Geheimwissenschaften*, p. 277, note 5.

The Pahlavi intermediacy in the transmission of these works was primary and decisive. Already before the ʿAbbāsid revolution we have information about translations of astrological texts from Persian into Arabic. The purpose of such translations was to ensure that, in the new political situation in which Persians lived under Arab rule and increasingly spoke Arabic, "this science," i.e., astrology, "should not fall into desuetude and its traces not be wiped away," as stated in "Zoroaster's" *Book of Nativities* which was translated into Arabic around 750 (see chapter 2.3). We have a report about an earlier translation, in all probability also from Persian, of an astrological text ascribed to Hermes, executed in 125/743.[3] These pre-ʿAbbāsid translations must be viewed as a continuation in Islamic times of Sasanian practices by Persian Zoroastrian groups with revivalist agenda like those of Sunbāḏ mentioned in "Zoroaster's" *Book of Nativities* (see chapter 2.5); the difference from those after the coming to power of the ʿAbbāsids is that the latter were made under caliphal patronage as part of imperial policy. The *Paranatellonta* of Teucer (Teukros) was translated into Pahlavi during the reign of Chosroes I Anūširwān around 540 AD, and then into Arabic before the middle of the ninth century, while the *Pentateuch* by Dorotheus (*K. al-Ḫamsa)* was translated by ʿUmar ibn-Farruḫān aṭ-Ṭabarī (d. 200/816) from a fifth-century Pahlavi redaction of a third-century Pahlavi translation.[4] So great was the demand for astrological material that the Pahlavi sources were soon depleted and recourse was had to the Greek. This same translator of Dorotheus from the Pahlavi, ʿUmar ibn-Farruḫān, not knowing Greek, commissioned this time al-Biṭrīq to translate into Arabic from the Greek the major astrological textbook of antiquity, Ptolemy's *Tetrabiblos*. The *Tetrabiblos* soon dominated astrological writing in Arabic, perhaps because of Ptolemy's fame also in astronomy and musical theory, and was translated for a second time by Ibrāhīm ibn-aṣ-Ṣalt, revised by Ḥunayn, and repeatedly commented upon.[5] Accordingly we witness in the earliest period of the ʿAbbāsid dynasty, from al-Manṣūr to al-Maʾmūn, the brilliant careers of some of the most famous astrologers of all time, Māšāʾallāh, Abū-Sahl ibn-Nawbaḫt, and Abū-Maʿšar, who, in addition to their deep involvement in the translation movement, were also responsible for the composition of independent

3 For details see *GAS* VII,50–4; Ullmann, *Geheimwissenschaften*, p. 290.
4 For the transmission details of these works see Ullmann, *Geheimwissenschaften*, pp. 279–80.
5 Ullmann, *Geheimwissenschaften*, pp. 282–3.

treatises and established astrology as a science in the nascent Islamic civilization. It is an indication of the profound mark left by their work on social attitudes, and of the value that was consequently attached to astrology by the ruling elite which adopted this translation culture, that a high standing military and political leader such as Ṭāhir ibn-al-Ḥusayn (d. 207/823), al-Ma'mūn's general and the founder of the Ṭāhirid dynasty, commissioned the translation from the Greek even of Aratus's *Phaenomena*.[6] With the demand unabated, there eventually developed an extensive astrological literature in Arabic of pseudepigraphic and anonymous works.[7]

The pattern that was set by astrology was to be repeated, in general terms, with all the other translated sciences. Political considerations, ideological or theoretical orientations, or practical need would initially occasion translations, their study and use would result in original Arabic compositions in that particular field, and the development of research on the particular subject in this way would further generate a need both for more accurate translations of texts already available and for translations of new texts. We are still a long way from being in a position to write the history of the development of each one of the scientific disciplines throughout the period of the translation movement; there are many texts that have yet to be edited, translated, and studied in all disciplines, and far too little research has been conducted on the philological details of the process of transmission and the gradual development of a technical vocabulary in each field. It is such details which we hope will eventually lead us, in the absence of any other evidence, to a correct understanding of the historical evolution of the disciplines.

3. THE NEEDS OF PROFESSIONAL EDUCATION: ADMINISTRATIVE SECRETARIES (*KUTTĀB*), INHERITANCE LAWYERS, ENGINEERS, ECONOMISTS

Other than astrology, which appears to have been of special importance in the earliest stages of the constitution of the ʿAbbāsid state, another major social need, or factor, that gave an impetus to the translation movement was the requirement for the education of the

6 Ullmann, *Geheimwissenschaften*, p. 278.
7 Ullmann, *Geheimwissenschaften*, pp. 286ff.

secretarial class that was to administer the empire just inherited by the ʿAbbāsids. That this class was to be educated, as far as secular training is concerned, along Sasanian models, was a foregone conclusion, given the orientation of the ʿAbbāsid rulers and the major administrators, like the Barmakids, whom they appointed as chiefs of the administration.

The subjects that the secretaries had to master in order to perform their functions had to do with practical matters: accounting, surveying, engineering, and time-keeping, for example, and it is in connection with these needs that the mathematical sciences – arithmetic, geometry, trigonometry, and astronomy – became the focus of the earliest translation activity. The best attestation to the practical needs for the education of the secretarial class and its Sasanian background is provided by the scholar who wrote the book, so to speak, on the subject, Ibn-Qutayba (d. 276/889): he composed his *Education of the Secretaries* (*Adab al-kātib*), about a century after the translation movement had begun, in support of proper philological training for the secretaries and possibly as a corrective against excessive infatuation with the foreign sciences. In the justly famous introduction, much commented upon by medieval scholars, he listed the subjects that the aspirant to a secretarial position must master:

> In addition to my works [which provide linguistic, literary, and religious training], it is indispensable for [the secretary] to study geometrical figures for the measurement of land in order that he can recognize a right, an acute, and an obtuse triangle and the heights of triangles, the different sorts of quadrangles, arcs and other circular figures, and perpendicular lines, and in order that he can test his knowledge in practice on the land and not on the [survey-]registers, *for theoretical knowledge is nothing like practical experience.*
>
> The Persians [i.e., the Sasanians] used to say that he who does not know the following would be deficient in his formation as state secretary: He who does not know the principles of irrigation [*iǧrāʾ al-miyāh*], opening access-canals to waterways and stopping breaches; [measuring] the varying length of days, the revolution of the sun, the rising-points [on the horizon] of stars, and the phases of the moon and its influence; [assessing] the standards of measure; surveying in terms of triangles, quadrangles, and polygons of various angles; constructing arched stone bridges, other kinds of bridges, sweeps with buckets, and noria waterwheels on waterways; the nature of the

instruments used by artisans and craftsmen; and the details of accounting.[8]

It is important to note that Ibn-Qutayba mentions here, in addition to the very specific kinds of knowledge in all the major mathematical sciences that a secretary ought to acquire, that it is necessary for him also to have the ability to apply this knowledge. This is a very significant statement which goes far in establishing that in the cultivation of the theoretical sciences, a significant amount of attention was directed to their application. Naturally not all sciences were equally applicable at all historical periods, and caution should be exercised to avoid generalizations. Nevertheless, such a statement by Ibn-Qutayba, who was writing at the very time when the Graeco-Arabic translation movement was in full force, clearly compels us to see correspondences between the translation and cultivation of the sciences at a theoretical level and the application of some of them by those classes who were professionally engaged in them. In this light, the translation of mathematical works to be discussed below gains in social relevance.

Pride of place in Ibn-Qutayba's enumeration of useful disciplines to be mastered by the prospective secretary is occupied by geometry. According to some acounts mentioned in Part I (chapter 2.2), Euclid's *Elements* was translated for the first time during the reign of al-Manṣūr, though we hear only of the two versions of al-Ḥaǧǧāǧ ibn-Maṭar done under Hārūn and al-Ma'mūn respectively. However this issue is ultimately resolved, and it will be decided on the basis of philological evidence, the practical usefulness of geometry for surveying, engineering, and irrigation works is clearly brought out by Ibn-Qutayba. In this connection it is relevant to notice that in the Arabic of the time, the word *muhandis*, an Arabic participial form from a word borrowed from Persian, meant both geometer and engineer. In the dictionary of technical terms for all the sciences compiled by al-Ḫwārizmī a century after Ibn-Qutayba, a geometer/engineer (*muhandis)* is defined, on the authority of none other than al-Ḫalīl, the father of Arabic lexicography, as someone who measures and

8 Ibn-Qutayba, *Adab al-kātib*, M. Grünert (ed.), Leiden, E.J. Brill, 1900, pp. 10–11, emphasis added; cf. the French translation by G. Lecomte, "L'introduction du *Kitāb adab al-kātib* d'Ibn Qutayba," in *Mélanges Louis Massignon*, Damascus, Institut Français de Damas, 1957, vol. 3, p. 60.

prepares plans (*yuqaddiru*) for the course of irrigation canals and the areas in which they are to be dug.[9]

Another mathematical science that developed very early and aimed to address practical needs was algebra. For its application to engineering and irrigation problems, it was useful to the secretaries very much like geometry. During early ʿAbbāsid times, however, Islamic law was also developing rapidly and algebra became an essential tool for working out all the intricate details of inheritance laws. Both of these applications are mentioned by Muḥammad ibn-Mūsā al-Ḫwārizmī himself in the introduction to his *Algebra*. Al-Ma'mūn, he says,

> encouraged me to compose a compendious work on algebra, confining it to the fine and important parts of its calculations, such as people constantly require in cases of inheritance, legacies, partition, law-suits, and trade, and in all their dealings with one another where surveying, the digging of canals, geometrical computation, and other objects of various sorts and kinds are concerned.[10]

The book is so structured that after an introductory section which is purely mathematical, the rest of the text is devoted to solving various problems of trade transactions, surveying, legacies, marriages, and slave emancipations, with specific representative cases discussed in each area.

Closely related to the mathematial sciences and astrology (though the responsibility of the court astrologer was outside the competence of the secretaries) was the development of mathematical astronomy. In this case there are significant pre-ʿAbbāsid translation activities, from both Pahlavi and Sanskrit this time, and of composition of works of astronomical tables and other useful astronomical and related literature, the so-called *zīǧ* (Arabic plural of the Persian word: *zīǧāt*), most notably the *Zīǧ aš-Šāh*, as it survived from the time of Chosroes I Anūširwān (r. 531–78) and Yazdiǧird III (r. 632–51), the *Zīǧ al-Arkand* from 735, and the *Zīǧ al-Harqan* from 742.[11] But the activity became officially adopted by the ʿAbbāsid state when an embassy arrived from Sind to Baghdad and the court of

9 Al-Ḫwārizmī, *Mafātīḥ al-ʿulūm*, G. van Vloten (ed.), Leiden, E.J. Brill, 1895, p. 202.9.

10 F. Rosen, *Algebra of Mohammed ben Musa*, London, Oriental Translation Fund, 1831; reprinted Hildesheim, Olms, 1986, p. 2 (text), p. 3 (translation, here slightly adapted).

11 D. Pingree, "The Greek Influence on Early Islamic Mathematical Astronomy," p. 37; cf. *GAS* VI,115, 120, and V,218.

al-Manṣūr in 154/771 or 156/773. The sources do not inform us about the purpose of this embassy; we are only told that an Indian scholar who was a member of the delegation brought with him a set of Sanskrit astronomical texts, a *siddhānta*, which was translated into Arabic by al-Fazārī, apparently by order of al-Manṣūr himself, and published under the Arabized calque title *Zīǧ as-Sindhind*. On the basis of this and the other sources mentioned above, al-Fazārī compiled his own set of annotated astronomical tables, the *Zīǧ as-Sindhind al-kabīr*, "in which he mingled elements from Indian, Pahlavi and Greek sources into a usable but internally contradictory set of rules and tables for astronomical computations."[12] The problems and questions raised by al-Fazārī's translation and his own work, explicitly referred to by the great al-Bīrūnī himself,[13] set in motion what in retrospect can be called an entire program of astronomical research which, in conjunction with all the other factors discussed in this book, yielded over the centuries the spectacular tradition of Arabic astronomy.

A similar pattern is seen in the translation of agricultural works. We have records that the *Eclogae* of Cassianus Bassus was translated into Arabic twice: initially from a Pahlavi translation dating not later than the seventh century (*Warz-nāma)*, and subsequently directly from the Greek, by Sirǧīs ibn-Hilīyā ar-Rūmī, who also translated the *Almagest* in 212/827.[14] The *Synagoge* of Anatolius was also translated twice. In 179/795, Yaḥyā ibn-Ḫālid ibn-Barmak commissioned a translation of it directly from the Greek from the Patriarch of Alexandria (apparently Politianus), the bishop of Damascus, and the monk Eustathius.[15] The second translation is

12 D. Pingree, "Sindhind," *EI* IX,641b; for the embassy see the references and discussion by D. Pingree, "The Fragments of the Works of Yaʿqūb ibn Ṭāriq," *Journal of Near Eastern Studies*, 1968, vol. 27, pp. 97–8; the passage from Ṣāʿid al-Andalusī which provides the most detailed extant description of the embassy is translated by Pingree in his "Fazārī," p. 105, fragment Z 1. In al-Yaʿqūbī, *Taʾrīḫ*, M. Houtsma (ed.), Leiden, E.J. Brill, 1883, vol. 2, pp. 433–4, we read that two delegations, one from India and the other from North Africa came to visit as-Saffāḥ, the first ʿAbbāsid caliph and al-Manṣūr's immediate predecesor, three days before his death in 754. This report would appear to be, given the context in which it is recounted, hagiographical legend having to do with the prophetic powers of ʿAlī ibn-Abī-Ṭālib.

13 See E. Sachau (transl.), *Alberuni's India*, London, 1888, reprinted Bombay, 1964, vol. 2, p. 15.

14 Ullmann, *Geheimwissenschaften*, pp. 434–5; *GAS* IV,317–18.

15 Ullmann, *Geheimwissenschaften*, pp. 430–1; *GAS* IV,315 says that this is not by Anatolius but by Ps.-Apollonius, Balīnās; see the summary of the discussion by Endress in *GAP* II,149, note 77.

known to have been from a Syriac translation of unknown date, though again one would presume that it was earlier than the Greek.[16] What these double translations would indicate is that with the means and the funds made available by the adoption of an official translation policy by the ʿAbbāsids, carriers of Sasanian culture who were interested in these fields for research and application purposes had the opportunity to acquire more accurate and more reliable texts. The educational needs of the secretaries are therefore seen from the very beginning as being instrumental in the gradual expansion of the translation movement.

4. ALCHEMY AND THE ECONOMY OF THE ʿABBĀSID STATE(?)

Another applied science that appears to have generated a distinct need for translated texts was alchemy. It has recently been brought to the attention of scholars that al-Manṣūr was informed about the benefits of alchemy. In a report preserved in Ibn-al-Faqīh al-Hamaḏānī's *Aḫbār al-buldān*, a work on cultural geography compiled in Baghdad around 290/903, ʿUmāra ibn-Ḥamza, al-Manṣūr's secretary, is said to have returned to Baghdad after a lengthy stay in Constantinople at the court of Constantine V (r. 741–75) and to have reported to the caliph how the Byzantine Emperor had transmuted, by means of a dry powder (τὸ ξηρίον = *al-iksīr* = elixir), lead and copper into silver and gold in his presence. ʿUmāra concluded his report with the words, "This was the reason that induced him [al-Manṣūr] to become interested in alchemy."[17] It is unknown whether al-Manṣūr also had alchemical texts translated, but the fact remains that numerous such texts, obviously translated, exist in Arabic, and they manifestly date from early ʿAbbāsid times.[18]

16 The Arabic translation is not extant independently but in later quotations; cf. Ullmann, *Geheimwissenschaften*, pp. 431–3.

17 See the two accounts of ʿUmāra's embassy in Constantinople by G. Strohmaier, "ʿUmāra ibn Ḥamza, Constantine V, and the invention of the Elixir," *Graeco–Arabica* (Athens), 1991, vol. 4, pp. 21–4; "Al-Manṣūr und die frühe Rezeption der griechischen Alchemie," *Zeitschrift für Geschichte der Arabisch-Islamischen Wissenschaften*, 1989, vol. 5, pp. 167–77. For Ibn-al-Faqīh see A.B. Khalidov, "Ebn al-Faqīh," *EIr.* VIII,23–5.

18 See the account by M. Ullmann, *Geheimwissenschaften*, pp. 148–52. It would appear, however, that some alchemical works were also transmitted via Pahlavi. Among the authorities cited by Abū-Sahl ibn-Nawbaḫt in his *K. an-Nahmuṭān* as preserved in the *Fihrist* there is a certain Phaedrus, apparently the protagonist in Plato's eponymous

Al-Manṣūr must have become quickly disillusioned with the potential of alchemy to provide funds for the state treasury,[19] but he may have unwittingly provided royal precedent for preoccupation with this "art."

5. THE NEEDS OF SCIENTIFIC RESEARCH AND THEORETICAL KNOWLEDGE

What these earliest translations indicate is that needs of applied research were at the basis of the translation movement from the very beginning, complementing the ideological imperial component discussed in Part I. When the impetus to the translation movement was given officially by al-Manṣūr and funds made available, it developed in two ways: first it expanded in the direction of scholarly precision and accuracy for the existing fields, and second into increasingly new areas and subjects considered worthy of translation. One has to keep in mind, in talking about the relationship between the translation movement and specialists in certain fields such as astrology and astronomy, that these experts antedated the foundation of Baghdad. These international scholars, as I called them in chapter 1.1, had been active in the Near East practicing their profession in whatever environment offered the best support and thereby transmitting much scientific knowledge without translation. Nawbaḫt, for example, did not develop his knowledge of astrology and astrological history overnight when al-Manṣūr decided to build Baghdad or indeed to adopt an imperial policy fashioned after that of the Sasanians. It was this development in official policy that allowed Nawbaḫt and other specialists to realize their research and application needs by providing institutionalized support and a focus for their scientific activities. This, in turn, generated a critical mass of specialists in Baghdad that formed the beginning of the Arabic scientific and philosophical enterprise. The impetus given to the translation movement by the demands of these specialists created an increasingly homogeneous

dialogue, who is credited with an extant astrological treatise: see p. 39 of this volume, passage C, §7 and note 21, and cf. Pingree, *Thousands*, p. 10 (cited as Cedros) and Ullmann, *Geheimwissenschaften*, pp. 156–7. Julius Ruska, the expert on Greek and Arabic alchemy of the previous generation, always maintained the Sasanian connection for Arabic alchemy, "aber bewiesen ist dies nicht," according to Ullmann, *Geheimwissenschaften*, p. 148.

19 See the story about the patriarch Isḥāq of Ḥarrān reported by Fiey, *Chrétiens syriaques sous les Abbassides*, p. 16.

body of scientific knowledge, in Arabic this time, which invited – and enabled – the participation of an ever-expanding number of scholars: astrologers and astronomers, mathematicians, physicians, and eventually philosophers. As these individuals proceeded with their research, they came across numerous problems for whose solution they felt the need to commission further translations. At this point, therefore, the translation movement became part of the scientific enterprise in Arabic and as such self-perpetuating: the patrons of translations were themselves scientists.

This can be witnessed in the cultivation of certain sciences which, given the nurturing context of the translation culture espoused by the early ʿAbbāsids and the intellectualism it fostered, either developed further or came into being in response to needs that were this time more strictly scholarly and theoretical. A case in point for the former instance is the astounding progress of the mathematical sciences beyond the mere needs of the instruction of administrative secretaries.

It is now possible to document aspects of the dialectic between research by international specialists, translation, further research, and renewed demand for translation in the case of mathematics. The famous book on algebra by al-Ḫwārizmī, which was to revolutionize mathematical studies forever, appeared some time between 813 and 830, i.e., about half a century after the translation of Euclid's *Elements*, as mentioned above. Al-Ḫwārizmī's demonstrations of different algebraic formulae for solutions are inspired by Euclid insofar as they rest on the idea of the equality of areas.[20] Al-Ḫwārizmī's work, in turn, and the further development of algebra, eventually occasioned the Arabic translation of the *Arithmetica* by Diophantus, and interestingly enough, though Diophantus's *Arithmetica* is a work on arithmetic, it was translated in the light of al-Ḫwārizmī's work on algebra and by means of technical terms borrowed from it. A similar example can be given from the related field of optics. The optical books by Diocles, Anthemius of Tralles, and Didymus were translated into Arabic as a result of the practical interest of scholars and rulers in burning mirrors. The legend of Archimedes setting fire to the flotilla of Marcellus during the siege of Syracuse, a legend known in Arabic as well, alerted mathematicians to the possibility of actually reproducing the feat. The available Greek works on the subject were thus tracked down, translated into Arabic, and al-Kindī wrote an independent treatise on the subject

20 See R. Rashed, "al-Riyāḍiyyāt," *EI* VIII,550b.

correcting and advancing in many ways the work of the Greek authors.[21]

The need for medicine has, obviously, different roots than those of the sciences discussed so far. Medicine was one of the earliest fields cultivated by scholars whose background lay in the Sasanian cultural field of influence. We need only remember that Ǧurǧīs ibn-Ǧibrīl ibn-Buḫtīšū', the physician who was called to Baghdad in 765 to treat the caliph al-Manṣūr, came from the Iranian city of Ǧundīsābūr, east of the Tigris, where he was director of the hospital. The physicians who came from there exhibited a high degree of sophistication in Hippocratic/Galenic medicine. The Buḫtīšū' family was to remain arguably the most influential medical family in Baghdad for a long time: generations of the descendants of Ǧurǧīs served as personal physicians to the caliphs: his son Buḫtīšū' served Hārūn ar-Rašīd, *his* son Ǧibrīl served Hārūn, al-Amīn and al-Ma'mūn, and *his* son Buḫtīšū' served al-Ma'mūn, al-Wāṯiq, and al-Mutawakkil. Just as important were other families of physicians originating in Ǧundīsābūr: the families of Māsawayh, of aṭ-Ṭayfūrī, and of Serapion. These families formed a closely knit social unit in Baghdad: their mother tongue was Persian, as Nestorian Christians their liturgical and scientific language was Syriac, and they intermarried with each other. In addition to practicing medicine in the 'Abbāsid court, however, they also engaged in medical research, wrote medical textbooks, and, most importantly, commissioned translations. They definitely had a stake in maintaining their scientific superiority because their high social status as caliphal physicians and the consequent wealth they amassed depended on their medical expertise. Their paramount concern was therefore the need for expert medical knowledge.

One of these men was the famous Yūḥannā ibn-Māsawayh, personal physician to al-Ma'mūn and his successors in Baghdad and Sāmarrā'. One can assume that he conducted his research in the course of his practice as chief physician in the hospital in Baghdad, but there was one area of medical research that was denied to him: this was the dissection of humans for the purposes of improved knowledge of anatomy. Although dissection as such was never formally forbidden in Islamic law, it seems not to have been practiced in medieval times; ibn-Māsawayh, in any case, as he says in the

21 R. Rashed, "Problems of the Transmission of Greek Scientific Thought into Arabic: Examples from Mathematics and Optics," *History of Science*, 1989, vol. 27, pp. 199–209.

passage cited below, was prohibited by the caliph.[22] Now ibn-Māsawayh had a son by a daughter of ʿAbdallāh aṭ-Ṭayfūrī. The woman, he tells us, was extremely beautiful, but also very stupid, and the son also turned out to be feeble-minded, receiving, in ibn-Māsawayh's words, his mother's and his father's worst qualities and none of the best. Then ibn-Māsawayh continues as follows:

> Had it not been for the meddling of the ruler and his interference in what does not concern him, I would have dissected alive this son of mine, just as Galen used to dissect men and monkeys. As a result of dissecting him, I would thus come to know the reasons for his stupidity, rid the world of his kind, and produce knowledge for people by means of what I would write in a book: the way in which his body is composed, and the course of his arteries, veins, and nerves. But the ruler prohibits this [Q 390–1].

Thus prevented from conducting dissections, ibn-Māsawayh had necessarily recourse to the best alternative: he commissioned the translations of Galen's anatomical books from his student and famous translator, Ḥunayn ibn-Isḥāq. Ḥunayn himself tells us in his bibliography of Galenic translations that he translated for ibn-Māsawayh no less than nine books by Galen on anatomy, two of which are precisely about the subjects in which ibn-Māsawayh wanted to do research: *On the Anatomy of Veins and Arteries*, and *On the Anatomy of Nerves*.[23]

There is finally philosophy, whose origin presents yet other aspects. It was clearly a discipline for which there was the least amount of practical need, in the sense that it was not "practical" in the same way that astrology, geometry, and medicine were practical. Nevertheless, socially relevant use could be made of it, and it appears that such were the considerations for its development. The introduction of philosophy into the Islamic world is indelibly linked with the name of al-Kindī (died ca. 870), the first philosopher in Arabic, and the circle of scientists and collaborators that he gathered around him. To understand this development it is important, first

22 For a review of the evidence on dissection see E. Savage-Smith, "Attitudes toward Dissection in Medieval Islam," *Journal of the History of Medicine and Allied Sciences*, 1995, vol. 50, pp. 67–110; for the incident discussed here see pp. 83–6.

23 *Kitāb fī tašrīḥ al-ʿurūq wa-l-awrād* (Περὶ φλεβῶν καὶ ἀρτηριῶν ἀνατομῆς, Kühn II,779–830), and *Kitāb fī tašrīḥ al-ʿaṣab* (Περὶ νεύρων ἀνατομῆς, Kühn II, 831–56).

of all, to keep in mind that al-Kindī was not a philosopher in the sense that he was only or primarily a philosopher. He was a polymath in the translated sciences and as such very much a product of his age. He wrote on all the sciences mentioned above: astrology, astronomy, arithmetic, geometry, medicine. This broad and synoptic view of all sciences, along with the spirit of encyclopedism fostered by the translation movement for the half-century before his time, led him to develop a research program whose aim was to acquire and complete the sciences that were transmitted from the ancients; the purpose of this approach, as al-Kindī says in a number of introductions to his essays, was to advance knowledge, not merely repeat it by rote memorization. Al-Kindī's goal was to approach mathematical accuracy in his argumentation and he held mathematical or geometrical proof to be of the highest order. In his philosophical writings, "he regularly employs certain proofs where his method is quite clearly derived from the *Elements* of Euclid."[24] Such was the influence of the translated scientific literature and the incipient original scholarship in Arabic that this ideal of unassailable proof was widespread in the ninth century and formed the model of many a discussion in the "humanistic" disciplines.[25] Second, al-Kindī's originality resides in his attempt to apply this approach to the theological and religious discussions of his time. In order to do so, he tried to gain access to the most "scientific," i.e., methodologically rigorous, discipline in these subjects, philosophy, and accordingly he had numerous translations of primarily metaphysical Greek texts made for him, foremost among which are Aristotle's *Metaphysics* and the selections from Plotinus and Proclus in Arabic known as the *Theology of Aristotle* and *The Pure Good* (*al-ḫayr al-maḥḍ*, which was to become known in the medieval Latin translation as *Liber de causis*) respectively (see further below, chapter 6.3). His recourse to these texts in itself, however, was again nothing extraordinary. Given the culture of translation prevalent, indeed dominant, in the Baghdad of his time, recourse to translations of Greek works for solutions to intellectual problems was standard procedure among intellectuals of the elite classes to which he belonged.

24 See the fundamental discussion by R. Rashed, from which this quotation is taken, in his article, "Al-Kindī's Commentary on Archimedes' 'The Measurement of the Circle'," *Arabic Sciences and Philosophy*, 1993, vol. 3, pp. 7–12.

25 See K. Samir and P. Nwyia, *Une correspondance islamo-chrétienne*, pp. 593 and 597, paragraphs 3 and 13 of Qusṭā's text where he states that Ibn-al-Munaǧǧim claimed to have used "geometrical proofs" (*burhān handasī*) to prove the prophethood of Muḥammad.

6

PATRONS, TRANSLATORS, TRANSLATIONS

1. PATRONS AND SPONSORS

That the translation movement enjoyed a very wide basis of support in early Baghdadi society is, in a general way, obvious through its sheer spread and longevity. However, if we are to gain a more precise understanding of the dynamics of this society that generated the need and support for it, and in the absence of a satisfactory theoretical framework to guide the investigation (cf. the Introduction), it is necessary to describe closely the significant social groups or strata that sponsored it. A useful place to start would be identifying the individuals who belonged to them. A comprehensive prosopography of eighth- and ninth-century Baghdad would thus be a primary desideratum in this case. We have perhaps more than enough information from the voluminous Arabic biographical dictionaries (if only it could be properly collected and interpreted), and several secondary studies on certain families and their affiliates, but nothing that approaches the exhaustiveness of, say, A.H.M. Jones's *The Prosopography of the Later Roman Empire (260–641)*.[1] Nothing of the sort can be attempted here. What I will try to do in this section is merely give a representative sample of the major groupings of sponsors and briefly comment on their relationship to the translation movement. At the same time I must emphasize that this is only a preliminary treatment of the subject; two centuries of continuous sponsorship of a social phenomenon such as the translation

1 Edited by A.H.M. Jones, J.R. Martindale, and J. Morris, 3 vols, Cambridge, Cambridge University Press, 1971–92. It even contains entries on early Muslim personalities, such as the caliph ʿUmar ibn-al-Ḫaṭṭāb, mentioned in Byzantine sources. Given the period covered by this work, an early Islamic prosopography would constitute a natural extension of it.

movement could not have been homogeneous and hence not to be accounted for by a few impressionistic examples.[2]

The bases for categorization that promise to be most productive for further analysis because they are indicated by our sources are, first, profession or social standing, and second, religious, ethnic, and indeed family affiliation. I will start with the first and incorporate in each segment information from the second. On the basis of social standing then, it is possible to identify four major groupings of sponsors or patrons of the translation movement: (a) ʿAbbāsid caliphs and their families; (b) courtiers; (c) officials of the state and military administration; (d) scholars and scientists.[3]

(a) ʿAbbāsid Caliphs and Their Families

Most of the discussion in Part I concentrated on the reasons that led the early ʿAbbāsid caliphs to promote and support the translation movement; thus its patronage during the first ʿAbbāsid century by various members of the ruling dynasty needs no additional documentation. If anything, there is too much of it, especially for al-Ma'mūn, who is credited with having written himself an extant treatise on medicine and agriculture [*GAS* IV,336]. After the end of al-Ma'mūn's policies under al-Mutawakkil, however, the historical and bibliographical sources do not give as clear a picture of sponsorship of the translation movement by the caliphs who followed him. This would appear to be due to a number of reasons, and it is important to interpret this fact accurately.

In the first place, it is obvious that there is a certain bias in these sources in favor of attributing all, or most, of the sponsorship of translations to the glorious line of the early caliphs. It is easy to see how achievements by a caliph in an area for which one of his predecessors has become famous can be attributed to the former man. Rulers like Hārūn ar-Rašīd and especially al-Ma'mūn had become associated in people's minds with the translation movement, due largely to the propaganda efforts of al-Ma'mūn himself, as discussed in chapter 4; it is thus a measure of the success of these public relations campaigns that subsequent activities in this field would be

2 Van Ess's *Theologie und Gesellschaft* presents, in effect, such an annotated prosopography of theologians of the eighth and ninth centuries; it would be desirable to do the same, following his example, for all those associated with the translation movement.

3 For a list of some of the sponsors of translations from the Greek see IAU I,205.25ff.

foisted upon them. An excellent example is provided by the case of al-Muʿtaṣim (r. 218/833–227/842), al-Ma'mūn's successor. This caliph followed implicitly the policies of his predecessor and indeed was the beneficiary of al-Ma'mūn's anti-Byzantinist ideology, scoring spectacular victories against the Byzantines in Asia Minor through the conquest of Amorium and Ankyra in 838. He also continued with the official policy of doctrinal inquisition (the *miḥna*) initiated by al-Ma'mūn. He appointed the philosopher and scientist al-Kindī as tutor to his son Aḥmad (about whom more below), and he himself was the addressee of a number of epistles by al-Kindī.[4] It would therefore have been remarkable had he not participated in the translation activity as sponsor, and yet the bibliographical sources are silent in this regard.[5] What we do find, however, is a report in Ibn-Ǧulǧul, writing some hundred and fifty years later, saying that Yūḥannā ibn-Māsawayh, the famous physician (d. 857), "was commissioned by *ar-Rašīd* to translate the ancient medical books that were found in Ankyra, Amorium, and Asia Minor after they had been captured by the Muslims."[6] The anachronism is striking. Apart from the fact that Yūḥannā was born during the reign of ar-Rašīd and was the personal physician to caliphs from al-Ma'mūn through al-Mutawakkil, the two cities mentioned specifically in the report were captured, as mentioned above, by al-Muʿtaṣim in 838; ar-Rašīd had only raided Ankyra in 806. Any commissioning of translations would thus have been done by al-Muʿtaṣim, but the report was foisted on ar-Rašīd as the better known of the two for his patronage of the ancient sciences.

Second, it is quite difficult to deny that even if the later caliphs did continue their patronage of the translation movement and related activities, the rate and vigor of such patronage had attenuated. In a general way it is observed that their activities of patronage correlate positively with the strength of the office of the caliph itself and the real power wielded by its successive holders. Real power, however, began to elude later caliphs following the disastrous policies of

4 See the references by Endress, *GAP* II,428 and note 86.

5 Al-Muʿtaṣim is said in the preface of the magical *aḏ-Ḏaḫīra al-Iskandariyya* to have asked the astrologer Muḥammad ibn-Ḫālid to translate it. The manuscript of the work was allegedly found in Amorium, after al-Muʿtaṣim had captured it; see Dunlop, "Al-Biṭrīq," p. 148. Given both the nature of the work itself and the association, in popular lore, of al-Muʿtaṣim with Amorium, this report can hardly be considered reliable.

6 Ibn Ǧulǧul, *Ṭabaqāt al-aṭibbā'*, Fu'ād Sayyid (ed.), Cairo, Institut Français d'Archéologie Orientale, 1955, p. 65, emphasis added.

al-Muʿtaṣim himself. His reorganization of the military and aggressive recruitment of Turkish troops, along with the consequent transferral of the military headquarters to Sāmarrā', had the effect of placing the office of the caliph under their control, a policy which ultimately cost the life of his son and second successor, al-Mutawakkil (r. 847–61), who tried to reverse it. After al-Mutawakkil, and until the advent of the Būyids in 945, the office of the caliph never regained its former ideological independence, political authority, and military and economic power. In this environment, it is clear that the translation movement was not or could not be used by the increasingly weaker caliphs for ideological purposes as it had been with the earlier ʿAbbāsids. Attenuated caliphal support, however, does not reflect the actual state of affairs, after the end of the *miḥna* under al-Mutawakkil, in the court in Baghdad where patronage of the translation movement and related literature remained dominant in cultural life.

As a matter of fact, it was precisely in the second ʿAbbāsid century that the translation movement reached its apogee with the work of Ḥunayn ibn-Isḥāq and his associates, and generated, because of its great success, two very significant developments: first, scholarship in all fields covered by the translation literature became so widespread and so profound in Baghdadi society that commissions for original works on scientific and philosophical subjects composed in Arabic became as current as commissions for translations from the Greek; and second, because of the spirit of research and analysis it inculcated, different fields of scholarly endeavor unrelated to the translations gained in sophistication, a plethora of ideas was available for ready consumption, and the areas covered by the translation literature were no longer the only ones to impress powerful minds. Intellectual debates of all sorts became the order of the day and patrons became interested not only in the *transmitted* knowledge from the Greeks but in the main problems posed by this knowledge and in the various ideological challenges to it. The century between the end of the *miḥna* and the advent of the Būyids (roughly between 850 and 950) is when *all* intellectual disciplines, those which came into being before the translation period and those because of it alike, attempt to rationalize and organize themselves both in terms of contents and method.

In this context, it makes no sense to talk about attenuated caliphal sponsorship of the translation movement as such as an indication of their aversion to it; to the contrary, the success and establishment of the translation movement made intellectuals, in broad terms, out of all members of the ruling elite so that we find numerous references in literary sources to caliphs after al-Ma'mūn commissioning works directly dependent on the translated literature, to say nothing, of course, of other subjects. Al-Ma'mūn's successor, al-Mu'taṣim, was briefly mentioned above. His successor, al-Wāṯiq, had scientific discussions with physicians and philosophers.[7] Al-Mu'taḍid (r. 279/892–289/902) appears to have been particularly interested in the Greek sciences. The son of a Greek woman, he could speak the Greek of his time,[8] but in addition he was on intimate terms with the luminaries of the translation movement, Isḥāq ibn-Ḥunayn and Ṯābit ibn-Qurra [*F* 272.10]. He commissioned a medical treatise from Yaḥyā ibn-Abī-Ḥakīm al-Ḥallāǧī, and a meteorological one from an-Nayrīzī.[9] His son, al-Muktafī, (r. 289/902–295/908) also commissioned from an-Nayrīzī an anthology on prognostications [*GAS* VII,156].

Other than caliphs, princes are frequently mentioned as patrons of scientific and philosophical activity, most famous among whom is Aḥmad, the son of al-Mu'taṣim, who was tutored by the philosopher and scientist al-Kindī himself and to whom were addressed numerous of his epistles.[10] Most specifically, Aḥmad is stated to have commissioned from al-Kindī the "correction," i.e., the stylistic improvement, of the stilted Arabic translation by Ibn-Nā'ima of the so-called *Theology of Aristotle*, extracts from the last three *Enneads* of Plotinus [*DPA* I,546]. Other than his association with al-Kindī, however, Aḥmad also commissioned from Qusṭā ibn-Lūqā the translation of mathematical and astronomical works: the *Spherics* (*K. al-Ukar*) by Theodosius, the *Rising and Setting [of the Fixed Stars]* (*K. aṭ-Ṭulū' wa-l-ġurūb*) by Autolycus, and the *Lifting-Screw* (*K. Raf' al-aṯqāl*) by Hero of Alexandria.[11] Aḥmad is sometimes confused in

7 See the references in *GAS* VII,267 #2, and the lost manuscript of his discussion with the philosophers, in A. Sidarus, "Un recueil de traités philosophiques et médicaux à Lisbonne," *Zeitschrift für Geschichte der Arabisch-Islamischen Wissenschaften*, 1990, vol. 6, p. 188.

8 The story is found in the account of 'Abbāsid court protocol and etiquette by Hilāl aṣ-Ṣābī, an insider and descendant of a family of translators. See E.A. Salem, *Hilāl aṣ-Ṣābi', Rusūm Dār al-Khilāfa*, Beirut, American University of Beirut, 1977, p. 71.

9 *Tadbīr al-abdān an-nahīfa allatī qad ġalabat 'alayhā ṣ-ṣafrā'*, *F* 298.5–6; IAU I,203,10–11; *GAS* III,263; *Aḥdāṯ al-ǧaww*, *F* 279.17.

10 See the references in the index, s.n. Aḥmad ibn-al-Mu'taṣim, in J. McCarthy, *At-Taṣānīf al-mansūba ilā faylasūf al-'Arab*, Baghdad, Maṭba'at al-'Ānī, 1382/1962, p. 119.

11 For these works and their manuscripts see, respectively, *GAS* V,154 (where the sponsorship of al-Musta'īn is attested by aṭ-Ṭūsī); *GAS* VI,73, no. 1; and *GAS* V,153, no. 4. For Qusṭā ibn-Lūqā fundamental remains the pioneering article by G. Gabrieli, "Nota

this connection with his nephew, al-Muʿtaṣim's grandson, Abū-l-ʿAbbās Aḥmad ibn-Muḥammad ibn-al-Muʿtaṣim, who ruled as caliph al-Mustaʿīn from 248/862 to 251/866, but the references in the manuscripts of these works are clearly to the *son* of al-Muʿtaṣim.[12]

About a century later, Ǧaʿfar, the son of the caliph al-Muktafī (r. 902–8), was knowledgeable in the history of astronomy, apparently having met in his youth the famous astronomer al-Battānī (d. 317/929), and acted as the informant of Ibn-an-Nadīm on these subjects (*F* 275.20–4, 279.21–4). Ǧaʿfar, moreover, appears to have known Greek, for Ibn-an-Nadīm quotes him on the nature of the letters of the Greek alphabet (*F* 16.7–16).[13]

Other members of the immediate families of caliphs who sponsored the translation movement and scientific production were ladies of the court. According to the *Fihrist* [294.29], al-Mutawakkil's slave concubine and mother of his son (one would like to think that this lady was the mother of al-Muʿtazz, nicknamed antiphrastically Qabīḥa, the ugly one, on account of her exceptional beauty),[14] commissioned from the great Ḥunayn himself a book on eight-month embryos (*K. al-Mawlūdīn li-ṯamāniyat aš hur*).

biobibliographica su Qusṭā ibn Lūqā," *Rendiconti della Reale Accademia dei Lincei*, Classe di Scienze Morali, Storiche e Filologiche, Ser. V, 1912, vol. 21, pp. 341–82; here pp. 353–4. A more recent and comprehensive account is the unpublished Ph.D. dissertation by Judith Wilcox, *The Transmission and Influence of Qusta ibn Luqa's "On the Difference between Spirit and Soul"*, The City University of New York, 1985, which I have not seen.

12 The confusion, which exists even in Arabic historical sources and led G. Gabrieli, "Qusṭā ibn Lūqā," p. 362, to identify al-Mustaʿīn as Qusṭā's patron, was cleared by F. Rosenthal, "Al-Kindī als Literat," *Orientalia*, 1942, vol. 11, p. 265, note 1 (Rosenthal's reference to the occurrence of Aḥmad ibn-al-Muʿtaṣim in al-Yaʿqūbī's *Taʾrīḫ*, ed. Houtsma, should be to pp. 584 and 591, not 514). It has nevertheless continued in secondary literature to this day; see the references in *GAP* II,429, note 96, to which is to be added Judith Wilcox, "Our Continuing Discovery of the Greek Science of the Arabs: The Example of Qusṭā ibn Lūqā," *Annals of Scholarship*, 1987, vol. 4.3, p. 58. The reference to al-Mustaʿīn in all these works is to be changed to Aḥmad b. al-Muʿtaṣim. Only Wilbur R. Knorr, in connection with his discussion of Theodosius's *Spherics*, rightly questioned – though for the wrong reason – the identification of the patron as al-Mustaʿīn ("The Medieval Tradition of a Greek Mathematical Lemma," *Zeitschrift für Geschichte der Arabisch-Islamischen Wissenschaften*, 1986, vol. 3, p. 233, note 7), but he failed to recognize in the manuscript reference to "Aḥmad, the son of the Amīr al-Muʾminīn" the pupil and companion of al-Kindī.

13 Ǧaʿfar Ibn-al-Muktafī-billāh died in 377/987; see Flügel, *Fihrist* II,131, note 9 to p. 275. He reports, apparently to Ibn an-Nadīm, about the career of al-Battānī from Ḥarrān.

14 Reported by aṯ-Ṯaʿālibī, *Laṭāʾif al-maʿārif*, translated by C.E. Bosworth, Edinburgh, Edinburgh University Press, 1968, p. 63.

(b) Courtiers

Among the intimates of the caliphs and their families should be placed the courtiers (including the so-called boon-companions, *nadīm, nudamā'*), individuals of learning, wit, and graceful manners who were sought after for their company. Their social function was significant, and will repay detailed study, insofar as they can be taken to represent the cultural attitudes of the learned elite as appreciated by the rulers and, conversely, the cultural predilections of the rulers as catered to by the elite.[15] One of the most famous boon-companions is arguably the disciple of al-Kindī and substantial philosopher and scholar in his own right, Aḥmad ibn-aṭ-Ṭayyib as-Saraḫsī (ca. 835–99). As-Saraḫsī was selected to serve as tutor to a prince, al-Mutawakkil's grandson, who was later to reign as al-Muʿtaḍid (r. 892–902). Upon al-Muʿtaḍid's accession, as-Saraḫsī was appointed boon-companion to his former pupil; eventually, however, he fell into disgrace and was executed in circumstances that are far from clear. The cause of his death is certainly not religious; he fell victim to court intrigues of the vizier's son al-Qāsim ibn-ʿUbaydallāh (later himself vizier) and the Turkish general Badr – plausibly because as-Saraḫsī had other candidates in mind to succeed ʿUbaydallāh. Stories which attribute atheism or lack of piety to Saraḫsī are later developments designed to account for his unexpected and inexplicable fall from grace. To the contrary, a surviving epistolary exchange of his, ridiculing religious narrow-mindedness and fanaticism, indicates that incidents of this sort were found amusing in the ʿAbbāsid court at the end of the ninth century; even more to the point, if, as Yāqūt claims, as-Saraḫsī concocted the correspondence in order to please al-Muʿtaḍid, this means that the caliph had an appreciation of the foreign sciences.[16]

15 For the subject see A. Chejne, "The Boon-Companion in Early ʿAbbāsid Times," *Journal of the American Oriental Society*, 1965, vol. 85, pp. 327–35, and G. Makdisi, *The Rise of Humanism in Classical Islam and the Christian West*, Edinburgh, Edinburgh University Press, 1990, pp. 284–7, especially for the variety of fields in which boon-companions were experts.

16 For as-Saraḫsī see the collection of fragments and study by F. Rosenthal, *Aḥmad b. aṭ-Ṭayyib as-Saraḫsī*, New Haven, American Oriental Society, 1943. The stories about as-Saraḫsī's death are analyzed in detail on pp. 26ff. The correspondence with Ibn-Ṭawāba is translated on pp. 86–94, as quoted by Yāqūt, whose judgment on the entire report is given on pp. 93–4. The story was copied by Yāqūt from at-Tawḥīdī's *Maṯālib al-wazīrayn* (now on pp. 157–63 of the edition by I. al-Kaylānī, Damascus, 1961).

Courtiers came from different backgrounds and were elevated to their status for different reasons. The two extremes are best represented by these examples. Al-Fatḥ ibn-Ḫāqān was the son of a Turkish soldier, the chief of al-Muʿtaṣim's guard. He was raised in court together with al-Muʿtaṣim's son, the future caliph al-Mutawakkil, with whom he became close personal friends. He remained so throughout al-Mutawakkil's reign (232/847–274/861) and ran a brilliant courtly salon for intellectuals. He gained lasting fame for his devotion to letters, his very rich personal library, and his profound promotion of scientific and literary learning.[17] At the other end of the spectrum there are the famous Banū-l-Munağğim, a Zoroastrian Persian family of intellectuals that traced its ancestry to ministers of Sasanian royalty. They were initially brought to the ʿAbbāsid court by al-Manṣūr as astrologers (whence their name, *Munağğim*) and remained in influential positions for over six generations – throughout, that is, the period of the translation movement, which they repeatedly patronized. It was a member of this family, ʿAlī ibn-Yaḥyā, who commissioned from Ḥunayn his famous *Risāla*, to which we are indebted for the inventory of translations of Galen's works.[18]

(c) Officials of the State and the Military

The secretaries of the ʿAbbāsid administration (*kuttāb*) and related state functionaries constituted from the very beginning one of the most important social groups who patronized and promoted the translations and works based on them. That the early ʿAbbāsid caliphs relied in this regard on Sasanian models has been amply discussed in the available literature and needs no special mention here. The Barmakids, with their unquestioned supremacy in these posts for the first half-century of the ʿAbbāsid dynasty, were naturally carriers of Sasanian practice and along with it of the concomitant culture of translation. They figure prominently as sponsors of the translation movement and, indeed, of works relating to astronomy [*F* 267.29ff.] and agriculture, as mentioned in chapter 5.3.[19] In addition, they were also interested in Indian material, translations of which they commissioned [*F* 303.6, 345.25ff.], and it is not

17 See the references in *GAP* II,427 note 80, and O. Pinto's article in *EI* II,837–8.

18 See the account of the entire family in the article by M. Fleischhammer, "Munadjdjim, Banu 'l-," *EI* VII,558–61, with further references, and cf. D. Pingree, "Banū Monajjem," *EIr.* III,716.

19 For the Barmakids in general see the articles in *EIr.* III,806 and *EI* I,1033ff.

far-fetched to assume that it was they who were responsible for the Indian embassy to the court of al-Manṣūr in 154/771 or 156/773, which resulted in the transmission and translation of the *Sindhind* (see chapter 5.3).

After the fall of the Barmakids (187/803) or, more specifically, after the assassination in 202/818 of their protégé and al-Ma'mūn's vizier, al-Faḍl ibn-Sahl, there is a manifest reorientation in the direction from which the ʿAbbāsid caliphs selected their viziers. Perhaps because the Barmakids and their circle presented, by al-Ma'mūn's time, an unacceptable image of *Zoroastrian* Persian proclivities (al-Faḍl ibn-Sahl was called by a modern scholar "the most Iranian of the viziers of the ʿAbbāsid caliphate"[20]), al-Ma'mūn's preferences were next directed to thoroughly Arabized Muslim Persians, the family of his general Ṭāhir Ḏū-l-Yamīnayn ibn-al-Ḥusayn (d. 207/823). The Ṭāhirids followed a cultural ideology of Arabization in order to avoid provocation such as the one that caused al-Faḍl ibn-Sahl's demise.[21] History bore out the success of their policy: theirs was the first semi-independent Muslim Persian dynasty to be formed and thrive within the bosom of the caliphate. Second, in addition to the Ṭāhirids, the attention of the ruling ʿAbbāsids turned also toward the Christians of ʿIrāq, Arabs and non-Arabs alike, from among whose numbers the high functionaries in the court were selected. Despite the new directions from which members of the secretarial classes were recruited from the time of al-Ma'mūn onward, their support for the translation movement continued unabated.

As representatives of the Arabized Muslim Persians come first of all the military men and political governors of the line founded by Ṭāhir, al-Ma'mūn's general. Ṭāhir himself was a significant patron of the translation movement and commissioned numerous translations.[22] Isḥāq ibn-Ibrāhīm ibn-al-Ḥusayn (d. 235/849–50), Ṭāhir's nephew, was governor of Baghdad (214/829–235/849–50) and a close friend and companion of al-Ma'mūn.[23] He commissioned from Ḥunayn a book on nutrition, which resulted in Ḥunayn's surviving Arabic work entitled *On the Properties of Nutriments* (*Fī quwā*

20 D. Sourdel, "al-Faḍl b. Sahl," *EI* II,731b.

21 For the Arabic culture espoused and promoted by the Ṭāhirids, see Bosworth, "The Ṭāhirids and Arabic Culture," pp. 45–79; the reasons behind this policy of theirs are discussed by Bulliett, *Conversion*, 46–8.

22 See the references in Endress, *GAP,* II,424 note 60; cf. above, chapter 5.2.

23 Bosworth, "The Ṭāhirids and Arabic Culture," p. 67.

l-aġdiya), based on Galen and other Greek writers.[24] Manṣūr ibn-Ṭalḥa ibn-Ṭāhir, Ṭāhir's grandson and governor of Marw and Ḫwārizm, was an acknowledged authority on philosophy, music, astronomy, and mathematics,[25] as well as the author of apparently a medical book, *K. al-wuǧūd*, which was criticized by the famous physician ar-Rāzī (Rhazes) [*F* 301.18]. ʿUbaydallāh ibn-ʿAbdallāh ibn-Ṭāhir, Ṭāhir's other grandson (d. 300/913), was also governor of Baghdad. His wisdom, familiarity with ancient philosophers, and his mastery of music and geometry were praised by Abū-l-Faraǧ al-Iṣfahānī.[26]

Another member of a line of thoroughly Arabized and Muslim Persians, hailing from Ǧīlān, is Muḥammad ibn-ʿAbd-al-Malik az-Zayyāt (d. 233/847), three times vizier under three successive caliphs, al-Muʿtaṣim, al-Wāṯiq, and al-Mutawakkil. Muḥammad presents an interesting case in the prosopography of patrons of the translation movement. His family had made money in the production and trade of oil (whence their name, az-Zayyāt, "dealer in oil") and had, already with his father, diversified into the manufacture of items for caliphal consumption: royal parasols, military tents, and equipment for swift riding camels.[27] Muḥammad's great ambition was to become a state secretary despite his clearly inferior social status. His ambition was realized through a combination of factors: his access to the court in his capacity as manufacturer, his unquestionable talents for finance and administration, and apparently his considerable fortune.[28] Muḥammad was clearly a social climber. Again despite his

24 Bergsträsser, *Galen-Übersetzungen*, p. 35.22. See the desciption of Ḥunayn's work by R. Degen, "The Kitāb al-Aghdhiya of Ḥunayn ibn Isḥāq," *Proceedings of the First International Symposium for the History of Arabic Science*, A.Y. al-Ḥassan *et al.* (eds), Aleppo, Institute for the History of Arabic Science, 1978, vol. 2, pp. 291–9; for the Ṭāhirid see p. 296.

25 *F* 117.9–14; cf. Bosworth, "The Ṭāhirids and Arabic Culture," p. 68.

26 Bosworth "The Ṭāhirids and Arabic Culture," p. 71; *F* 117.

27 Aṭ-Ṭabarī, *Taʾrīḫ*, ed. M.J. de Goeje et al., Leiden 1879–1901, vol. III, p. 1183; English translation by C.E Bosworth, *Storm and Stress along the Northern Frontiers of the ʿAbbāsid Caliphate* [The History of al-Ṭabarī, vol. 33], Albany, State University of New York Press, 1991, p. 31.

28 For his administrative career see Sourdel, *Vizirat*, pp. 254–70, and the article "Ibn al-Zayyāt" in *EI* III,974b, also by Sourdel. Al-Marzubānī, *Muʿǧam aš-šuʿarāʾ*, Cairo, 1960, p. 365, mentions explicitly that he came from Persia, while the *Fihrist* (338.16–77) has a report that he was presumably Manichean (*zindīq*). Ǧamīl Saʿīd, "Muḥammad b. ʿAbd-al-Malik az-Zayyāt, al-Wazīr, al-Kātib aš-Šāʿir," *Maǧallat al-Maǧmaʿ al-ʿIlmī al-ʿIrāqī*, 1986, vol. 37.3, pp. 189–90 denies his Persian descent and claims that he was Arab. For interesting light cast on his character see the essay by al-Ǧāḥiẓ addressed to him, *R. fī l-ǧidd wa-l-hazl*, "On Jest and Earnest," summarized and partly translated by C. Pellat, *Jāḥiẓ*, pp. 207–16.

humble origins, he had pretensions to being a poet and, what is of interest to us, a patron of the translation movement. There are reports that he would spend 2000 dīnārs per month on translators and scribes [IAU I,206.16–20]. Ḥunayn relates the interesting episode that Muḥammad, whom he describes as "a man of intelligence" (*ḥusn al-fahm*), commissioned him to translate into Arabic Galen's *On Voice* (Περὶ φωνῆς, *Fī ṣ-ṣawt*), and that when Ḥunayn was finished Muḥammad set about to changing many expressions in the translation according to what he thought was better.[29] Muḥammad ibn-az-Zayyāt's case thus presents us with an excellent example for the fact that the translation movement had become one of the defining characteristics of the cultural life of the ʿAbbāsid elite and indeed of the state functionaries. Not born to the class or the profession, he managed to make himself accepted through his considerable talents, and in his attempts to prove that he belonged by right to his newly acquired status he spent excessively on the translators without being himself a scientist.

The Christians of ʿIrāq constitute the second major pool of talent drawn upon for administrative posts during the second ʿAbbāsid century. Among them there were Nestorian Arabs who converted to Islam in office, like the illustrious Wahb family of secretaries, viziers, and scholars who claimed to be Christians from Nağrān in south Arabia and who actually served as secretaries to the Umayyads.[30] The brilliant administrator and courtier al-Qāsim ibn-ʿUbaydallāh ibn-Sulaymān ibn-Wahb (d. 291/904), vizier to al-Muʿtaḍid and al-Muktafī, employed in his service Isḥāq ibn-Ḥunayn [*F* 285.24–5]. From him he commissioned the final and best translation of Aristotle's *Physics*, the one extant today,[31] as well as a brief history of Greek medicine, also extant.[32] His brother, Abū-Muḥammad al-Ḥasan, also a state secretary,[33] was apparently a sort of mathematician and wrote an essay on a problem in Euclid [*F* 273.5–7]. Their

29 Bergsträsser, *Galen-Übersetzungen*, p. 24.17ff.; *F* 290.11.

30 Sourdel, *Vizirat*, pp. 312ff.; *F* 122.

31 A catalogue of the Escorial library written in 1577 lists a manuscript, subsequently destroyed by fire in 1671, which contained a *Physics* translation done by Ḥunayn for "the vizier al-Qāsim ibn-ʿUbaydallāh." The reading "Ḥunayn ibn-Isḥāq" in the destroyed manuscript is manifestly an error for Isḥāq b. Ḥunayn, especially since al-Qāsim is referred to as "vizier," an office he held long after Ḥunayn's death. See J. Brugman and H. Drossaart Lulofs, *Aristotle. Generation of Animals*, Leiden, E.J. Brill, 1971, p. 67.

32 See F. Rosenthal, "Isḥāq b. Ḥunayn's Taʾrīḫ al-Aṭibbāʾ," *Oriens*, 1954, vol. 7, pp. 72–3.

33 Sourdel, *Vizirat*, pp. 338, 737.

first cousin, finally, Isḥāq ibn-Ibrāhīm ibn-Sulaymān ibn-Wahb – a branch of the family that apparently converted to Shīʿism – and also a secretary, wrote after 335/947 a book on rhetoric, *K. al-Burhān fī wuǧūh al-bayān*, which has been described as an "attempt to apply Greek, Muʿtazilī and Imāmī doctrines to Arabic rhetoric."[34]

Other Nestorian Christians were Arabized Persians who subsequently converted to Islam, like the al-Ǧarrāḥ family of secretaries. They hailed from Dayr Qunnā on the lower Tigris, a center of traditional Nestorian education which was the home, in addition to numerous high officials of the state, also of the philosopher Abū-Bišr Mattā ibn-Yūnus, the founder of the Aristotelian school of Baghdad and teacher of al-Fārābī.[35] Abū-Muḥammad al-Ḥasan ibn-Maḫlad ibn-al-Ǧarrāḥ (d. after 269/882),[36] three times vizier to al-Muʿtamid, was interested in medical matters and commissioned from Qusṭā ibn-Lūqā a treatise on sexual hygiene[37] and another on medicine for pilgrims, recently edited.[38] The most famous members of this family, however, are al-Ḥasan's relatives from a different branch, the "good vizier" ʿAlī ibn-ʿĪsā (d. 334/946),[39] and his son ʿĪsā ibn-ʿAlī (d. 391/1001). With regard to the father, it is worth noting that he had studied Prophetic traditions (*ḥadīṯ*), theology, mysticism, Qurʾānic commentary, and grammar with the leading scholars of his day, to which one is to add his interests in all other disciplines from poetry to history, including the translation literature. The *Fihrist* reports, as a matter of fact, that the translator Abū-ʿUṯmān ad-Dimašqī was attached to his service [*F* 298.24–5]. It was his son, however, ʿĪsā ibn-ʿAlī, who made a name for himself as the unparalleled scholar of his time in the ancient sciences [*F* 129.8]. He studied philosophy with Yaḥyā ibn-ʿAdī and held intellectual sessions in his salon; one such session, the *Fihrist* reports, was devoted to a discussion about the origins of philosophy, in the course of which ʿĪsā ibn-ʿAlī

34 See the article "Ibn Wahb" by P. Shinar in *EI*, Supplement, fascicles 5–6, p. 402a.

35 See the references in the article "Dayr Ḳunnā" by D. Sourdel, *EI* II,197b; and cf. Sourdel, *Vizirat*, p. 304.

36 Sourdel, *Vizirat*, pp. 313–15 and index, s.n.

37 *Risāla fī aḥwāl al-bāh wa-asbābihī*; IAU I,244.27.

38 *Fī tadbīr al-badan fī s-safar;* see *GAS* III,270 #10, edited by G. Bos, *Qusṭā ibn Lūqā's Medical Regime for the Pilgrims to Mecca*, Leiden, E.J. Brill, 1992.

39 One of the few ʿAbbāsid personages for whom a monograph has been written. See H. Bowen, *The Life and Times of ʿAlī ibn ʿĪsā, the Good Vizir*, Cambridge, Cambridge University Press, 1928. Cf. Sourdel, *Vizirat*, pp. 520ff. and the article "ʿAlī b. ʿĪsā" in *EIr*. I,850–1.

displayed detailed knowledge of Porphyry's *Philosophos historia* and the number of its books that had been translated into Arabic [*F* 245.12–15].[40]

(d) Scholars and Scientists

Equally significant as the support of the political and social elite was the active sponsorship of scientists and scholars of all groups who commissioned the translation of Greek texts for their practice and research. Physicians were among the most prominent and significant of these patrons, and in particular the medical elite of the Nestorians hailing from Ǧundīsābūr, the families of Buḫtīšūʿ, Māsawayh, and Ṭayfūrī, to name the most famous. They dominated medical practice and scholarship in Baghdad and in the ʿAbbāsid court throughout the period of the translation movement and were responsible for the translation, commissioned from Ḥunayn and his associates, of a great number of the works of Galen.[41]

All the translated sciences, and the mathematical sciences in particular, found perhaps their greatest sponsors in the three sons of Mūsā ibn-Šākir, a former highwayman (!) and astronomer of unknown pedigree who befriended al-Ma'mūn already in Marw, before the latter's accession to the caliphal throne in 813. The three sons of Mūsā (the Banū-Mūsā) grew up in Baghdad under the guardianship of al-Ma'mūn and received the best scholarly education of their time. They also prospered economically and spent a significant portion of their wealth on the sponsorship of translations and scientific activities. According to the *Fihrist* [243.18–20], Abū-Sulaymān as-Siǧistānī said that the Banū-Mūsā used to pay monthly 500 dīnārs to Ḥunayn, Ḥubayš, and Ṯābit ibn-Qurra "for full-time translation" (*li-n-naql wa-l-mulāzama*). This statement is confirmed by Ḥunayn's very long list of medical works translated by him and his nephew Ḥubayš under commission from Muḥammad ibn-Mūsā (d. 259/873). The brothers themselves, and especially Muḥammad,

40 For a fuller discussion of the accomplishments of ʿĪsā ibn-ʿAlī and references to the sources see J.L. Kraemer, *Humanism*, pp. 134–6.

41 See the entries in Ullmann, *Medizin*, pp. 108–15; *GAS* III, index, s.nn.; cf. J.C. Sournia and G. Troupeau, "Médecine Arabe: biographies critiques de Jean Mésué (VIII° siècle) et du Prétendu 'Mésué le Jeune' (X° siècle)," *Clio Medica*, 1968, vol. 3, pp. 109–17. For a proper appreciation of the function of these Baghdadi families and other individuals in the context of medicine in Islamic lands in general see Endress, *GAP* II, pp. 440–8.

were highly competent scientists in astronomy, mathematics, and mechanics, as attested by their surviving works.[42]

As a patron of philosophy and all the sciences during the translation period none is more important than the Muslim Arab aristocrat, al-Kindī (d. ca. 256/870). Much has been written about him, but what needs to be mentioned in the context of the present discussion is, first, that he commissioned translations of scientific subjects about which he also wrote independent essays; second, that he attempted to achieve scientific certainty in the discussion of ideological issues such as theology and he accordingly made himself be informed about Greek philosophy, in particular physics and metaphysics; third, that in order to promote his interest mentioned in the preceding item, he gathered around him a wide circle of individuals capable of advising him on these texts and translating them; and, fourth, that as a result of these activities it seems clear that he developed an overarching vision of the unity and interrelatedness of all knowledge and its research along verifiable and rational lines (*more geometrico*).[43]

Finally, among the scholars who sponsored the translation movement mention should also be made of the translators themselves. Ḥunayn, much sought after to translate into both Syriac and Arabic, clearly had to work in combination with others to meet the demand. In his *Risāla* he repeatedly refers to Galenic books which, rendered by him into Syriac, were translated into Arabic by one of his associates, including his son Isḥāq, his nephew Ḥubayš, and ʿĪsā ibn-Yaḥyā.[44]

The results of this brief and necessarily impressionistic survey of the patrons of the translation movement are rather negative in that sponsorship appears not to have been restricted to any readily identifiable group; the sponsors came from all ethnic and religious groups: Arabic, Syriac, and Persian speakers, and Muslims, Christians of all sorts, Zoroastrians, and pagans. Certainly the ruling ʿAbbāsid family and its most intimate advisors appear to have supplied the initial impetus and a significant amount of the subsequent support, but had it not been for the active involvement of

42 See the complementary accounts by D. R. Hill, article "Mūsā, Banū," in *EI* VII,640–1, and D. Pingree, article "Banū Mūsā," *EIr.* III,716–17. Cf. further Rashed, "Transmission of Greek Scientific Thought."

43 For a concise orientation on him and references to further bibliography see Endress, *GAP* II,428.

44 See Bergsträsser, *Galen-Übersetzungen*, index, s.nn.

the other groups discussed above it is certain that the translation movement would not have lasted as long as it did, or had the same impact. Certainly, also, some religious groups were more involved than others; in medicine, for example, the Nestorian Christians were more prominent than, say, the Orthodox, but this fact is due to specific historical circumstances and in itself has no hermeneutic value for the problem at hand: the Nestorians were prominent in medicine in Ǧundīsābūr already before al-Manṣūr invited the first member of the Buḫtīšū' family to Baghdad, and yet nothing comparable to the translation movement ever took place there. The same objection would apply to any argument that would consider as significant the prominence of one ethnic group over another in some scientific activity, such as the strong Persian presence in astrological and astronomical studies during the first 'Abbāsid century. With regard to the question of patronage, therefore, it appears relatively clear that the translation movement was a result of a common effort of the majority, if not the totality, of *economically and politically* significant – actually, dominant – groups in Baghdad during the first two 'Abbāsid centuries, regardless of ethnic and religious background, because it served their various purposes both individually and collectively, as discussed in chapters 2–5.

However, distinctions have to be made, and these are based on the emphasized words in the preceding formulation. That is to say, it is also clear that the movement was strongly associated with the financially well-off and the political elite (among whom one might also count the leaders of the military). This is true especially insofar as the two went together: Baghdad, after all, was the capital city of the empire from the very beginning, and any member of the society gaining prominence would inevitably have done so either through the one or the other means. As the culture of the economic and political elite, the translation movement imposed itself upon high society and to a large extent percolated downwards to the literate but not so affluent strata of the population. Ibn-an-Nadīm's *Fihrist* is the best indicator of the wide diffusion of books on all subjects in tenth-century Baghdad, with the implication that in order to read the translated sciences one did not need to have a fortune to spend on a translator like Ḥunayn but merely enough to pay a scribe for the transcription of a few books. However, the differentiating factor in the social promotion and consumption of the cultural goods of the translation movement would appear to be, throughout its duration, political and primarily economic status, and future research on the social history of Baghdad will have to concentrate on the extent of its diffusion among the poorer strata, and the social and cultural significance of that.

2. TRANSLATORS AND TRANSLATIONS

The translations of non-Christian Greek works into Arabic were done either from the Greek originals, or from Syriac or Persian (Pahlavi) intermediaries.[45] The translators of the Pahlavi material were accordingly Persians, presumably converted to Islam. Although many Nestorian Christians who lived within the borders of the former Sasanian empire also spoke Persian and were involved with the translation movement – primarily the medical families from Ǧundīsābūr – we have no record of their having translated Pahlavi translations of Greek works into Arabic.

The translators of Greek and Syriac texts present a more variegated picture. A few of them were Syriac-speaking pagans, the Ṣābi'an scholars of Ḥarrān, who also knew Greek as *their* religious language, that of late pagan spirituality. The vast majority, however, were Aramaic (Syriac)-speaking Christians (some of whom were Arabs, like Ḥunayn) who knew Greek as a liturgical language and, given the pre-Islamic Graeco-Syriac scientific translations, in some cases, also as a scientific language. These translators from Greek and Syriac themselves belonged to the Christian churches dominant in the Fertile Crescent: Melkites or Orthodox, like the Biṭrīq father and son and Qusṭā ibn-Lūqā (who was a native Greek speaker); Jacobites, like ʿAbd-al-Masīḥ ibn-Nāʿima al-Ḥimṣī and Yaḥyā ibn-ʿAdī; and Nestorians, like the family of Ḥunayn ibn-Isḥāq, and Mattā ibn-Yūnus.

After the initial translation of Greek works through the Sasanian Pahlavi intermediaries, for which Persian-speaking translators were readily available due to the Pahlavi–Arabic translations done before the ʿAbbāsid revolution (see chapter 1.3), it is clear that when sponsors wanted to have books translated directly from the Greek, specialists

45 Although there were translations of some Greek literature into Coptic and there are traces in Sanskrit of Greek astronomy, we have at present no documentation for translations from Coptic into Arabic of scientific material, while the Arabic translations from Sanskrit of astronomical and medical works are only remotely related to any Greek sources. Lists of translators from all languages into Arabic are given by Ibn-an-Nadīm, *F* 244.1–245.10, and IAU I,203–5.

were not readily available. That is to say, although it has to be assumed, on the basis of the demography of the Near East in the second half of the eighth century, that there were enough Greek speakers in Syria and Palestine, there were no Graeco-Arabic translators by profession. This is clear from the reports we read about the earliest such attempts. Al-Mahdī, for example, had to have recourse, for the translation of Aristotle's *Topics*, to the best person *he* knew, Timothy I, the Nestorian patriarch. For his part, Timothy must have felt inadequate insofar as he had to have the help of Abū-Nūḥ, another cleric (chapter 3.1). Similarly, when the Barmakid Yaḥyā ibn-Ḫālid wanted to have an Arabic translation from the Greek of the *Synagoge* by Anatolius, he employed the talents of the patriarch of Alexandria and other churchmen (chapter 5.3). Thus, most of the early translators from the Greek were apparently clerics, doubtless because ʿAbbāsid patrons could approach them in their official capacity. Presumably the ʿAbbāsid patrons did not ask the high-standing church officials *themselves* to do the translations but simply addressed their requests to them with the understanding that the task would be delegated to appropriate individuals. One should therefore list with caution the names of these clerics among the translators. After such beginnings forced by circumstances, however, and as the demand for Graeco-Arabic translations grew because of the needs of scientists and philosophers (chapter 5.5), so did the supply and competence of translators.

It is important to emphasize this point. It was the development of an Arabic scientific and philosophical tradition that generated the wholesale demand for translations from the Greek (and Syriac and Pahlavi), not, as is commonly assumed, the translations which gave rise to science and philosophy. That the demand was primary in both time and substance is clearly indicated by the poor quality of the *Arabic style* (not necessarily of the contents) of the earliest translations: the social and scientific need on the part of the patrons, as described in chapter 5.1, for the early translations was so great that they were willing to tolerate Arabic styles that were vastly inferior to what their contemporary grammarians and stylists were extolling as proper Arabic. For example, the translator Yaḥyā ibn-al-Biṭrīq had a reputation for his bad style; Ibn-al-Qifṭī says [Q 379.18–19] that although "he was a reliable translator and rendered the concepts [of the original] well, he used broken Arabic" (*alkanu;* see *WKAS* II, ii,1265.32–5). These early translations, much maligned by al-Ǧāḥiẓ, had accordingly to be retouched and corrected stylistically (*iṣlāḥ*) by speakers of correct Arabic, like the philosopher al-Kindī.[46]

There is accordingly a corresponding development in the quality of the translations both in style and substance. Initially, when the clerics and other *ad hoc* translators were called upon by their various sponsors to translate Greek works into Arabic, they had the pre- and early Islamic Graeco-Syriac translations to fall back on as models; however, this proved of limited usefulness. The Graeco-Syriac translations of non-Christian texts did not cover the wide range of subjects in demand for translation into Arabic, and, having been made for scholarly purposes in completely different circumstances than those calling for the translations into Arabic, they were not subjected to keen criticism and demand for precision. This is best indicated by Ḥunayn's sharp criticism of earlier Syriac translations in his *Risāla*, something which is clearly not self-promotion. It is therefore inaccurate to say or infer that Greek culture "flourished" in the monasteries and Christian centers before and during the first century of Islam, and that the Graeco-Arabic translation movement simply drew upon the pre-existing knowledge of Greek of the Christians.

The translators were forced to improve their knowledge of Greek beyond the level of previous Syriac scholarship. This is most likely how one is to interpret the romantic story of Ḥunayn's rebuff by Yuḥannā Ibn-Māsawayh, his disappearance for three years, and his return with a good enough knowledge of Greek as to recite Homer by heart.[47] The Greek of the Syriac schools was not sufficient for the new standards required by the rich sponsors of the translations, and translators accordingly invested time and effort into learning Greek well because by then it had become a lucrative profession. As mentioned in the preceding section, the Banū-Mūsā used to pay monthly 500 dīnārs "for full-time translation." At that time a dīnār was 4.25 grams of almost pure gold; the monthly salary, in other words, was 2125 grams, or almost 75 ounces, of gold, or in today's price (about $320 per ounce), 24,000 US dollars. Such levels of compensation naturally attracted the best talent of the time. An excellent example is provided by the case of the Syro-Palestinian Greek, Qusṭā ibn-Lūqā, or Constantine the son of Loukas. Bio-

46 See the passages from al-Ǧāḥiẓ, *Kitāb al-Ḥayawān*, cited by Endress, *GAP* III,4. Sometimes translators appear to have worked in tandem with speakers of correct Arabic; cf. *F* 244.16.

47 See the references and discussion by G. Strohmaier, "Homer in Bagdad," *Byzantinoslavica*, 1980, vol. 41, pp. 196–200.

graphical reports about him state that he left his native Baʿlabakk (in contemporary Lebanon) and went to Baghdad in search of fame and fortune as a translator. He even took books with him, namely, Greek manuscripts that he estimated rich patrons in Baghdad would wish to have translated [*F* 243.18]. Eventually Qusṭā went to Armenia, where he continued to ply his trade.

That translation cost a lot of money is also indicated by the following incident told by Ḥunayn in his *Risāla*. Aḥmad ibn-Muḥammad ibn-al-Mudabbir asked Ḥunayn to translate Galen's commentary on Hippocrates' *Aphorisms*. After Ḥunayn had translated the first book, however, Aḥmad asked him not to translate any more until he, Aḥmad, had read the first book. Obviously Aḥmad wanted first to test the quality and possibly usefulness of whatever it was that he was buying before he decided to spend more money on it; in other words, the sum would have been substantial and worth such precautions as Aḥmad took.[48] Of course, not all translations were made directly for financial gain; Ḥunayn mentions numerous times in his *Risāla* that he prepared some translations for his son, Isḥāq,[49] from whom, presumably, he did not take any money. These were all into Syriac, as far as we can tell, and so apparently intended either for instruction or, more plausibly, further translation into Arabic for some other patron. The ultimate purpose was thus again financial. The translators were professionals and they worked as private individuals unaffiliated with any institution (for the *bayt al-ḥikma* see chapter 2.6).

Translations therefore improved with time not only because translators became more experienced, but primarily because their knowledge of Greek improved; and their knowledge of Greek improved because they had become, due to the increased demand, professional translators. The fostering of a translation culture in the first ʿAbbāsid century generated demand for better knowledge of Greek and created in the second a group of professional translators whose Greek surpassed by far that of the educated clerics of an earlier generation like the patriarch Timothy I. A scientist and translator like al-ʿAbbās ibn-Saʿīd al-Ǧawharī (d. after 843) knew Greek so well that he had memorized *in Greek* the books on logic and could recite them by heart.[50] Ḥunayn learned not only Greek as a language but

48 Bergsträsser, *Galen-Übersetzungen*, p. 40.9–13.

49 Bergsträsser, *Galen-Übersetzungen*, pp. 28.18; 34.6; 44.17; 47.1; *F* 290.10–11.

50 K. Samir and P. Nwyia, *Une correspondance islamo-chrétienne*, pp. 78–9, §12; see also *GAS* V,243–4; VI,138–9.

Greek culture in general in order better to understand the context of what he was translating. The same can be said of the next generation of translators: Qusṭā ibn-Lūqā, whom I just mentioned, was a Greek to begin with, Ṯābit ibn-Qurra, whose translation of Nicomachus's *Arithmetic* is a masterpiece of translation by any standards, and Isḥāq ibn-Ḥunayn, who presumably was taught by his father. Ḥunayn himself tells us about his expertise in the style and ideas of some authors – Homer, especially – and not others. In a note to Galen's *On Medical Names* (*De nominibus medicinalibus*), he says the following:

> In the following passage Galen quotes Aristophanes. However, the Greek manuscript, from which I translated this work into Syriac, contains such a large number of mistakes and errors that it would have been impossible for me to understand the meaning of the text had I not been so familiar with and accustomed to Galen's Greek speech and acquainted with most of his ideas from his other works. But I am not familiar with the language of Aristophanes, nor am I accustomed to it. Hence, it was not easy for me to understand the quotation, and I have, therefore, omitted it.
>
> I had an additional reason for omitting it. After I had read it, I found no more in it than what Galen had already said elsewhere. Hence, I thought that I should not occupy myself with it any further, but rather proceed to more useful matters.[51]

The second reason Ḥunayn adduces in this passage is also very informative about the theoretical assumptions that underlay the work of translation and the prevailing concepts, in this context, of "source text" and "target text." They indicate that, according to Ḥunayn's understanding, the primary quality that defined what a "(source) text" is was not the physical form (i.e., the precise and unique concatenation of words) given to it by its author, but rather its contents and the use for which it was consulted. This would also seem to be indicated by Ḥunayn's stressing, at the very beginning of his *Risāla*, that it is important to know for whom some work was translated in order to evaluate its quality.[52] The obligation of the

51 Rosenthal, *Classical Heritage*, p. 19. Elsewhere, Ḥunayn explains Homeric allusions in Galenic texts; see the examples cited by Strohmaier, "Homer in Bagdad."

52 Bergsträsser, *Galen-Übersetzungen*, p. 2.23f.

"target text," accordingly, would be to reproduce *these* features, and not a presumed "integrity" of the source text, as we assume today. Such expert knowledge of Greek and capacity for translation acquired by Ḥunayn was not something that was routinely available in the Christian monasteries where presumably most of these translators were educated, but something which the *translation movement itself generated.*

The high level of translation technique and philological accuracy achieved by Ḥunayn, his associates, and other translators early in the fourth/tenth century was due to the incentive provided by the munificence of their sponsors, a munificence which in turn was due to the prestige that Baghdadi society attached to the translated works and the knowledge of their contents. Better long-term investment was perhaps never made, for the result was spectacular for the Arabic language and Arabic letters. The translators developed an Arabic vocabulary and style for scientific discourse that remained standard well into the present century.[53]

3. TRANSLATION COMPLEXES AND THEIR STUDY

After its initial steps during the reign of al-Manṣūr, the translation movement progressed apace for more than two centuries, following a path and traversing stages dictated both by the needs of research and capacity for scholarship that it developed from within and by prevalent ideological tendencies and policies that supported it from without. Accordingly, the subject of the stages of the translation movement can be studied in its two major aspects, technical and socio-historical. The first concerns the philological nature of the translations and the translation techniques they represent. The second investigates the kinds of work selected for translation, the

53 Cf. M. Ullmann, "Nicht nur . . . sondern auch . . .," *Der Islam*, 1983, vol. 60, pp. 34–6, and his remarks in *WKAS* II,ii, pp. ix-xi. A survey of the language of the translations at all stages and of the development of scientific Arabic is given by Endress, *GAP* III,3–23. Specific studies on the development of Arabic technical terminology, on the basis of the translation literature, in the fields of logic, philosophy, astronomy, and medicine are collected in D. Jacquart, *La formation du vocabulaire scientifique et intellectuel dans le monde arabe* [Études sur le Vocabulaire Intellectuel du Moyen Age VII], Turnhout, Brepols, 1994. Graeco-Arabic historical glossaries are appended to a number of editions of translated Greek works. See now *GALex*, especially Fasc. 1, Introduction and List of Sources.

social and research needs which they covered, and the implications of this for social history. The two are naturally interrelated in different ways.

Discussion of the technical aspect of the Graeco-Arabic translations has dominated scholarly interest to the point of exclusivity since, it would seem, the very beginning; the great Arab littérateur al-Ǧāḥiẓ, a contemporary of Ḥunayn himself, makes numerous observations relating to the enterprise and process of translation.[54] What is most frequently quoted on the subject by an Arab scholar, however, has been the statement by the fourteenth-century polymath, Ḫalīl ibn-Aybak aṣ-Ṣafadī (d. 764/1363). He claimed that there are two methods of translation, a literal one (*ad verbum*) and one according to sense (*ad sensum*), and cited Ibn-al-Biṭrīq and Ibn-an-Nāʿima as representatives of the former and Ḥunayn ibn-Ishāq and al-Ǧawharī of the latter, which he also claimed to be superior.[55] Given the appeal of this simplistic formulation and the great fame of Ḥunayn, this report received more attention than it ever deserved, but it has now been shown to be completely baseless – indeed, if generalizations could at all be descriptive of the technical aspects of the Graeco-Arabic translations it would be truer to say that the tendency was toward greater literalness after Ḥunayn.[56] It is also misleading because, by the very fact that Ibn-al-Biṭrīq and Ibn-Nāʿima lived before Ḥunayn and al-Ǧawharī, aṣ-Ṣafadī generates the impression of a *temporal* progression in the development of translation styles – first come the clumsy, literal translations, followed by the more polished free ones. This in turn has facilitated the widely held assumption that the translation movement has developed in *successive* phases or stages of increasing refinement and sophistication in the translation technique. Three such phases have been by and large identified: the literal "old" translations (the *veteres*), the more

54 Primarily in his book on animals (*Kitāb al-Ḥayawān*); for a sampling of his remarks in English translation see Pellat, *Jāḥiẓ*, p. 133.

55 The full text is translated in Rosenthal, *Classical Heritage*, p. 17, where related comments by other scholars are also cited. Hugonnard-Roche, "Les traductions du grec," p. 141, note 28, cites a similar sentiment by Maimonides.

56 See the detailed comparison between two translations of the same Greek text, one from the circle of al-Kindī and the other by Isḥāq ibn-Ḥunayn, by J.N. Mattock, "The Early Translations from Greek into Arabic: An Experiment in Comparative Assessment," in G. Endress (ed.), *Symposium Graeco-arabicum II*, Amsterdam, 1989, pp. 73–102. Further examples by Hugonnard-Roche, "Les traductions du grec," pp. 143–4, with reference to similar earlier views by F. Zimmermann and G.L. Lewis.

polished intermediate phase of Ḥunayn and his circle, and the later ones (the *recentiores*) of the Baghdad philosophical school which, being predominantly revisions of the earlier ones, exhibit mastery of philological and scholarly detail.[57]

The reality is infinitely more complicated, and a chronological paradigm of successive stages, each necessarily differentiated from the rest by a specific characteristic, the style of translating – literal, free, revisionist – is not helpful for analysis. This is due to the fact that the chronological paradigm is inflexible with regard to style both synchronically and diachronically. Synchronically, because different styles of translating can be witnessed in translations that belong to the same phase: for example, the *Metaphysics* translation by Usṭāṯ is slavishly literal, as opposed to that of the *Enneads*, i.e., the *Theology of Aristotle;* and yet not only were both of these translations contemporary, but they were also executed for the same purposes and in the same circle (of al-Kindī; see further below). Thus, if the early style of the translations is assumed to be either literal or free, one or the other of the two cases just mentioned cannot be explained; and if it is assumed to be both, then the paradigm loses its classificatory value with style as its criterion. Diachronically, because the same style of translating is witnessed in more than one phase, in which case the same arguments as in the preceding instance will have the same invalidating effect.

The chronological paradigm based on differences of style is completely inadequate to represent the reality of the actual course of the translation movement with regard to the nature of the translations as translations. It is much more fruitful to discuss the problem in terms of *complexes* of translations, rather than stages or phases, because such a schema allows us to examine them in their concrete manifestations, without theoretical presuppositions, and can accommodate all the specific facts about each complex which may not be shared by other complexes. For the specific characteristics of translations are many and they are present in complexes of translations in different combinations. Among the variable characteristics that may present themselves in different combinations the following are the most obvious: (a) The languages from which the Arabic translation was made varied: some of the earliest translations of Greek works were done from Persian (intermediaries), Syriac remained to the very

57 This view is most clearly stated by F.E. Peters in his *Aristotle and the Arabs*, New York, 1968, pp. 59–61, who also used the Latin terms given above in parentheses.

end of the translation period an intermediate stage that was constantly in use, while many others were done directly from the Greek. (b) Repeated translations were often not "new" but revisions of existing ones. Such revisions would naturally exhibit a mixture of styles and terminology. Revised versions on occasion also exhibit contaminations: both (c) theoretical, from the commentatorial tradition, and (d) applied, from terminology and usage based on the actual research of scholar sponsors. (e) Competences of translators varied, both in general and in regard to a particular subject; the *Fihrist* is full of judgments about translators, and even Ḥunayn tells us that he could not translate the work of Aristophanes (see section 6.2). (f) The approach and purpose of the translator, finally, also varied: a paraphrastic version was frequently a goal, not an accident of incompetence.[58]

Analysis on the basis of complexes of translations allows us to take into consideration all of the above, decide their relevance to the complex under investigation, and present a description of the complex that would at the same time account *historically* for its having taken this particular aspect. What is clearly called for is identification of circles, subjects, orientations among the translators and scientists, and study of the specifics of each such identified unit. Research has made some progress along these lines and it is possible to have an idea of how the translation complexes actually worked.

To begin with, an obvious complex of translations is constituted by the Galenic and Hippocratic works translated by Ḥunayn and his associates. In the identification of these works we are fortunate to have Ḥunayn's own account, as preserved in his *Risāla*, a work that has already been frequently quoted. The Arabic versions of Ḥunayn, however, are different from those of Ḥubayš or ʿĪsā ibn-Yaḥyā, and the pioneering linguistic analyses by G. Bergsträsser of their translations paved the way for differentiating among them.[59] More recent work by H.H. Biesterfeldt along the same lines defined in even greater detail the characteristics of the translations by Ḥubayš.[60] On the basis of this work, it has been possible to extend research into the translations by Ḥunayn and his associates that are not covered by his

58 For a detailed exposition of the problems involved in the analysis of the translations see Endress, *GAP* III,5–6.

59 G. Bergsträsser, *Ḥunain ibn Isḥāḳ und seine Schule*, Leiden, E.J. Brill, 1913.

60 H.H. Biesterfeldt, *Galens Traktat 'Dass die Kräfte der Seele den Mischungen des Körpers folgen' in arabischer Übersetzung*, Wiesbaden, F. Steiner, 1973, pp. 15–28.

Risāla. On the basis of the Arabic versions of some of the essays by Alexander of Aphrodisias, H.-J. Ruland provided useful criteria, in the form of a Graeco-Arabic "translation grammar" (*Übersetzungsgrammatik*), for discerning the different layers of translation work with regard to some of the points I mentioned in the last-but-one paragraph.[61] As the most famous translator, numerous translations are falsely ascribed to Ḥunayn in both the Arabic bibliographical literature and the manuscripts. In the case of the famous dream book of Artemidorus, it has been possible, on the basis this time of analysis of Ḥunayn's vocabulary, to disprove the ascription.[62]

A second complex of translations, and one of the highest importance for the origins of Arabic philosophy, is that of al-Kindī and his circle, identified and described in a series of publications by G. Endress. On the basis of linguistic similarities, Endress identified the following works as belonging to this complex: Aristotle's *Metaphysics* in the translation of Eustathius (Usṭāṯ), otherwise unknown; a paraphrastic selection from Plotinus's *Enneads* (Books IV–VI), known as the *Theology of Aristotle*, translated by ʿAbd-al-Masīḥ ibn-Nāʿima and corrected by al-Kindī himself; a selection of propositions from the *Elements of Theology* by Proclus, some of which were eventually reworked, possibly by al-Kindī himself, into the compilation known as *The Pure Good* (translated into medieval Latin as *Liber de causis)*; *Introduction to Arithmetic* by the Neopythagorean Nicomachus, translated by Ḥabīb ibn-Bihrīz and corrected by al-Kindī; paraphrases of certain Platonic dialogues, like that of the *Timaeus* done by Yaḥyā ibn-al-Biṭrīq, a Byzantine *patrikios*, and that of the *Symposium*, apparently done by a Ṣābi'an scholar; Aristotle's *De caelo, Meteorology*, and zoological works, also translated by Yaḥyā; and a compendium, influenced by the interpretation of Ioannes Philoponus, of Aristotle's *De anima*.[63] All of these texts display certain

61 H.-J. Ruland, *Die arabische Übersetzung der Schrift des Alexander von Aphrodisias über die Sinneswahrnehmung* [Nachrichten der Akad. der Wiss. in Göttingen, Philol.-Hist. Klasse, 1978, Nr. 5], Göttingen, 1978, pp. 164, 196–202 [6, 38–44], based also on the same author's exhaustive analyses in his dissertation, *Die arabischen Fassungen von zwei Schriften des Alexander von Aphrodisias Über die Vorsehung und Über das liberum arbitrium*, unpublished Ph.D. dissertation, University of Saarbrücken, 1976, pp. 107–32, 148–9.

62 M. Ullmann, "War Ḥunain der Übersetzer von Artemidors Traumbuch?" *Die Welt des Islams*, 1971, vol. 13, pp. 204–11.

63 G. Endress, "The Circle of al-Kindī," in G. Endress and R. Kruk (eds), *The Ancient Tradition in Christian and Islamic Hellenism*, pp. 52–8, with references to his other publications.

characteristics of translation which define this complex; Endress calls them "guide fossils" and lists them as follows [p. 59]:

- the use of loan-words and transliterated Greek (also some Aramaic and Persian) terms;
- the use of loan-translations (calques);
- the transition from pre-scientific *ad hoc* use of Arabic equivalents (sometimes coined on Syriac calques) to a systematic and consistent terminology;
- the formation of abstract nouns and other neologisms;
- the concurrent use of several terms or sets of terms by contemporary translators or groups of translators;
- the stylistic influence of the Alexandrian lecture-course in the phraseology of the translators, where an inventory of introductory, summarizing, transitional and connecting phrases is one of the most striking features of some of these texts;[64]
- a tendency towards interpretation with a markedly Neoplatonic preference, but at the same time eliminating in the Neoplatonic texts themselves the plurality of divine hypostases.

The last point made by Endress here is very significant for it points to an understanding of translation activity as a creative process that only now is beginning to be fully appreciated. The changes and additions that we frequently see in the translated text vis-à-vis the Greek original were either amplificatory and explanatory, or systematic and tendentious.[65] This means that some of the translations were deliberately not literal because they were made for a specific purpose and to serve certain theoretical positions already held. Thus, just as certain Greek texts were selected for translation because they were expected to provide information and arguments in discussions in progress in ʿAbbāsid society, the ideological or scientific orientation of these very discussions influenced the way in which the texts were translated. This circularity is the best evidence we have of the organic nature of the translation movement in early ʿAbbāsid intellectual life; we have seen an example of it from mathematics in the translations of Diophantus (above, chapter 5.5), while an example from philosophy

64 For examples of such phrases and their relation to the underlying Greek original see *GALex*, Fasc. 2, pp. 176–8, *iḏā* 8.1.

65 For a detailed list of them in the Arabic translation of Proclus's *Elements of Theology* see G. Endress, *Proclus Arabus*, Beirut, F. Steiner, 1973, pp. 194–241.

has recently been provided by the analysis of some translations of Alexander of Aphrodisias executed in the circle of al-Kindī.[66]

The complex of translations of the Aristotelian *Organon* is one of the great achievements of the translation movement both for its influence and philosophical content. A detailed study would require a book of its own, divided according to the different stages of its evolution, from the earliest Syriac translations to the final phase as represented in the scholarship of the Baghdad Aristotelians, recorded in the Paris manuscript of the texts (Bibliothèque Nationale, ar. 2346). The manuscript contains all nine treatises of the Alexandrian *Organon*, starting with Porphyry's *Eisagoge* and including the *Rhetoric* and the *Poetics*. They were all copied from the autograph of al-Ḥasan ibn-Suwār (d. ca. 421/1030), who had copied some of them from the autograph of his teacher, Yaḥyā ibn-ʿAdī (d. 363/974), who in turn had collated his own copy of the *Categories* and *De interpretatione* with the autograph of the translator, Isḥāq ibn-Ḥunayn (d. 298/910). Moreover, all the treatises were collated again with a number of other versions, ranging from the copies of Ibn-Zurʿa (d. 398/1008), another student of Yaḥyā ibn-ʿAdī, to the autographs of other translators like Abū-ʿUṯmān ad-Dimašqī (d. after 302/914). In addition, the manuscript contains a very great number of both marginal and interlinear notes of a philosophical nature, the result of repeated recourse to earlier Syriac translations and of analysis on the basis of philosophical discussions in the school of al-Fārābī to which they all belonged.[67] The manuscript is a one-volume encyclopedia of the history of Arabic logic in Baghdad for over a century, a history which has yet to be written out.[68]

A fourth and equally significant translation complex is that of Euclid's works and in particular his *Elements*. The situation is

66 S. Fazzo and H. Wiesner, "Alexander of Aphrodisias in the Kindī-Circle and in al-Kindī's Cosmology," *Arabic Sciences and Philosophy*, 1993, vol. 3, pp. 119–53.

67 See the discussion and examples given by H. Hugonnard-Roche, "Remarques sur la tradition arabe de l'*Organon* d'après le manuscrit Paris, Bibliothèque Nationale, ar. 2346," in C. Burnett (ed.), *Glosses and Commentaries on Aristotelian Logical Texts*, pp. 19–28, correcting the philologically reductionist views of R. Walzer, "New Light on the Arabic Translations of Aristotle," *Oriens*, 1953, vol. 6, pp. 91–142, reprinted in his *Greek into Arabic*, Oxford, Bruno Cassirer, pp. 60–113.

68 The numerous articles by H. Hugonnard-Roche are fundamental in this respect. See, in general, his "La formation du vocabulaire de la logique en arabe," in D. Jacquart (ed.), *La formation du vocabulaire scientifique et intellectuel dans le monde arabe*, pp. 22–38, and his references to his other works there.

extremely complicated and no theory of a linear development of increasingly more faithful translations will help clear the situation. The *Fihrist* informs us that al-Ḥaǧǧaǧ ibn-Yūsuf ibn-Maṭar made two translations, one during the reign (or the commission) of Hārūn and the other during the reign of al-Ma'mūn, and that it was translated yet again by Isḥāq ibn-Ḥunayn and corrected by Ṯābit ibn-Qurra [*F* 265]. There were numerous Arabic commentaries. This information has been difficult to verify on the basis of the existing texts, which display a bewildering variety.[69] What is more, there is no mention by the bibliographers of the earlier translation made during the reign of al-Manṣūr, about which we are informed by the historians (see above, chapters 2.2 and 5.5). The complexity of the situation is obviously due to the fact that the translations were not made to be stored on shelves and forgotten – in which case it would have been a simple matter to trace their genealogy – but to be used by scholars in their research, in the course of which there were constant elaborations and revisions. The study of the Arabic translations of the *Elements*, therefore, cannot be accomplished without a parallel study of the development of mathematical sciences during the time of the translations. A parallel but different instance of complexity is presented by the text of Euclid's *Optics*. On the basis of the medieval bibliographical information, its translation and transmission appeared simple. The detailed investigation by R. Rashed of all the earliest extant Arabic treatises on the subject, however, has revealed that the extant Arabic translation of the *Optics* is not the one used by al-Kindī, who appears to have used an earlier one. Both of these translations, moreover, reflect recensions of the Greek text that are also different from the two extant Greek recensions, called the "original" and that "of Theon" by Heiberg.[70] Continued research, both philological and scientific, on these mathematical texts, perhaps also in conjunction with the translations of Ptolemy's *Almagest*,[71] are needed before a clearer picture emerges.

69 See the textual probes in a number of articles by S. Brentjes, in particular "Textzeugen und Hypothesen zum arabischen Euklid," *Archive for History of Exact Sciences*, 1994, vol. 47, pp. 53–92.

70 See R. Rashed, *Oeuvres philosophiques et scientifiques d'al-Kindī. Volume I. L'Optique et la Catoptrique*, Leiden, E.J. Brill, 1997, pp. 6–45, reprinted independently as "Le commentaire par al-Kindī de l'*Optique* d'Euclide: un traité jusqu'ici inconnu," *Arabic Sciences and Philosophy*, 1997, vol. 7, pp. 9–56.

71 For these consult P. Kunitzsch, *Der Almagest. Die Syntaxis Mathematica des Claudius Ptolemäus in arabisch-lateinischer Überlieferung*, Wiesbaden, F. Steiner, 1974, pp. 6–71.

In each of the four examples just given, the translation techniques and their progression are unique to them and cannot be generalized for all. Obviously in each complex there were early, middle, and late translations, but these terms would mean different things for the different complexes. Chronologically, first of all, there is frequently significant disparity: the Kindī circle complex of translations, for example, was finished before that of the Baghdad *Organon* even began. Genetically, the Kindī circle translations would seem to have been done directly from the Greek; the Baghdad *Organon*, as we have it in the Paris manuscript, relied almost entirely on Syriac intermediaries – indeed, it relied on the very rich and long tradition of Syriac logical works that goes chronologically back to the seventh century. Substantively, there appears to be little concern, for ideological reasons, in the Kindī circle complex, for philological exactitude in fidelity to the original: as we saw, "interpretive" translation was a feature of this complex. The Baghdad *Organon* by contradistinction (also because of the nature of the subject matter treated, logic), paid great attention to philological detail, as Walzer showed, if only to arrive at better philosophical understanding, as Hugonnard-Roche rightly added.

These examples should suffice to give an understanding of the infinite complexity and richness of the translations themselves, the futility of trying to see them as mechanically progressing from a "literal" to a "sophisticated" phase, and their significance, when properly studied, for a deeper understanding of intellectual developments in Baghdad during the translation movement. Seen from such a perspective of translation complexes, with their own history of development in accordance with the set of problems proper to each individual complex, many misconceptions not only about the translation movement itself but also about the development of Arabic science and philosophy will be eliminated of themselves. One such very prevalent misconception is that the translation movement went through two major stages, a "receptive" one, roughly through the time of al-Ma'mūn, and a "creative" one subsequently.[72] Study of

72 The notion of "receptive" and "creative" stages is used by F. Sezgin as applied to Arabic science in general and not specifically to the translation movement. Sezgin takes this notion from W. Hartner, "Quand et comment s'est arrêté l'essor de la culture scientifique dans l'Islam?" in *Classicisme et Déclin culturel dans l'histoire de l'Islam*, Paris, Besson-Chantermerle, 1957; reprinted Maisonneuve et Larose, 1977, p. 322. He applies it, though, to the Banū-Mūsā, the great patrons of translations, with whom ostensibly the "creative" period begins (*GAS* V,246). G. Strohmaier also talks about a "receiving" culture as opposed

the translation complexes, as the example of the Kindī circle complex of translations shows, invalidates by itself even the very posing of the question in such a way: translations are seen from the very beginning as part of research processes stemming from intellectual currents in Baghdad and as such creative responses to the rapidly developing Arabic scientific and philosophical tradition. Study of the complexes emancipates one from the perennial but moot problems of essentializing conceptualizations and explanations, such as the extent of the "originality" of Arabic science and philosophy, or the "creativity" or lack thereof of Arabs and Semites.

to the "providing" culture, and he views the Arabs still to be the receivers, and the Byzantines the providers in the eighth century: "Byzantinisch-arabische Wissenschaftsbeziehungen in der Zeit des Ikonoklasmus," in H. Köpstein und F. Winkelmann (eds), *Studien zum 8. und 9. Jahrhundert in Byzanz* [Berliner Byzantinistische Arbeiten 51], Berlin, Akademie Verlag, 1983, pp. 179–83. More quaint formulations of this theme include the use of the metaphor of plant irrigation to explain the two phases: "At the end of the IIIrd/IXth cent., the bulk of the Greek philosophical . . . writings . . . was accessible in good Arabic translations. The result was that of a fertilizing rain: hundreds of Muslim scholars eagerly began to study and to appropriate Greek learning . . ." J. Schacht and M. Meyerhof, *The Medico-Philosophical Controversy between Ibn Butlan of Baghdad and Ibn Ridwan of Cairo* [The Egyptian University, Faculty of Arts Publication no. 13], Cairo, 1937, p. 7. Variations of this theme can be found throughout the literature.

7

TRANSLATION AND HISTORY

Developments from the Translation Movement

1. THE END OF THE TRANSLATION MOVEMENT

All our information indicates that after a vigorous course for over two centuries, the translation movement in Baghdad slowed down and eventually came to an end around the turn of the millennium. In order to be understood properly, however, this observation needs to be qualified in a number of ways. In the first place, an inference that cannot be drawn from it is that there was an attenuation of interest in the translated sciences, or that, as a corollary, there was a diminution in the number of scholars able to translate from the Greek. Quite to the contrary, an efflorescence of scientific activity is witnessed toward the end of the tenth century with the foundation of the ʿAḍudī hospital in Baghdad (372/982) and the scholars affiliated with it. One of the physicians in their midst, Naẓīf ibn-Yumn(or Ayman?) ar-Rūmī, the Melkite, translated, apparently in addition to medical works, book A (and possibly also book M) of Aristotle's *Metaphysics,*[1] and told Ibn-an-Nadīm, the author of the *Fihrist*, that he had come across a Greek version of the tenth book of Euclid's *Elements* which contained an additional forty figures and that he was planning to translate it [*F* 266.2–4]. His colleague Ibrāhīm ibn-Bakkūš al-ʿAššārī, a well-known physician, translated from the Greek *The Causes of Plants* and *On Sense Perception* by Theophrastus, and from Ibn-Nāʿima's Syriac version Aristotle's *Sophistici elenchi.*[2] Ibn-Abī-Uṣaybiʿa, who mentions that Ibrāhīm's

1 M. Bouyges, *Averroès. Tafsir ma baʿd at-tabiʿat. Notice*, Beyrouth, Dar el-Machreq, 1952, reprinted 1972, pp. cxxii, lvi. See further the references in *GAP* II,443 note 103, and the discussion in Kraemer, *Humanism*, pp. 132–4.

2 See the references by Ullmann, *Geheimwissenschaften*, pp. 73–4.

son ʿAlī was also a physician and translator, specifies that his translations were much appreciated [IAU I,244.13]. Unrelated (?) to this activity, Ṣābi'an scholars like Ṯābit ibn-Ibrāhīm aṣ-Ṣābi' (d. 369/980) continued to translate Greek medical works [*GAS* III, 154–6; *EI* VIII,673–4].

These and numerous other examples make it abundantly clear that interest in translations and the translated sciences in Būyid Baghdad not only had not diminished since the the first two ʿAbbāsid centuries but had arguably increased. The cultural efflorescence of the Būyid era has been richly described in recent studies, and in particular by J.L. Kraemer's *Humanism in the Renaissance of Islam*, so that there is no need for further elaboration. And if the interest and the financially supported sponsorship were there, then had they been directed toward Greek works, translators capable of rendering them – the theoretical descendants of a Naẓīf or an Ibrāhīm ibn-Bakkūš – could always have been found. In this context, the waning of the Graeco-Arabic translation movement can only be seen to be due to the fact that it had nothing to offer; in other words, it had lost its social and scientific relevance. It had nothing to offer not in the sense that there were no more secular Greek books to be translated, but in the sense that it had no more Greek books to offer that were relevant to the concerns and demands of the sponsors, scholars and scientists alike. In most fields, the crucial main texts had long before been translated, studied, and commented upon, and as a result, each discipline had advanced beyond the stage represented by the translated works. The Greek works thus lost their scholarly currentness and the demand was now for up-to-date research. Patrons commissioned increasingly not the translation of Greek works but original Arabic compositions. This process had been long in the making, and it has already been observed during the second ʿAbbāsid century (cf. chapter 6.1a). With the Būyid era, it reached the point where it became so prevalent that translations were no longer commissioned. From this vantage point, the translation movement stopped or came to an end because the Arabic philosophical and scientific enterprise which had created the need for it from the very beginning became autonomous.

Let us consider: long before the end of the Būyid period (1055), and thus before the final waning of the translation movement, the following scholars had already written their major works which revolutionized science: in medicine, ʿAlī ibn-ʿAbbās al-Maǧūsī (Haly Abbas, d. toward the end of the fourth/tenth century) and Avicenna (d. 428/1037); in astronomy, al-Battānī (d. 317/929) and al-Bīrūnī (d. 440/1048); in mathematics, al-Ḫwārizmī (first half of third/ninth century) and in physics, Ibn al-Hayṯam (d. after 432/1041); in philosophy, al-Fārābī (d. 339/950) and Avicenna again, etc. The works of these scholars not only engaged and eventually superseded, from a scientific point of view, the translated literature, but they were also composed in a style, form, and attitude that responded to contemporary attitudes in the Islamic world. Representative examples are such explicitly critical books as Rhazes' *Doubts about Galen* (*aš-Šukūk ʿalā Ǧālīnūs*) and Ibn-al-Hayṯam's *Doubts about Ptolemy* (*aš-Šukūk ʿalā Baṭlamyūs*). To these one might add a book such as Avicenna's *Eastern Philosophy* (*al-Ḥikma al-mašriqiyya*), an expository distillation of his major areas of disagreement with Aristotle which, for all practical purposes, could have been called "Doubts about Aristotle."[3] It is not so much the influence of these specific books that exposed the inadequacies of the three pillars of Greek science – Galen, Ptolemy, Aristotle – (which they did) that is important in the final analysis, but the attitude of scholars and scientists who, through their active interest in the advancement of their respective disciplines made possible an intellectual climate in which such books could be written and appreciated. In this context, the translated works lost their relevance and became part of the history of science.

As a matter of fact, in the tenth and eleventh centuries the composition of original scientific and philosophical treatises in Arabic that advanced beyond the level of the translated Greek works became so dominant and widespread that it generated its own "purist" reaction. Certain scholars with a pedantic bent, whose approach to science and philosophy was scholastic and legalistic rather than experimental and creative, reacted against this development, which they considered a dilution of the teachings of "infallible" Greek scientists, and advocated, in word and deed, a return to the original Greek works (in their Arabic translation, of course). This movement was most widespread in al-Andalus, where Averroes objected to the development of philosophy in the hands of Avicenna and sought to return to an understanding of "pristine" Aristotle, and where the astronomer al-Biṭrūǧī found not only Arabic astronomers but also Ptolemy unfaithful to Aristotelian principles and created bizarre astronomical theories in order to accommodate Aristotle's

3 Cf. the discussion in my *Avicenna and the Aristotelian Tradition*, Leiden, E.J. Brill, 1988, pp. 125–7.

theory of uniform circular motion of the celestial bodies.[4] In the East also such a reaction can be witnessed in the writings of ʿAbd-al-Laṭīf al-Baghdādī (d. 629/1231) who advocated rejecting original Arabic scholarship (Avicenna) and going back to Aristotle, Hippocrates, and Galen in a book significantly entitled *Two Pieces of Advice* (*Kitāb an-Naṣīḥatayn*), i.e., on philosophy and medicine. The reactionary nature of such attempts, in the face of the great advances of Arabic sciences and philosophy, is evident from the fact that such scholars exercised almost no influence in subsequent Arabic letters.

In a parallel development and along with the political fragmentation in the tenth century that is characteristic of the Būyid era and the creation of a "Muslim commonwealth,"[5] the scientific and philosophical activities disengaged themselves from their original locus, Baghdad, and spread throughout the Islamic world. Decentralization of power also meant decentralization of cultural patronage, but just as the model of political power remained Baghdad and the caliphate, the model of culture, to be emulated by all aspiring provincial rulers, remained the scientific and philosophical tradition and the translation culture of the Baghdadi elites. Of the scholars named above for purposes of illustration, al-Bīrūnī and Avicenna worked in Central Asia, Avicenna (later in his life) and al-Maǧūsī in the Iranian world, al-Battānī in ar-Raqqa (eastern Syria) and Ibn-al-Hayṯam in Cairo, while the Andalusian caliph ʿAbd-ar-Raḥmān III (r. 300/912–350/961) imported the translated sciences into his court and sponsored a new translation of Dioscurides' *Materia medica*, complete with a translator on loan from the Byzantine emperor.[6]

The spread of the scientific and philosophical tradition had a felicitous side effect. As the centers of political power and hence of culture multiplied, so did patronage and hence scientific and philosophical work itself. This will help explain why the Būyid era might seem to some scholars as a "renaissance" in the sense of a cultural revival. Actually, however, the real renaissance, in the original sense of revival of classical Greek learning, took place in the first two centuries of ʿAbbāsid rule in Baghdad. But even in this sense it is

4 See A.I. Sabra, "The Andalusian Revolt against Ptolemaic Astronomy," in E. Mendelsohn (ed.), *Transformation and Tradition in the Sciences*, Cambridge, Cambridge University Press, 1984, pp. 133–53.

5 As called by H. Kennedy, *The Prophet and the Age of the Caliphates*, London and New York, Longman, 1986, pp. 200ff.; cf. Kraemer, *Humanism*, p. 53 and note 61.

6 Ullmann, *Medizin*, p. 260.

possible to make a discrimination, in that though the early ʿAbbāsid and European renaissances may share an interest in classical learning for its use value – i.e., for its application to real problems – the philological aspect of classical studies, which also has its modern origin in the European Renaissance, was wholly absent in the Arabic counterpart. There are some semblances of scholarly and philological scholasticism, with regard to Aristotelian studies, that would appear to set in with the Baghdadi school of Yaḥyā ibn-ʿAdī and his students,[7] but the hurricane of Avicenna's philosophy quickly swept such tendencies away.

2. CONTEMPORARY REACTIONS TO THE TRANSLATION MOVEMENT

The massive infusion of translated works was decisive in the formation of classical Arabic culture in the ninth and tenth centuries. Like any movement in history, it was, as described in the preceding pages, initiated, favored, and promoted from within the early ʿAbbāsid society by certain social groups and strata for the advancement of their causes, interests, and policies; without such internal sponsorship translation activity, the talented and learned Syriac-speaking Christians notwithstanding, would have remained the incidental scholarly occupation of the eccentric few, socially and historically insignificant.

Since the translation movement was a social and historical phenomenon in this sense, it is only natural to expect that it would also have corresponding consequences. These were manifold and took various forms throughout Islamic history. The historical delineation and serious study of them have not yet begun; if anything, they have been hampered and set back by the almost universal and completely unfounded assumption of a unified and undifferentiated Islamic "orthodoxy" that was allegedly inimical to the ancient sciences. Reactions to the translation movement there certainly were, but they need to be described and studied in concrete detail for every age and social context within Islamic history. In this section I will present the more salient of them during the period of the translation movement;

7 This is perhaps best exemplified by the *Categories* commentary of Abū-l-Farağ ibn-aṭ-Ṭayyib, an exact replica of what was written in Alexandria five centuries earlier, reproduced apparently just in imitation of tradition; cf. my *Avicenna*, p. 227, note 12.

in the following section I will discuss the alleged "orthodox" opposition in subsequent centuries and the actual historical record.

The initial reactions to the influx of the translated sciences came essentially from two directions, one from outside the ʿAbbāsid intellectual circles in Baghdad and the other from inside. The reaction from outside came, understandably, from the adherents and nostalgists of the defeated Umayyad dynasty. After the victory of the ʿAbbāsid revolution in 750, the sole surviving Umayyad prince, ʿAbd-ar-Raḥmān, established himself as caliph in al-Andalus and North Africa. The Mālikī school of law, which had already spread in the region, took up the defense of the fallen dynasty. In what can only be described as an apologetic account of the fall of the dynasty, one of the main fathers of Mālikī law, ʿAbdallāh ibn-abī-Zayd of Qayrawān in Tunisia (310/922–386/998), the "second Mālik ibn-Anas" [*GAS* I,478–81] said the following:

> God have mercy on the Umayyad dynasty! There was never a caliph among them who instituted a [heretical] innovation in Islam. Most of their governors and administrators of their provinces were Arabs. But when the caliphate passed from them and devolved upon the ʿAbbāsid dynasty, their state was based upon the Persians, who held positions of leadership, while the hearts of most of the leaders among them were filled with unbelief and hate for the Arabs and for the Islamic state. They introduced within Islam currents that would permit the destruction of Islam. Had it not been for the fact that God Almighty had promised His Prophet that his religion and its adherents would be victorious on the Day of Judgment, they would have abolished Islam. They did, however, make breaches on it[s walls] and damage its pillars, but God will fulfill His promise, God willing!
>
> The first current which they introduced was to export in Islamic lands the books of the Greeks which were then translated into Arabic and circulated widely among the Muslims. The reason of their being exported from the land of the Byzantines into the Islamic territories was Yaḥyā ibn-Ḫālid ibn-Barmak.

ʿAbdallāh ibn-abī-Zayd then went on to provide the following story in explanation of Yaḥyā's acquisition of Greek books. The Byzantine emperor, in whose land the Greek books were to be found, was afraid that if the Byzantines examined these books they would abandon Christianity and revert to the religion of the Greeks, thereby ruining his empire. He thus collected all the ancient books and had them interred in a secret building. When Yaḥyā ibn-Ḫālid the Barmakid took effective control of the ʿAbbāsid state, he heard the story about the interred books and requested to borrow them from the Byzantine emperor. The emperor was delighted at this request because, as he said to his assembled bishops, all his predecessors were afraid that should these books fall into the hands of Christians and be read by them it would spell the ruin of Christianity. He therefore suggested that the books be sent to Yaḥyā with the added request that they be not returned; in this way, he said, "the Muslims will be afflicted with these books and we shall be rid of their evil. For I am not sure that there will not come someone after me who will dare to make these books public to the people, in which case they will fall into what we are afraid of." ʿAbdallāh ibn-abī-Zayd then ends with the following moral: "Very few people ever applied themselves to the study of this book [on logic] and were saved from heresy (*zandaqa*). Then Yaḥyā established in his house disputations and dialectical argumentation on matters that should not [be discussed], and every adherent of a religion began to discuss his religion and raise objections against it relying on himself [alone, i.e., disregarding revelation]."[8]

This can only be interpreted as "associationist" opposition to the Greek sciences: they are to be disapproved of not because of themselves, but because they are associated with the hated ʿAbbāsids who introduced them; to the fallen Umayyads, nothing the ʿAbbāsids did could ever be good. The story of the Byzantine emperor and the books is offered as proof of the incompetence and gullibility of the ʿAbbāsids who are consequently shown to be unfit to lead the Muslim community.

The reaction from within the ʿAbbāsid intellectual world in Baghdad and ʿAbbāsid society in general came from different quarters, each operating independently of the other and for its own reasons. In trying to understand the very complex social situation in Baghdad during the period of the translation movement it is necessary to heed a word of caution in order not to have a distorted and anachronistic historical outlook. In the first place, there was no such thing as "Islamic orthodoxy" in the period under discussion, in the

8 Quoted by as-Suyūṭī, *Ṣawn al-manṭiq wa-l-kalām ʿan fann al-manṭiq wa-l-kalām*, ʿAlī Sāmī an-Naššār (ed.), Cairo, 1947, pp. 6–8.

general (or, for that matter, in any) sense of the term. There were ideological policies espoused and promulgated by the caliphs, certainly, but these had primarily religious content or orientation to varying degrees and with varying intensity. Of the three such policies that I discussed in the previous chapters, al-Manṣūr's was the least "religious" as such, al-Mahdī's was religious (Islamic) only in a polemical sense, i.e., it defended Islam by opposing non-Muslims both in argument and through persecution, without, however, defining what "Islam" was, and only al-Ma'mūn's was religious in the sense that it enforced a specific religious dogma: it raised the religious element as the principal one in his political ideology and made religion the pre-eminent ideological expression of his political agenda, taking to heart the Testament of the Sasanian Ardašīr. Caliphal ideology, however, though on occasion wishing to impose a belief that it would like to present as orthodoxy, is not what is understood by the term. Other than the ideologies from the top, ʿAbbāsid society seen from below was a great amalgam of competing groups with widely varying ideologies, religious beliefs, and practices that also wished, like the rulers, to project their views as "orthodox" and win for them a central position in the society. The period of the translations thus is a formative period in which no *religious* view had crystallized to an extent that it could be called "orthodoxy"; if anything, and if we are to judge by the support for the translation movement from the totality of the political and economic elite of Baghdadi society (cf. chapter 6.1), it came as close to being a *majority* ideology – even if not a religious view – as one could wish, and it certainly was such in the succeeding Būyid century (945–1055).

Second, throughout this period there was no confrontation between what Western scholars call "reason" and "faith." The question of how faith is to be defined certainly played a key role in the theological developments of the period, but it was not opposed to "reason"; if anything, reason was used as a tool in all these discussions. Furthermore, reason was not something championed exclusively by the scholars in favor of Greek sciences as opposed to the "faith" of the benighted Muslims (this dichotomy is a distinctly Western theologoumenon that has nothing to do with Islamic realities). One frequently finds, in discussions of the philosophical and scientific traditions in Islamic societies, the following enlightened observation of al-Kindī:

> We ought not to be ashamed of appreciating the truth and of acquiring it wherever it comes from, even if it comes from races

> distant and nations different from us. For the seeker of truth nothing takes precedence over the truth, and there is no disparagement of the truth, nor belittling either of him who speaks it or of him who conveys it. [The status of] no one is diminished by the truth; rather does the truth ennoble all.[9]

What one does not find mentioned at all is precisely the similar view expressed by his contemporary Ibn-Qutayba (d. 276/889), a traditional scholar with no interest in the translated sciences. In the introduction to his literary compilation, *Choice Narratives*, he says the following:

> This book, although not on the subject of the Qur'ān and *sunna* [Prophetic tradition], the religious law or the knowledge of what is lawful and forbidden, yet points to sublime things and shows the correct way to noble character; it restrains from baseness, diverts from the disreputable, and incites to right personal conduct, fair management [of others], mild administration [of government], and to making the land prosperous. For the way to Allāh is not one nor is all that is good confined to night prayers, continuous fasting, and the knowledge of the lawful and the forbidden. On the contrary, the ways to Him are many and the doors of the good are wide. . . .
>
> Knowledge is the stray camel of the believer; it benefits him regardless from where he takes it: it shall not disparage truth should you hear it from polytheists, nor advice should it be derived from those who harbor hatred; shabby clothes do no injustice to a beautiful woman, nor shells to their pearls, nor its origin from dust to pure gold. Whoever disregards taking the good from its place misses an opportunity, and opportunities are as transient as the clouds. . . . Ibn-ʿAbbās [the Prophet's uncle] said: "Take wisdom from whomever you hear it, for the non-wise may utter a wise saying and a bull's eye may be hit by a non-sharpshooter."[10]

9 From al-Kindī's *Fī l-falsafa al-ūlā*, in *Rasā'il al-Kindī al-falsafiya*, M.'A. Abū-Rīda (ed.), Cairo, 1950, vol. 1, p. 103, translated by A.L. Ivry, *Al-Kindī's Metaphysics*, Albany, State University of New York Press, 1974, p. 58.

10 Ibn-Qutayba, *'Uyūn al-aḫbār*, Cairo, 1923–30 (repr. 1973), vol. 1, pp. 10.11–15 and 15.11–17.

What these quotations indicate is that we witness in the ninth century in Baghdad a richly textured society in which there was a great wealth of ideas and attitudes in circulation. Well-defined boundaries around intellectual and ideological positions had not then been drawn, and no movement or set of beliefs had managed to gain a clearly dominant position. On any given subject one could find any number of varying opinions, and it is therefore methodologically unsound to isolate the positions of some group, party, or class as "orthodox" or as representing either "faith" or "reason." The approaches to ninth-century Islamic societies must be as textured as the societies themselves. An excellent example about our subject is provided by the way in which attitudes about it are reflected in poetry composed in the same time and place. Both favorable and disparaging views of the translated sciences, and especially of philosophy, are represented, as in the poems of two contemporary literary men from Nīsābūr who lived toward the end of the translation movement. They are both quoted in the works of the great critic aṯ-Ṯaʿālibī (d. 429/1038) who was also from Nīsābūr. The first, Abū Saʿīd ibn-Dūst (d. 431/1040; *GAS* VIII,237), says,

> You who seek religion, avoid the paths of error,
> Lest your religion be snatched from you unawares.
> Shīʿism is destruction, Muʿtazilism is innovation,
> Polytheism is infidelity, and philosophy is a lie.

The opposite view is expressed by Abū-l-Fatḥ al-Bustī (d. after 400/1009; *GAS* II,640):

> Fear God, and seek the guidance of His religion,
> Then, after these two, seek *falsafa* (philosophy),
> In order not to be taken in by people who approve
> A religion of falsehood and "*falsafa*";
> Ignore people who criticize it,
> For a man's *falsafa* is the blunting of ignorance.[11]

11 Quoted in the translation by E.K. Rowson, "The Philosopher as Littérateur: al-Tawḥīdī and His Predecessors," *Zeitschrift für Geschichte der Arabisch-Islamischen Wissenschaften*, 1990, vol. 6, p. 86 and note 128. The poetic fragments are taken from aṯ-Ṯaʿālibī's *Ḫāṣṣ al-ḫāṣṣ*, Beirut, 1966, pp. 72f., and the same author's *Yatīmat ad-dahr*, Cairo, 1956, IV,314. The last hemistich contains al-Bustī's famous pun (referred to also by Goldziher, p. 35, note 3/p. 215 note 138, in the publication discussed in the next section, note 22), *al-falsafatu fallu s-safahi*, "philosophy is the blunting of ignorance."

With these caveats in mind, it is possible to see, in the analysis of the social dynamics of ninth-century ʿAbbāsid society, that the single most significant factor in initiating a process that was *eventually* to lead to a polarization between the translated sciences, with all they eventually came to represent, and the Qur'ānic and traditional sciences was al-Ma'mūn's policy of the *miḥna*; in historical terms, it had the opposite effect of the one intended. Because it made a theological position, the createdness of the Qur'ān, the central point of contention, it antagonized the supporters of traditionally transmitted religious knowledge (the literal understanding of the Qur'ān and *ḥadīṯ*) and helped them coalesce into a well-defined group and develop a fideist theology of the eternity of the Qur'ān;[12] in particular, it made a martyr of Aḥmad ibn-Ḥanbal (d. 241/855), whose person subsequently provided the traditionists with a focus and a rallying point.

This did not affect the translation movement directly or immediately, as I emphasized in the preceding paragraph, for it continued to flourish for the rest of the ninth and throughout the tenth century; in essence, it had nothing to do with the *miḥna* nor was it perceived as such by contemporaries. But it was again al-Ma'mūn's policies that made the association possible: his use of the translation movement as the basis of a rationalistic theology, Muʿtazilism, to be wielded for the purpose of concentrating religious authority in the hands of the caliph and his intellectual elite (see above, chapter 4). It was this that affected the traditionists intimately, because it meant the corresponding loss of their claim to religious knowledge and religious authority. Their objection to the *miḥna*, therefore, was in essence an opposition to the theology that imposed it, Muʿtazilism – both to its contents, philosophical theology, and to its method, dialectic disputation – and not to the translated or "foreign" sciences.

An event that took place about forty years after the end of the *miḥna* appropriately illustrates this point. The historian aṭ-Ṭabarī reports the following for the year 279/3 April 892–22 March 893:

> Among the events taking place, the authorities decreed in Baghdad that no popular preachers, astrologers, or fortune-tellers should sit (and practice their trade) in the streets or in

12 See the detailed exposition of this development by W. Madelung, "The Origins of the Controversy Concerning the Creation of the Koran," in *Orientalia Hispanica* [Festschrift F.M. Pareja], J.M. Barral (ed.), Leiden, E.J. Brill, 1974, pp. 504–25.

> the Friday Mosque. Moreover, the booksellers were sworn not to trade in books of theology (*kalām*), dialectical disputation (*ǧadal*) or philosophy (*falsafa*).[13]

This event took place at the very end of al-Muʿtamid's reign and apparently before al-Muʿtaḍid's accession,[14] during a period of great political and social upheaval; the war against the Zanǧ had just concluded (270/883), while the danger of the Qarmaṭians was just beginning (278/892), and various factions of the military were fighting in Baghdad. Clearly, then, as Fields notes in the Foreword to his translation, the "censorship on preachers and booksellers was implemented to prevent provocative theological debates and fermentation in Baghdad" [p. xv]. Specifically it was intended to prevent people from gathering in public places, apparently in connection with some unpopular measure that the caliph was contemplating. Such a connection is clearly stated in a similar prohibition issued five years later, in 284/897, when al-Muʿtaḍid was planning to have Muʿāwiya, the first Umayyad caliph, cursed from the pulpit, and he wanted to forestall public demonstrations.[15] This implies that the subjects dealt with in the books whose sale was prohibited did cause such gatherings. The purpose of this censorship (which appears to have been very short lived) was thus to maintain public order and has no doctrinal content; specifically it does not indicate any inherent "Islamic" opposition to the foreign sciences or to their study. What it does indicate, though, is that these subjects were contentious and

13 Aṭ-Ṭabarī, *Ta'rīḫ*, III,2131 de Goeje; translated by P.M. Fields, *The ʿAbbāsid Recovery* [The History of al-Ṭabarī, vol. 37], Albany, State University of New York Press, 1987, p. 176. I have added the Arabic terms in parentheses and changed Fields's translation for *ǧadal* from "polemics" to "dialectical disputation."

14 Both Ibn-Kaṯīr, *al-Bidāya wa-n-nihāya*, Cairo, 1932, XI,64–5 and aḏ-Ḏahabī, *Duwal al-Islām*, Hyderabad, 1364/1945, I,123, who also report this event, mention that the ruling caliph at the time was al-Muʿtaḍid. Aṭ-Ṭabarī, however, clearly has it under the caliphate of al-Muʿtamid, and it is difficult to see how the authority of aṭ-Ṭabarī for this particular event, which he must have witnessed personally, can be impugned. In this connection it is also worth noting the personal biases of subsequent authors. Though both Ibn-Kaṯīr and aḏ-Ḏahabī were contemporary Syrian traditionists and historians, the former mentions the three subjects in question with the same words that aṭ-Ṭabarī does while the latter omits *kalām* (Islamic theology) and changes *ǧadal* (dialectic disputation) into the generic term *manṭiq* (logic).

15 Aṭ-Ṭabarī, *Ta'rīḫ*, III,2165 de Goeje; translated by F. Rosenthal, *The Return of the Caliphate to Baghdad* [The History of al-Ṭabarī, vol. 38], Albany, State University of New York, 1985, p. 47; cf. van Ess, *Theologie und Gesellschaft*, IV,728–9.

the authorities, interested in political quietism, avoided them. The traditionists who were the victims of the *miḥna* opposed philosophical theology and dialectical disputation, the very subjects mentioned in the measures of 279/892. The selection of these particular subjects in the measures, therefore, can only be explained with reference to the *miḥna*. The *miḥna* obviously had made these subjects controversial, creating the polarization I mentioned at the outset. It must be emphasized, however, that this polarization in subsequent centuries in various Islamic societies is not static or an essential given, and this imposes the obligation to analyze in specific and concrete detail the dynamics of its occasional appearance.

The traditionists' opposition to Muʿtazilism and to these subjects had consequences in later educational policy because it was the traditionists who eventually formed the curriculum of formal legal education in Islamic societies. In this curriculum they did not include, as was to be expected, these subjects, but neither did they include any of the other translated sciences. This is to be explained partly by the fact that the translated sciences did not represent their concerns and were not, in the final analysis, relevant to the subject matter, and partly by the association generated in people's minds, because of al-Ma'mūn's ideological campaigns, between dialectical theology and the translated sciences. The scholarship that the translation literature generated thus remained initially in the private sphere.[16]

This separation of areas of concern or applicability was recognized as proper not only by the traditionists but also by scholars of the translated sciences. Toward the end of the translation period, a significant philosopher and direct disciple of al-Fārābī and Yaḥyā ibn-ʿAdī, Abū-Sulaymān as-Siǧistānī, criticized in a famous passage the "Brethren of Purity" (*Iḫwān aṣ-Ṣafāʾ*) for attempting, unsuccessfully, to coalesce Greek philosophy and Islamic law. Their failure, he stressed, came from the inherent and fundamental incompatibility of the two domains:

> They claim that perfection is achieved when Greek philosophy and Arab [Islamic] law [*aš-šarīʿa*] are brought together in an orderly arrangement. . . .
>
> They thought they could insert philosophy . . . into Islamic

16 See discussion of this subject in the works of George Makdisi, especially *The Rise of Humanism*, pp. 67–70.

> law and attach Islamic law to philosophy. This, however, is an aspiration on the way to which there are insurmountable obstacles [*marāmun dūnahu ḥadadun*]: . . . Islamic law is derived from God, by means of an ambasssador between Him and humans, by way of revelation.[17]

After the fourth/tenth century and the end of the translation movement, when law was firmly entrenched in Islamic social life, some of the subjects opposed by the traditionists, and the related translated sciences, were gradually reintegrated into the curriculum, through numerous compromises on all sides. In the case of theology (*kalām*), as investigated by Makdisi, it gained legitimacy only by affiliating itself with the legal schools and by recasting its past history as one of dispute among the emergent legal schools (*maḏāhib*).[18] Logic and dialectics were fully integrated in law and *kalām*, primarily but not exclusively through the efforts of al-Ġazālī (d. 505/1111), while Aristotelian philosophy, as developed by Avicenna, both maintained its independence and continued to inform discussions and understanding of theology and mysticism in different Islamic societies in ways that have yet to be studied in detail.

For the most part, however, reaction to the incursion of Greek sciences during the period of the translation movement took the form of emphasizing the achievements of pre-Islamic and Muslim Arabs as equal to, or better than, those of the Greeks. This understandable reaction to what may have been an excessive zeal in promoting the case of Greek letters by the proponents of the translation movement should not, however, be misinterpreted as an *opposition* to the Greek sciences; its aim was not to *exclude* the Greek works from the canon of acceptable sciences but merely to offer an alternative or more comprehensive and correct tradition. Representative of the earliest reactions of this sort that we have is again Ibn-Qutayba. In the introduction to his book on traditional Arab astronomy and meteorology (*Kitāb al-anwā'*), i.e., astronomy and meteorology not in the curriculum of Aristotelian studies, he says the following about the reasons that prompted him to compose the work:

17 At-Tawḥīdī, *al-Imtā' wa-l-mu'ānasa*, Aḥmad az-Zayn and Aḥmad Amīn (eds), Cairo, 1951 (reprinted Beirut, n.d.), vol. 2, pp. 5–6.

18 Makdisi, "The Juridical Theology of Shāfi'ī," pp. 21–2.

> My purpose in everything that I reported [here] has been to confine myself to what the Arabs know about these matters and put to use, and to exclude that which is claimed by those non-Arabs who are affiliated with philosophy and by mathematicians/astronomers [*aṣḥāb al-ḥisāb*]. The reason is that I consider the knowledge of the Arabs to be knowledge that is plain to sight, true when put to test, and useful to the traveler by land and sea. God says, "It is He who has appointed for you the stars, that / by them you might be guided in / the shadows of land and sea."[19]

In the following century, the theologian ʿAbd-al-Qāhir al-Baghdādī (d. 429/1037), talking about zoology, went one step further than Ibn-Qutayba and claimed, following the lead of al-Kindī who had asserted that Yūnān and Qaḥṭān (the mythical forefathers of Greeks and Arabs respectively; see chapter 4.2) were brothers, that philosophy plagiarized ancient Arab knowledge:

> The [Greek] philosophers never mentioned anything on this subject [i.e., the nature of animals] that was not stolen from the Arab sages who antedated the philosophers, namely the Ḥimyarite tribes of Qaḥṭān, Ǧarham, Ṭasmiya, etc. The Arabs mentioned in their poems and proverbs all the natural characteristics of animals although in their time there was neither a Bāṭinī around nor anyone claiming to be a Bāṭinī.[20]

Similar sentiments were widespread in the third–fourth/ninth–tenth centuries, and constituted part of both the linguistic reaction to anti-Arab sentiment (*Šuʿūbiyya*) discussed by Goldziher and of the social reaction to it elaborated by Gibb (though with reference only to its Persian background).[21] It seems clear that the translation movement, though itself largely due to the Sasanian culture of

19 Ibn-Qutayba, *Kitāb al-anwāʾ*, C. Pellat and M. Hamidullah (eds), Hyderabad, 1375/1956, §2, pp. 1–2. Cf. also the French translation by C. Pellat, "Le traité d'astronomie pratique et de météorologie populaire d'Ibn Qutayba," *Arabica*, 1954, vol. 1, p. 87. The Qur'ānic quotation, from Sūra 6.97, is in Arberry's translation.

20 Al-Baġdādī, *Al-Farq bayna l-firaq*, Beirut, 1977, p. 295.

21 I. Goldziher, *Muslim Studies*, C.R. Barber and S.M. Stern (translators), London, Allen & Unwin, 1967 [original German edition 1889], vol. 1, pp. 137–98; Gibb, "Social Significance of the Shuubiya." For the most recent bibliography and discussion of various interpretations of the *Šuʿūbiyya* see the article by S. Enderwitz in *EI* IX,513–16.

translation, was influential on its own in generating consciously Arabocentric positions.

3. THE LEGACY TO POSTERITY: ARABIC PHILOSOPHY AND SCIENCE AND THE MYTH OF "ISLAMIC" OPPOSITION TO THE GREEK SCIENCES

The translation movement as such came to an end around the turn of the first millennium as the scientific and philosophical research that provided most of the demand in Baghdad and elsewhere became autonomous (chapter 7.1). This scientific and philosophical work in Arabic is increasingly receiving the scholarly attention it deserves, but tracing its history in the millennium since then clearly lies outside the scope of this study. Nevertheless, because previous scholarship has generated the misconception that the "old Islamic orthodoxy" was opposed to the translated Greek sciences, i.e., to this scientific and philosophical tradition, it is necessary to comment briefly on the subject as an aid to future research.

The single most influential study to generate this misconception has been the essay by Ignaz Goldziher, "The Attitude of the Old Islamic Orthodoxy toward the Ancient Sciences." First published in German in 1916, it has been constantly referred to as the expert opinion on the subject, and was translated into English in 1981 under the wrong (and misleading) title, "The Attitude of Orthodox Islam toward the Ancient Sciences."[22] Two major criticisms can be leveled at this work of otherwise great erudition, and both have their starting point in the title, the two assumptions of which are never addressed in the body of the work: what, precisely, Islamic "orthodoxy" is, and, within that, what "old" orthodoxy is. In the absence of explicit specification, the answers necessarily have to be derived from the contents and import of the essay.[23]

22 I. Goldziher, "Stellung der alten islamischen Orthodoxie zu den antiken Wissenschaften," *Abhandlungen der Königlich Preussischen Akademie der Wissenschaften*, Jahrgang 1915, Philosophisch-historische Klasse, no. 8, Berlin, Verlag der Akademie, 1916. Translated by M.L. Swartz in his *Studies on Islam*, Oxford, Oxford University Press, 1981, pp. 185–215. I refer both to the original and to the translation, in that order.

23 For a broader set of criticisms to Goldziher's essay, more charitably put, see Sabra, "Greek Science in Medieval Islam," pp. 230–2.

To start with the second, and ultimately less significant, problem of the study: the identity of the "old orthodoxy." "Old orthodoxy" is obviously to be contrasted to some "new" orthodoxy, and this is identified as Islam in Goldziher's day, which he mentions in his very last sentence: "Contemporary Islamic orthodoxy in its modern development offers no opposition to the ancient sciences, nor does it see an antithesis between itself and them."[24] This statement points to the source of Goldziher's rationalist and even political bias. His intention clearly appears to be to portray as anti-rationalists those Muslims who opposed the ancient sciences, the representatives, that is, of what he calls "old orthodoxy." Since most of the anti-rationalists he mentions were Ḥanbalīs, or, more appositely, non-Ḥanafīs (as I will discuss later in the section), they are as a consequence presented in a negative light while by implication the Ḥanafīs, representatives of "Islamic orthodoxy in its modern development," are shown to be rationalists in agreement with the spirit of the ancient sciences. The anti-Ḥanbalī bias of Goldziher, which has misled not a few scholars writing after him, is well known and has been discussed, notably by George Makdisi.[25] In the political realities of Goldziher's day, as Makdisi has shown,[26] the Wahhābīs of Saʿūdī Arabia were the (neo-)Ḥanbalīs while their enemies, the Ottoman Turks, were the Ḥanafīs. Given this tendentiousness, the import of his study is the light it throws on Goldziher's ideology and the political climate of Europe in his time rather than on the attitude of a presumed "old Islamic orthodoxy" to the ancient sciences.[27]

24 "Die neuzeitliche islamische Orthodoxie setzt den antiken Wissenschaften in ihrer modernen Fortbildung keinen Widerstand entgegen und fühlt sich nicht im Gegensatz zu ihnen"; p. 42. I have adapted Swartz's translation: he reads "Orthodox Islam" for "Contemporary Islamic orthodoxy," and adds "study of" before "ancient sciences" (p. 209). The pleonastic "neuzeitliche" in the first phrase is significant for the concern it shows on the part of Goldziher to differentiate the contemporary and modern orthodoxy from the "old."

25 See, for example, his brief survey of the influence of Goldziher's bias in his "The Hanbali School and Sufism," *Boletin de la Asociacion Española de Orientalistas*, Madrid, 1979, vol. 15, pp. 115–26, reprinted in his *Religion, Law and Learning in Classical Islam*, Hampshire, Variorum, 1991, no. V.

26 In his detailed study of the anti-Ḥanbalism of nineteenth-century Western orientalism, "L'Islam Hanbalisant," *Revue des Études Islamiques*, 1974, vol. 42, pp. 213ff., translated also by Swartz, *Studies*, pp. 219ff.

27 Of course, Goldziher's essay retains its value as a list of quotations by various Muslim scholars on the subject of the ancient sciences.

To add a contemporary note on the continuation of this tendentiousness, M.L. Swartz in his translation omits from the title of the essay the word "old" ("alte"), eliminating even this minimal differentiation among the various epochs in Islamic history. Admittedly Goldziher added it for the purpose just mentioned, but Swartz should have been aware of Goldziher's anti-Ḥanbalī bias since he also translated, in the same volume, Makdisi's article that exposes it; omitting the word "old" in the English context makes all "orthodox Islam" appear opposed to the study of the ancient sciences.

The other, more grave problem of Goldziher's study is his failure to identify the "orthodoxy" of his title, and as a result the impression generated in the reader is that the "orthodox" must be the representatives of those schools whose opinions against the ancient sciences are cited *in extenso* in the essay. But there are two difficulties here: first, the question of the very notion of "orthodoxy" in Islamic societies, which is never a given, and second, the identification of a number of individuals, on the mere basis of their pronouncements against the ancient sciences, as "orthodox."

To begin with, as Goldziher himself doubtless knew, "orthodoxy" is not something in Sunnī Islam that is legislated by a centralized religious authority (as in the Orthodox and Catholic Christian Churches) – there are no such authorities; at most what one could claim is the prevalence of a certain religious approach at a specific time and in a specific locality.[28] But even this has to be qualified by stating to *whom*, among the different strata of society, this approach belonged, because an assumption of "prevalence" as meaning "majority view" is not necessarily always true. For example, in the tenth century the Fāṭimids gained control of Egypt. The Fāṭimids were ardent Ismāʿīlīs, an offshoot of Shīʿism, and conducted energetic missionary campaigns not only within Egypt but throughout the Islamic world. And yet the Ismāʿīlī Fāṭimid ruling class was a minority; the majority of the Muslim population in Egypt was and remained Sunnī (sometimes even in the face of persecution), to say nothing of the considerable segments of the indigenous population (possibly, in the early tenth century, more than half overall) that were

28 For the problematics of the concept of "orthodoxy" in Islamic societies see now the extensive discussion by van Ess, *Theologie und Gesellschaft*, IV,683ff.

Christian and Jewish. In this context, who were the "orthodox"? And is it possible to use the term meaningfully about the Fāṭimids without further definition and contextualization? For, to revert to Goldziher's subject, the Fāṭimids were great patrons of Greek science and philosophy, which literally flourished during their time. Thus, the scattered reports of alleged enmity to the sciences of the ancients that Goldziher mentions are, without specification and contextualization, meaningless at best and gravely misleading at worst.

For example, on pp. 17–18/193–4, Goldziher lists the great linguist Ibn-Fāris (d. 395/1005; *GAS* VIII,209) as a representative of "the feeling of the majority of traditional religious circles" opposed to the Greek sciences, and especially to geometry, and states that he so expressed himself in the introduction of one of his books which he dedicated to the well-known Būyid vizier Ṣāḥib ibn-ʿAbbād who, he adds, was "an enemy of the sciences of the ancients" ("Feind der *awāʾil*-Wissenschaften"). To make such a statement, however, is unconscionably misleading without also mentioning at the same time, indeed stressing, that all this was happening in Rayy (outside of modern Tehran) and Baghdad under the Būyids (945–1055), the period during which the study and cultivation of the ancient sciences were, by universal acknowledgment, pursued by the overwhelming majority of all intellectuals and dominated cultural life in most of its manifestations. Naturally there were dissenting views – there are dissenting views on all subjects in all societies – and Ibn Fāris's was one such, but it constituted, during the Būyid period, a distinct minority.[29]

Furthermore, not every instance of hostility to the Greek sciences one may find attested in the sources is attributable to religious causes or traceable to a defense of an "orthodox" position. A case in point is the dedicatee of Ibn-Fāris's essay, the Ṣāḥib Ibn-ʿAbbād. His hostility to the Greek sciences (cited by Goldziher on p. 26/199) did not stem from excessive – or any – piety, for it was no secret to his contemporaries, as at-Tawḥīdī reports, that he had little religion; the very Ibn-Fāris, the linguist cited by Goldziher, calls him an "enemy of religion." Finally, at-Tawḥīdī's reproach of such an attitude on the part of the Ṣāḥib can have meaning only if addressed to an

29 For a panoramic view of the spread and depth of classical learning in Būyid Baghdad see Kraemer, *Humanism*, and its companion volume, *Philosophy in the Renaissance of Islam*, Leiden, E.J. Brill, 1986.

audience that would consider it reprehensible, as indeed was the case with Būyid intellectuals.[30]

Second, with regard to the identification of certain scholars as "orthodox" by implication, what is seriously missing from Goldziher's presentation is an analysis of the historical and social circumstances surrounding the pronouncements cited against the ancient sciences. The majority of the authorities he quotes and the most severe in their pronouncements are the great Ḥanbalī and Šāfiʿī scholars of Baghdad and Damascus in the seventh/thirteenth and eighth/fourteenth centuries, and are associated with two very specific and extraordinary historical circumstances. Those active in Baghdad were the Ḥanbalī ʿAbd-al-Qādir al-Ǧīlānī (p. 13/191, d. 561/1166) and Ibn-al-Ǧawzī (p. 14/191, d. 597/1200), and the Šāfiʿī ʿUmar as-Suhrawardī (d. 632/1234), the propagandist of the ʿAbbāsid caliph an-Nāṣir li-Dīn-Allāh (r. 575–622/1180–1225). The policies of this caliph, which formed the culmination of those of his predecessors (like al-Mustanǧid, cited by Goldziher on p. 15/192) were related to his efforts to consolidate a decaying caliphate against all sorts of attacks, including ideological. As it turned out, the efforts proved fruitless and Baghdad fell to the Mongols thirty-three years after his death.[31]

The second group of authorities cited by Goldziher are all Damascene scholars of the late Ayyūbid and early Mamlūk period: the Šāfiʿī Ibn-aṣ-Ṣalāḥ (pp. 35–9/204–6, d. 643/1245), aḏ-Ḏahabī (p. 11/189, d. 748/1348) and Tāǧ-ad-Dīn as-Subkī (pp. 11, 40/189, 207, d. 771/1370), and the famous Ḥanbalī Ibn-Taymiyya (p. 40/207, d. 728/1328). Syria, or more generally, the Mamlūk state, during this time was facing two major crises that had threatened its very existence: the Christian Crusades and the Mongol onslaught, two powers that at one moment actually were in alliance (669/1271). The barbarism, aggressiveness, and incomprehensible insistence of

30 For at-Tawḥīdī's report on the Ṣāḥib's religiosity see his *Maṯālib al-wazīrayn*, pp. 82 and 212. In the latter reference, Ibn-Fāris says that he can judge that the Ṣāḥib is an enemy of God because he has "little religion" (*li-qillati dīnihi*). Informative portraits of both at-Tawḥīdī and the Ṣāḥib Ibn-ʿAbbād are sketched by M. Bergé and C. Pellat respectively in the Cambridge History of Arabic Literature, *ʿAbbāsid Belles-Lettres*, J. Ashtiany *et al.* (eds), Cambridge, Cambridge University Press, 1990, pp. 96–124.

31 Politics and culture in late ʿAbbāsid Baghdad are discussed in detail by A. Hartmann in her *An-Nāṣir li-Dīn Allāh (1180–1225). Politik, Religion, Kultur in der späten ʿAbbāsidenzeit*, Berlin, W. de Gruyter, 1975. The results of the book are summarized in her article "Al-Nāṣir li-Dīn Allāh" in *EI* VII,996–1003. Hartmann is currently working on an edition and study of ʿUmar as-Suhrawardī's work against the Greek sciences.

the Christians to steal foreign lands in the name of "religion" necessarily generated a reaction in the people of Palestine and Syria toward a less tolerant version of Islam; the great Mamlūk ruler who defeated the Crusaders and stopped the Mongols, Baybars I (r. 1260–77), is presented in Arabic historiography as a true hero as opposed to the ambivalent attitude of the historians to Saladin who, despite his liberation of Jerusalem, had a more accommodating attitude toward the Crusaders. The Mongol invasions of Syria after 1258 and especially their siege of Damascus in 699/1300 simply exacerbated a bad situation and called for a more aggressive ideological attitude – hence Ibn-Taymiyya, who played an active role in the Mongol–Syrian negotiations, and hence the return to a "conservative" traditionalism, championed by the Ḥanbalīs and the reconstructed or reformed Aš'arism of Šāfi'ī scholars after al-Ġazālī.

Why, then, are these scholars identified as members of the "old" orthodoxy, and why are such views, generated in societies under extreme pressure, supposed to represent "Islamic" orthodoxy? For the historical record, consulted in its entirety, is otherwise, and even within Mamlūk lands, the heartland of Ḥanbalī and Šāfi'ī "old orthodoxy," as Goldziher's study would lead us to believe, the ancient sciences flourished. The examples are numerous and now much better known (or acknowledged) than during Goldziher's time. The physician Ibn-an-Nafis (d. 687/1288), a Šāfi'ī, studied medicine in Damascus and later taught it there and in Cairo where he became chief physician. He wrote numerous commentaries on Hippocratic works as well as on the *Canon* of Avicenna, which he also epitomized in a work that subsequently became a popular textbook. His great achievement was to describe, against the authority of both Galen and Avicenna, the lesser circulation of the blood through the lungs. The astronomer Ibn-aš-Šāṭir (d. 777/1375), employed as the official timekeeper (*muwaqqit*) at the Umayyad Mosque in Damascus, was one scientist in the long line of astronomers attempting to revise Ptolemy. He produced models of planetary orbits which were both based on uniform circular motion and corresponded to actual astronomical observations. His models reappear two centuries later, through channels that only recently are becoming clear, in the work of Copernicus and thus stand at the very beginning of modern astronomy.[32]

32 For Ibn-an-Nafis see the article in the *EI* and *DSB* and the references cited there. For Ibn-aš-Šāṭir and Arabic astronomy and Copernicus see the articles collected by G. Saliba in his *A History of Arabic Astronomy*, pp. 233–306.

Again during the time of the Mongol incursions into the Near East, there was established in Marāġa in Āḏarbāyǧān an observatory that was to prove highly significant for the development of astronomy not only in Arabic but also, through translations (back) into Greek, in Byzantine astronomy. The founders of this observatory, which was sponsored by the Mongol Hūlāgū, were well known scholars and scientists. They include, among numerous others, Naṣīr-ad-Dīn aṭ-Ṭūsī (d. 672/1274; *GAL* I,508), a Twelver Shīʿī, and Naǧm-ad-Dīn al-Kātibī (d. 675/1276; *EI* IV,762), a Sunnī Šāfiʿī, and the author of two of the most influential textbooks of Arabic philosophy, one on logic (*ar-Risāla aš-Šamsiyya*) and the other on physics and metaphysics (*Ḥikmat al-ʿayn)*.[33] During the high time of the period when Muslim "orthodoxy" was supposed to be at its most inimical to the ancient sciences, a very significant ancient science was not only cultivated in Islam but also institutionalized through the foundation of an observatory.

The same can be observed in the same period also in philosophy. The work of Avicenna early in the eleventh century gave rise in the succeeding three centuries to a torrent of philosophical discussion, argumentation, and counter-argumentation – and a corresponding literary output – among Sunnī and Shīʿite Muslims in the central Islamic lands.[34] This period of Arabic philosophy, almost wholly unresearched, may yet one day be recognized as its golden age.

During the very same centuries in ʿIrāq and Iran, under the leadership of Twelver Shīʿites, a new intellectual system was actively being constructed out of Greek philosophy as reworked by Avicenna, Muʿtazilite theology, and Sufism.[35] The official integration of Avicennan Aristotelianism into mainstream Twelver thought that was to begin with Naṣīr-ad-Dīn aṭ-Ṭūsī just when the Mongols were devastating ʿIrāq was to continue throughout the centuries and

33 On the Marāġa observatory see the classic study by A. Sayılı, *The Observatory in Islam*, Ankara, Türk Tarih Kurumu, 1960, reprinted 1988, chapter 6. More recent scholarship is discussed by Saliba, *A History of Arabic Astronomy*, pp. 245–90.

34 The fourteenth-century Egyptian scholar Ibn-al-Akfānī, in his survey guide of the sciences (*Iršād al-qāṣid*), gives a minimal list of this philosophical output. See the translation in my "Aspects of Literary Form and Genre in Arabic Logical Works," in C. Burnett (ed.), *Glosses and Commentaries on Aristotelian Logical Texts*, pp. 60–2.

35 See the brief synthesis by Madelung in depicting the background of the work of a Twelver scholar, "Ibn Abī Ǧumhūr al-Aḥsāʾī's Synthesis of *kalām*, Philosophy and Sufism," in *Actes du 8ème Congrès de l'Union Européenne des Arabisants et Islamisants* (Aix-en-Provence, 1976), Aix-en-Provence, 1978, pp. 147–8, reprinted in his *Religious Schools and Sects in Medieval Islam*, London, Variorum, 1985, no. XIII.

witness a particular efflorescence in Iran under the Safavids in the sixteenth and seventeenth centuries.[36]

Nor was this an exception; Ḥanafī Islam was equally receptive to Greek philosophy and sciences at all times, including during the high centuries of Ottoman civilization.[37] Avicennan philosophy and its subsequent development found eager cultivators among Ottoman scholars of the sixteenth through the eighteenth centuries. The great historian and bibliographer Kātib Čelebi (Ḥāǧǧī Ḫalīfa, 1017–67/1609–57) says the following in his entry on the history and development of philosophy in Islam:

> Philosophical sciences (*al-falsafa wa-l-ḥikma*) also found a brisk market in Asia Minor (*ar-Rūm*) after the Muslim conquest until the middle period of the Ottoman state. During that era a man's nobility was commensurate with the extent to which he could acquire and encompass both the intellectual and the traditional sciences. In their age there lived great masters who could combine philosophy and Islamic law, like the most learned Šams-ad-Dīn al-Fanārī (d. 834/1431; *EI* II,879a), the excellent Qāḍī-zāda ar-Rūmī (d. ca. 840/1435),[38] the most learned Ḫwāǧa-zāda (d. 893/1488; *GAL* II,230), the most learned ʿAlī al-Qūšǧī (d. 879/1474; *EI* I,393), the excellent Ibn-al-Mu'ayyad (d. 922/1516; *GAL* II,227), Mīram Čelebi (d. 931/1524; *GAL* II,447), the most learned Ibn-Kamāl (d. 940/1533; *EI* IV,879–81), the excellent Ibn-al-Ḥinnā'ī (= Qınālızāde ʿAlī Čelebi, d. 979/1572; *GAL* II,433), who was the last of them [ḤḪ I,680].

The translation activities in the Ottoman Empire from the fifteenth to the eighteenth centuries consitute a major chapter in its history that has yet to be fully studied. Translations into Arabic were

36 The credit for bringing this entire tradition to the attention of Western audiences in this century belongs to H. Corbin; see in particular his *En Islam Iranien*, 7 parts in 4 vols, Paris, Gallimard, 1971–2.

37 For an excellent example of a highly respected Ḥanafī legal and religious scholar, Ṣadr-aš-Šarīʿa of Buḫārā (d. 747/1347), who wrote a very sophisticated astronomical treatise, see the recent edition and study by A. Dallal, *An Islamic Response to Greek Astronomy*, Leiden, E.J. Brill, 1995.

38 *GAL* II,212 gives the erroneous date of death of 815/1412. For the correct date and other references see N. Heer, *The Precious Pearl. Al-Jāmī's al-Durrah al-Fākhirah*, Albany, State University of New York Press, 1979, p. 24, note 6.

made from a number of languages, but primarily from Greek and Latin: the historian I just mentioned, for example, Kātib Čelebi, as well as his younger contemporary, Ḥusayn Hezārfenn (d. ca. 1089/1678–9), had Greek and Latin sources translated for them for their historical works.[39] Most importantly, however, the Sultan Meḥmed II Fātiḥ, the Conqueror (r. 855–86/1451–81), is famous for his "cultural catholicity" and his interest in Greek letters. It is known that he viewed Alexander the Great as a model; what remains to be investigated is the extent to which he may have seen himself as another al-Ma'mūn, who was perceived, in later tradition that he himself helped generate (see chapter 4.2), as the great patron of the translation movement and the ancient sciences. Numerous Greek manuscripts copied in the court of Meḥmed II, some for his personal use, have been identified; one of them is Arrian's *Anabasis of Alexander the Great*, another, interestingly, is the Greek translation by Demetrios Kydones (d. 1397/8) of Thomas Aquinas's *Summa contra gentiles* (Vat. gr. 613). Meḥmed II also requested Arabic translations of Greek works, including Ptolemy's *Geography* (translated by Amiroutzes) and the *Chaldean Oracles* by the last Byzantine pagan, Georgios Gemistos Plethon (d. 1452).[40] He commissioned, finally, Arabic works on philosophy deriving directly from the tradition initiated by the Graeco-Arabic translation movement: he held a competition for the best refutation of Averroes' *Refutation* (*Tahāfut at-tahāfut*) of al-Ġazālī, which was won by the *Tahāfut* by Ḫwāğa-zāda mentioned by Ḥāğğī Ḫalīfa in the passage cited above,[41] and asked the famous poet and scholar al-Ǧāmī (d. 898/1492) to

39 See the article on Hezārfenn by Ménage in *EI* III,623, and O. Şaik Gökyay's articles "Kâtip Çelebi" in *İslâm Ansiklopedisi* and "Kātib Čelebi" in *EI* IV,760–2. Further details about the editions used by Kātib Čelebi are provided by V.L. Ménage, "Three Ottoman Treatises on Europe," in C.E. Bosworth (ed.), *Iran and Islam. A Volume in Memory of Vladimir Minorsky*, Edinburgh, Edinburgh University Press, 1971, pp. 421–33.

40 See the valuable article by J. Raby, "Mehmed the Conqueror's Greek Scriptorium," *Dumbarton Oaks Papers*, 1983, vol. 37, pp. 15–34 (with 41 figures), especially pp. 22–5. One of the manuscripts of the Arabic translation of Ptolemy's *Geography* (Aya Sofya 2610) was published in facsimile reproduction by F. Sezgin, Frankfurt am Main, Institut für Geschichte der Arabisch-Islamischen Wissenschaften, 1987. The Arabic translation of Plethon's *Chaldean Oracles* has now been published together with the Greek text: B. Tambrun-Krasker, *Oracles Chaldaïques. Recension de Georges Gémiste Pléthon* [Corpus Philosophorum Medii Aevi 7], Athens, The Academy of Athens, 1995; the Arabic text was edited by M. Tardieu.

41 The three *Tahāfuts* were studied by M. Türker, *Üç tehâfüt bakımından felsefe ve din münasebeti*, Istanbul, Türk Tarih Kurumu, 1956.

write a treatise evaluating the respective merits of theology, mysticism, and philosophy.[42]

To round up the record finally with some further translation activities that are as interesting as they are almost completely unresearched: during the Tulip Period in the first quarter of the eighteenth century, and under the patronage of the Grand Vizier Dāmād Ibrāhīm Pāšā, the Ottoman scholar Asʿad al-Yanyāwī (d. 1134/1722; *GAL* II,447, *GALS* II,665), dissatisfied with the early ʿAbbāsid translations of Aristotle, learned Greek from certain Greek functionaries in the administration and translated anew into Arabic some Aristotelian treatises, including the *Physics*, and wrote logical commentaries on the *Organon*. His student Aḥmad from Skopje copied the manuscript, now in Istanbul, Hamidiye 812, which contains the full course of al-Fārābī's summaries of the *Organon*.[43] The scholarch of the Academy of the Patriarchate in Constantinople, Nikolaos Kritias of Prusa (Bursa), who died in 1767, translated into Arabic, or possibly into Turkish, the work on logic by the prominent Aristotelian Theophilos Korydaleus.[44] This Graeco-Arabic (or possibly Graeco-Turkish) translation activity in the Ottoman Empire well into the eighteenth century went hand in hand with a contemporary and flourishing Aristotelianism by Greek scholars that is only recently beginning to come to light.[45]

4. THE LEGACY ABROAD: THE TRANSLATION MOVEMENT AND THE FIRST "BYZANTINE HUMANISM" OF THE NINTH CENTURY

Translation requires originals from which to be made; no matter how favorable all factors conducive to a translation activity may be, it

42 See the exemplary translation and study by N. Heer, *The Precious Pearl*.

43 See the references in M. Türker, "Fārābī'nin 'Şerā'it ul-yaḳīn'i," *Araştırma*, 1963, vol 1, pp. 151–2, 173–4; cf. Gutas, "Aspects of Literary Form and Genre in Arabic Logical Works," p. 62 note 158.

44 Λίνος Γ. Μπενάκης (Linos G. Benakis), "Ἕνα ἀνέκδοτο Ἑλληνοαραβικὸ λεξιλόγιο Ἀριστοτελικῆς λογικῆς ὁρολογίας τοῦ Βησσαρίωνος Μακρῆ (1670)" (An unpublished Graeco-Arabic glossary of Aristotelian logical terminology by Vissarion Makris), Νεοελληνικὴ Φιλοσοφία 1600–1950 [Πρακτικὰ τῆς Γ′ Φιλοσοφικῆς Ἡμερίδας Ἰωαννίνων, Μάρτιος 1988 (Proceedings of the 3rd Philosophical Congress of Ioannina, March 1988)], Thessaloniki, 1994, p. 108.

45 See the references by Benakis to his own work in the article cited in the preceding note, pp. 97f., note 1.

cannot take place unless these archetypal texts are available. This raises immediately the question of the status of Greek manuscripts containing secular works in the eighth century, in areas accessible to the translators, i.e., in the Islamic realm and Byzantium.

Students of Byzantium have devoted a significant amount of attention to this question, though for different reasons. For them, the eighth century is the time when the minuscule hand of Greek writing first came into current and standard use, the time of the devastating upheavals of the iconoclastic controversy, the time of the "dark ages" of Byzantium. In the general dearth of information for the study of this crucial century, manuscripts present one of the few reliable sources, and they have accordingly been studied relatively intensively. Although there are individual variations among Byzantinists in emphasis and nuance, there is a general consensus, first, that we know little about the period, and second, that the little we know paints a rather bleak picture about the status of Greek secular manuscripts during the period when these works were busily being translated into Arabic. Understandably, for Byzantinists ignorant of Arabic, the Graeco-Arabic translation movement has not figured in such discussions.

In the first place, all existing Greek manuscripts containing secular works until the middle to the end of the eighth century, i.e., until the beginning of the Graeco-Arabic translation movement, were written in uncials, the Greek majuscule hand. The minuscule came into use by about this time, and it took some considerable time before Greek scribes in Byzantium transcribed manuscripts into minuscule. The distinction between uncial and minuscule manuscripts is important for gauging their number and availability. The old, large hand is neat but cumbersome, and it takes more space than the cursive and smaller minuscule hand. This means that it took longer to transcribe codices in uncials than in minuscule, and that accordingly uncial manuscipts would be more expensive than minuscule. The writing material was inevitably animal skins, i.e. parchment. Papyrus was also used, but primarily in Egypt; outside of Egypt its usefulness was curtailed due its greater perishability in more humid climates.

Due to these circumstances it is understandable that during this period (and in this case, throughout the ninth century as well) there appears to have been no book trade in Byzantium to speak of. Book production was laborious and costly and therefore the acquisition of even a very modest private library of a few dozen books was beyond the means of most, if not all, rich intellectuals.[46]

Second, we know relatively little about libraries in the Byzantine world because there is scanty information on the subject. We know next to nothing particularly for the earlier period until the ninth century, which is of relevance for our purposes here. But if one may extrapolate with caution from the situation existing after the ninth century, the major collections of books can be expected to have been in monasteries, in the libraries of high officials of Byzantine government (including the imperial library), and in private collections.[47]

This picture is in agreement with the general tenor of the eighth century in the history of Byzantium, the so-called "dark age," and its devastating effect on the survival of classical culture. In particular, this was a period, starting already from the middle of the seventh century, when interest in and production of secular literature had completely disappeared.[48] Consequently, no manuscripts of secular content were copied; there was no demand for them, and there were no scholars and scientists demanding them. The period of the iconoclastic controversy is singularly devoid of men of any eminence

46 See N.G. Wilson, "Books and Readers in Byzantium," *Byzantine Books and Bookmen* [Dumbarton Oaks Colloquium, 1971], Washington, DC, Dumbarton Oaks, 1975, p. 4. This is in sharp contrast with the situation during the very same time in the Islamic world, and especially in Baghdad, where, in addition to a flourishing book trade (Ibn-an-Nadīm, who apparently handled most of the thousands of books he lists in his *Fihrist*, was a bookseller), there are reports of private libraries of thousands of books.

47 See the discussion by N.G. Wilson, "The Libraries of the Byzantine World," *Greek, Roman and Byzantine Studies*, 1967, vol. 8, p. 53, reprinted in D. Harlfinger (ed.), *Griechische Kodikologie und Textüberlieferung*, Damstadt, Wissenschaftliche Buchgesellschaft, 1980, p. 276.

48 The case is most succinctly and emphatically presented in the works of J.F. Haldon:

> There is, after the late 620s and early 630s, and up until the later eighth or early ninth century, a more or less complete disappearance of secular literary forms within the [Byzantine] Empire. . . . Similarly, this period provides no examples of geographical, philosophical, or philological literature. . . . Interest in the secular, pre-Constantinian, much less the pre-Christian, culture of the past was, for a century or so, a rarity,

in "The Works of Anastasius of Sinai: A Key Source for the History of Seventh-Century East Mediterranean Society and Belief," in A. Cameron and L.I. Conrad (eds), *The Byzantine and Early Islamic Near East*, pp. 126–8. The social and cultural reasons behind this development in the Byzantine Empire are discussed in his *Byzantium in the Seventh Century: The Transformation of a Culture*, Cambridge, Cambridge University Press, 1990, pp. 425–35.

in sciences and philosophy. Then, after the turn of the ninth century, there is a gradual re-emergence of scholarly activity and its development into what Paul Lemerle called "the first Byzantine humanism." In his classic book by this title, Lemerle argued that the causes of this "renaissance" are to be sought in developments within Byzantium itself and specifically rejected the theories that had been proposed about Arab influence.[49] Lemerle is right, of course, in the general sense that outside influences affect a society only if there are internal and innate factors that make it receptive to such outside influences – a proposition that has been documented, I hope, in the present book. But he is wrong in assuming, in order to establish the purity of the ninth-century Byzantine renaissance, a hermetically sealed society without connection to or knowledge of events beyond its borders. The Byzantines were quite aware of the scientific and translation movement in Bagh̲dad and it is obvious that it influenced the ninth-century renaissance in significant ways.

Evidence of this influence is scarce and mostly anecdotal in the historical sources. On the Arabic side we have some references to missions sent by caliphs or scholars to Byzantium in search of Greek manuscripts. We also have reports about Greek books acquired after the sacking of a city, most famously Amorium (in 223/838) by al-Muʿtaṣim. Such reports in the historical sources may or may not be true, but ultimately they are worthless because they are not specific enough for our purposes. Obviously, for all those Greek writings which were translated into Arabic, the translators had the Greek originals from which to work, and they got them from somewhere. But unless we know the precise provenance and date of the Greek archetype manuscript, information that a particular caliph sent a scholar to "Byzantium" to get it does not improve our knowledge.

Usefully interpreting such reports means identifying the sources of the Greek manuscripts used by the Arabic translators. In this regard scholarship by Arabists has not been as diligent as that by Byzantinists, though admittedly there is very little information and material to work with. We do not have Arabic manuscripts dating from the translation period, nor have the Greek manuscripts of the

49 Lemerle, *Le premier humanisme byzantin*; all my references are to the English translation by H. Lindsay and A. Moffatt, *Byzantine Humanism*. For Lemerle's arguments against "The Hypothesis of a Link through Syria and the Arabs," see pp. 17–41.

ninth and tenth centuries been investigated to ascertain whether they have been used for translation into Arabic.[50] The Arabic bibliographical literature, finally, is also of no help, again with the only and partial exception of Ḥunayn's *Risāla*, in which he mentions on occasion the cities where he found Greek manuscripts. With regard to Galen's *De demonstratione*, for example, he says the following:

> None of our contemporaries has up to this point [i.e., ca. 863] come across a complete Greek manuscript of [Galen's] *De demonstratione*, despite the fact that Ǧibrīl [ibn-Buḫtīšūʿ] spent an enormous amount of effort looking for it, just as I myself searched for it most intensively. I traveled in its search in northern Mesopotamia, all of Syria, Palestine, and Egypt until I reached Alexandria. I found nothing except about half of it, in disorder and incomplete, in Damascus.[51]

Other cities Ḥunayn mentions in connection with Greek manuscripts are Aleppo and Ḥarrān.[52] It is interesting to note that he does not mention once any city under Byzantine jurisdiction, and especially not Constantinople. Given the tenor of the *Risāla*, in which Ḥunayn tries to present himself as an indefatigable philologist and strict critic of other translators, it is difficult to believe that he would not have mentioned the fact had he indeed found a Greek manuscript in Constantinople. The nature of this information is in accord with the little that we know, as mentioned above, about libraries containing Greek manuscripts in the seventh through the ninth centuries. We can only guess, in this case, that Ḥunayn looked for those manuscipts in monasteries and churches and in private libraries.[53]

50 The only exception would seem to be illustrated Greek manuscripts used by artists to copy the illustrations in corresponding Arabic manuscripts, as in the case of the *Materia medica* of Dioscurides. But these Arabic illustrations concern later copies of the Arabic translations made in the ninth and tenth centuries, and thus we do not get direct information about the provenance of the Greek manuscript at the time it was actually translated.

51 Bergsträsser, *Galen-Übersetzungen*, p. 47,12 (text), pp. 38–9 (translation).

52 Bergsträsser, *Galen-Übersetzungen*, p. 33,17 (text), p. 27 (translation); Bergsträsser, *Neue Materialien*, p. 11.

53 Thus emphasizing the importance of what Byzantinists call the "provincial" libraries. It is, however, only natural to expect to find manuscripts in the "provinces": the areas that were conquered by the Arabs in Southeast Asia Minor, Syria, Palestine, and Egypt constituted, perhaps more than Constantinople, the major centers of Hellenism. Thus important eastern centers like Mount Sinai and St Saba near Jerusalem doubtless contained valuable resources, but we have no concrete information for the eighth century. Cf. Wilson, "Libraries," pp. 291, 300.

On the Byzantine side we have a similar anecdotal report in *Theophanes continuatus* about Leo the Philosopher (or the Mathematician): how one of his students, captured by al-Ma'mūn, impressed the caliph with his knowledge of geometry acquired from Leo, and how al-Ma'mūn, dazzled by Leo's mathematical knowledge, sought to recruit him in his service. The Byzantine emperor, the story goes, made a counter offer, which resulted in Leo's obtaining a public teaching post with a salary. Impossibly, Byzantinists give credence to this fairy tale.[54] Al-Ma'mūn, of course, could have had no use of Leo, who allegedly taught himself mathematics on the Aegean island of Andros(!); he, al-Ma'mūn, had Muḥammad al-Ḫwārizmī, the founder of classical algebra, right there in his court, along with many other brilliant scientists.[55] The value of this story lies precisely in indicating the extent to which the Byzantines in Constantinople were aware of the scientific work being done in Baghdad, and indeed in the court of al-Ma'mūn. Other than this, the report is useless.

The only reliable evidence for the problem comes from two sources. One is the report by an astrologer, and the other comes from the analysis of Greek manuscripts. The astrologer is Stephanus the Philosopher [*GAS* VII,48], who was active in Baghdad during its first decades and apparently an associate of Theophilus, al-Mahdī's astrologer [*GAS* VII,49]. In an apology for astrology written in the 790s in Constantinople, he states that he found the city to be devoid of astronomical and astrological sciences, but because of the political and imperial benefits of astrology (echoing the argument for political astrology that was current in Baghdad, as discussed in chapter 2.5), he thought it necessary "to renew this useful science among the Romans and to implant it among the Christians so that they might be

54 See J. Irigoin, "Survie et renouveau de la littérature antique à Constantinople (IXe siècle)," *Cahiers de Civilisation Médiévale, X[e]–XIIe Siècles*, 1962, vol. 5, pp. 290ff., reprinted in D. Harlfinger (ed.), *Griechische Kodikologie*, pp. 179ff., referring also to Bréhier (note 36); Lemerle, *Byzantine Humanism*, pp. 174–7 (also for references to the sources), p. 197; and N. G. Wilson, *Scholars of Byzantium*, London, Duckworth, 1983, pp. 79–80. Wilson even goes so far as to say, in support of the verisimilitude of the tale, that "the episode occurred shortly before the Arabs obtained their excellent knowledge of Greek mathematics through the translations of Hunain ibn Ishaq" (p. 80), thus eliminating in one sentence both al-Ḫwārizmī and Ibn-Turk [*GAS* V,229–42], two of the greatest algebraists in Arabic. They essentially worked before the time of Ḥunayn who, in any case, translated few if any mathematical works.

55 For Leo's mathematical competence and al-Ma'mūn see the comments by D. Pingree, "Classical and Byzantine Astrology in Sassanian Persia," p. 237b.

deprived of it nevermore." Stephanus brought with him to Constantinople from Baghdad not only news of scientific developments there but also concrete mathematical and astrological information: an astrological technique described in a work by Theophilus was used in 792 by Pancratius, the astrologer of Constantine VI, to cast a horoscope.[56]

Evidence from manuscripts comes from the fact that after a hiatus of apparently over one hundred and fifty years, Greek secular manuscripts began to be copied again around 800.[57] The expert and detailed work accomplished by generations of Byzantine scholars has identified those manuscripts which survive from the first three-quarters of the ninth century. These manuscripts have received repeated attention from Byzantinists because, in addition to being the major hard evidence for the ninth-century renaissance, they were for the most part written in the new minuscule hand in the context of a movement, aimed at transcribing the old uncial manuscripts, that is responsible for the preservation of most classical literature.[58] A brief look at a listing of them makes it immediately apparent that the vast majority, indeed almost all of them, are scientific and philosophical. The question that forces itself upon us in the context of the subject of this book is, naturally, how these manuscripts correlate with the translation movement going on in Baghdad at the very moment these manuscripts were being copied. The following table presents the information in synoptic form, juxtaposing the works contained in all the known manuscripts from this period with the status and date of their translation into Arabic. The second

56 For Theophilus and Stephanus, and the translation of the quotation cited, see Pingree, "Classical and Byzantine Astrology in Sassanian Persia," pp. 238–9. Pingree had signaled the eighth-century transmission of astrology to the Byzantines through the Arabs already in 1962: "The early ʿAbbāsid astrologers, many of whom were Iranians, introduced Sasanian theories of the possibility of interpreting history astrologically to the Arabs, and they were passed on almost immediately to the Byzantines"; in his "Historical Horoscopes," *Journal of the American Oriental Society*, 1962, vol. 82, p. 488a.

57 The objections to this picture by Irigoin, "Survie et renouveau," pp. 89ff. (reprinted pp. 177ff.), namely, that some pagan literature was read during this period, are mostly impugned by his own evidence. Some rhetorical progymnasmata, pieces on grammar and prosody, fables, some Homer and some Aristotelian categories seem to be all that were copied, and these hardly make up a classical curriculum. Besides, the total absence of manuscripts from this period shows that no complete copies of any of these works were commissioned, even if students and schoolteachers may have had some portions copied for their use. Cf. the remarks by J.F. Haldon quoted above, note 48.

58 See the concise and useful summary by Wilson, *Scholars of Byzantium*, pp. 85–8.

Date	*U/M*	*Author*	*Work*	*Greek MS*	*Earliest attested Arabic transl.*[59]
800–30	M	Theon	Comm. on Ptolemy's *Almagest*	Laurentianus 28, 18	"old transl." *F* 268.29;*GAS* V,186
800–30	M	Pappus	Comm. on Ptolemy's *Almagest*	Laurentianus 28, 18	* *GAS* V,175
800–30	U	Ptolemy	*Almagest*	Parisinus gr. 2389	transl. before 805; *GAS* VI,88
800–30	U	Dioscurides	*Materia Medica*	Parisinus gr. 2179	tr. Steph. b. Basil; *GAS* III,58
800–30	M	Paul Aegin.		Paris. suppl. gr. 1156,	before 814; *GAS* III,168
800–30	M	Paul Aegin.		Coislin. 8 and 123	before 814; *GAS* III,168
800–30	U	Aristotle	*Sophistici Elenchi*	Paris. suppl. gr. 1362	before 785; *DPA* I,527
813/20	U	Ptolemy	*Almagest*	Vaticanus gr. 1291	transl. before 805; *GAS* VI,88
813/20	U	Ptolemy	*Almagest*	Leidensis B.P.G. 78	transl. before 805; *GAS* VI,88
813/20	U	Theon	Comm. on *Almagest*	Leidensis B.P.G. 78	(see first entry above)
830–50	M	Ptolemy	*Almagest* and other works	Vaticanus gr. 1594	transl. before 805; *GAS* VI,88
830–50	M	Euclid	*Elements*	Vaticanus gr. 190	before 800; ch. 6.3 above
830–50	M	Euclid	*Data*	Vaticanus gr. 190	ca. 850; *GAS* V,116
830–50	M	Theon	Comm. on Ptolemy's *Canons*	Vaticanus gr. 190	before Yaʿqūbī; *GAS* V,174, 185
830–50	M	Theodosius	*Sphaerica*, etc.	Vaticanus gr. 204	*GAS* V,154–6
830–50	M	Autolycus	*Sphaerica*, etc.	Vaticanus gr. 204	*GAS* V,82
830–50	M	Euclid		Vaticanus gr. 204	before 800; ch. 6.3 above
830–50	M	Aristarchus		Vaticanus gr. 204	*GAS* VI,75
830–50	M	Hypsicles	*Anaphorica*	Vaticanus gr. 204	*GAS* V,144–5
830–50	M	Eutocius		Vaticanus gr. 204	*GAS* V,188
830–50	M	Marinus	Comm. on Euclid's *Data*	Vaticanus gr. 204	? but cf. Euclid
830–50[60]	M	Aristotle	*PA, IA, GA, Long. vit., De Spir.*	Oxon. Corp. Chr. 108	ca. 800; *DPA* I,475
ca. 850	M	Aristotle	*Physics*, ff. 1r–55v	Vind. phil. gr. 100[61]	by 800 (ch. 3.2 above)
ca. 850	M	Aristotle	*De caelo*, ff. 56r–86r	Vind. phil. gr. 100	by 850 (ch. 6.3 above)
ca. 850	M	Aristotle	*De gen. et corr.*, ff. 86v–102r	Vind. phil. gr. 100	? but cf. *Physics*
ca. 850	M	Aristotle	*Meteorology*, f. 102v–133v	Vind. phil. gr. 100	by 850 (ch. 6.3 above)

ca. 850	M	Aristotle	*Metaphysics*, ff. 138–201	Vind. phil. gr. 100	by 842: *DPA* I,529
ca. 850	M	Theophrastus	*Metaphysics*, ff. 134r–137	Vind. phil. gr. 100	before 900[62]
ca. 850	M	Aristotle	*Hist. anim.* VI,12–17:ff. 13–14	Paris. suppl. gr. 1156[63]	ca. 800; *DPA* I,475
850–80	M	Ptolemy	[*Almagest?*]	Vat. Urbinas gr. 82	transl. before 805; *GAS* VI,88
850–80	M	Plato	*Tetralogies* VIII and IX	Paris. gr. 1807	never translated in full(?)
850–80	M	Maximus Tyr.		Paris. gr. 1962	?
850–80	M	Albinus		Paris. gr. 1962	never translated(?)
850–80	M	Proclus	Comm. on the *Timaeus*	Paris. suppl. gr. 921	*
850–80	M	Olympiodorus	Comm. on Plato	Marcianus gr. 196	never translated(?)
850–80	M	Simplicius	Comm. on the *Physics* V–VIII	Marcianus gr. 226	*
850–80	M	Philoponus	*Contra Proclum*	Marcianus gr. 236	*GAP* III,32, note 52
850–80	M	Damascius	Comm. on *Parm.* = *De principiis*	Marcianus gr. 246	never translated(?)
850–80	M	Alex. Aphrod.	*Quaest.*; *De an.*; *De fato*	Marcianus gr. 258	*DPA* I,132–3
850–80	M	Proclus	Comm. on the *Republic*	Laurentianus 80,9	*
850–80	M	Proclus	Comm. on the *Republic*	Vaticanus gr. 2197	*
850–80	M	Varii	geographies, doxographies	Palat. Heidelb. gr. 398	various translations
IX cent.		Aristotle	*De interpr.*17a35–18a16	Damascus[64]	9th c.; *DPA* I,514

59 An asterisk (*) in this column means that though this particular book by an author is not mentioned in Arabic bibliographies and does not survive in independent ms tradition, other books by the same author on the same or related subjects were translated into Arabic.

60 Most scholars, though, date this ms significantly later; see *DPA* I,479.

61 Irigoin "L'Aristote de Vienne," 8 top.

62 The extant manuscript ascribes the translation to Isḥāq ibn-Ḥunayn (d. 298/910): I. Alon, "The Arabic Version of Theophrastus' Metaphysica," *Jerusalem Studies in Arabic and Islam*, 1985, vol. 6, p. 164.

63 Irigoin "L' Aristote de Vienne," 9 top.

64 Palimpsest discovered in the Umayyad mosque in Damascus; see Harlfinger, *Griechische Kodikologie*, p. 452.

column indicates whether the Greek manuscript is in U[ncials] or M[inuscule] hand.[65]

The table shows an almost perfect positive correlation between the works translated into Arabic and the first Greek secular manuscripts copied during the first fifty years of the ninth century. This evidence can be interpreted by taking into consideration the following factors, taking the top half of the ninth century first: (a) all the works copied, with the single exception of the uncial fragment of the *Sophistici Elenchi*, are scientific in nature, and indeed predominantly mathematical and astronomical; in medicine there is only Dioscurides and the medical/biological compilation in Paris. suppl. gr. 1156: Paul's encyclopedia and the zoological *Historia animalium* of Aristotle;[66] (b) we have absolutely no information that any Byzantine scholar, at the very beginning of the ninth century, was either interested in or had sufficient training and mathematical knowledge to be able to study these works: Stephanus the philosopher, who came to Constantinople in the 790s just before these manuscripts were copied, found precisely these sciences to be completely wanting; (c) Stephanus transmitted demonstrably some astrological knowledge from Baghdad to Constantinople, as discussed above; and (d) all of these texts (with the possible exception of Pappus's commentary on the *Almagest* and Marinus's on Euclid's *Data*, though Arabist research is only just beginning on these subjects) had been translated into Arabic and studied intensively by the middle of the ninth century; astronomy and mathematics, as we saw above (chapter 5.2), were among the first sciences to be cultivated and rapidly developed in Arabic.

It seems clear that the correlation is causally related. There are two basic alternatives: either the Greek manuscripts were copied in

65 The table is drawn primarily on the basis of information and dating provided by the study of Irigoin, "Survie et renouveau"; other studies consulted were T.W. Allen, "A Group of Ninth Century Greek Manuscripts," *Journal of Philology*, 1893, vol. 21, pp. 48–55; A. Dain, "La transmission des textes littéraires classiques de Photius à Constantin Porphyrogénète," *Dumbarton Oaks Papers*, 1954, vol. 8, pp. 33–47, reprinted in D. Harlfinger (ed.), *Griechische Kodikologie*, p. 206–24; J. Irigoin, "L' Aristote de Vienne," *Jahrbuch der Österreichischen Byzantinischen Gesellschaft*, 1957, vol. 6, pp. 5–10; Wilson, *Scholars of Byzantium*, pp. 85–8. Some fragments in palimpsest from the ninth century, mentioned by Lemerle, *Byzantine Humanism*, p. 83 (citing R. Devreesse), may contain interesting clues, but the evidence is very tenuous and needs expert analysis; they have not been taken into account.

66 Cf. Irigoin, "Survie et renouveau," pp. 288–9 (reprinted p. 176): "dans cette période (first third of the ninth century), seuls les textes scientifiques ou techniques de l'antiquité grecque sont connus et diffusés."

imitation of or as a response to the Arabic translations of these works (however this "imitation" or "response" is to be understood as stemming organically from Byzantine society – a problem for Byzantinists to resolve), or they were copied because of specific Arab demand and under commission for these works. It may not be a matter of choice between the two insofar as both may have been operative.

What seems to be relatively clear, though, in general lines, is the following: by the year 800, i.e., before the end of the reign of Hārūn ar-Rašīd, the translation movement was well under way in Baghdad, concentrating primarily on astrology, astronomy, and mathematics. Through various means such as embassies (cf. above chapter 5.4, on alchemy), but particularly through traveling scholars, intellectuals in Constantinople were informed about developments in Baghdad: they heard about scientific advances in Arabic (and in the case of astrology, as in the case of Pancratius, learned some of it), and they knew about the demand for manuscripts of secular Greek works. In this context, the manuscripts would have been copied for a variety of reasons. Financially, copying Greek manuscripts to supply Arab demand would be a lucrative enterprise; we know that the pay was good. And if an educated young man like Qusṭā ibn-Lūqā could leave his home town for Baghdad deliberately carrying manuscripts as part of his capital (above, chapter 6.2), there is no reason why Greek scribes, both within and without the borders of the Islamic empire, should not have sought to benefit financially from the situation. News of the demand would certainly travel fast. Ḥunayn reports that he visited the entire Fertile Crescent and Egypt in search of manuscripts. In each city he visited one would expect him to go where such manuscripts could be found: the Syriac- and Greek-speaking Christian communities, monasteries, Christian notables with private libraries, as discussed above. From these communities, news of the demand – and, one would expect, Ḥunayn's standing orders – would easily reach Asia Minor and Constantinople. A sociological explanation of the renewed Byzantine interest in copying secular manuscipts would be to interpret the myth about Leo the Philosopher and al-Ma'mūn as an expression of the awareness by Byzantine intellectuals of the scientific superiority of Arabic scholarship and the wish to emulate it.[67] This would also be very close to

67 Cf. Pingree, "Greek Influence on Early Islamic Mathematical Astronomy," p. 33: After the Emperor Heraclius, astronomical studies in Constantinople were abandoned, "not to be revived in Byzantium till the ninth century, when their restoration seems to have been due to the stimulus of the desire to emulate the achievements of the Arabs."

the truth if we keep in mind that in subsequent centuries, and well into the thirteenth, numerous Arabic and Persian scientific works were translated from Arabic into Byzantine Greek. Foremost among the subjects translated were astrology, astronomy, medicine, alchemy, and dream interpretation.

With regard to the Greek manuscripts in the table that were copied during the second half of the ninth century, the evidence presents striking differences. The subjects covered are almost entirely philosophical, and the correlation with Arabic translations of the same works is only partial. The Aristotelian works and commentaries were certainly translated into Arabic, but the Platonic commentaries most probably were not. This differentiation between the Arabic philosophical scholarship in the second half of the ninth century and the renewed Byzantine interest in classical studies with Photius and Arethas is significant for both the Arabic and the Byzantine side. On the Arabic side, neglect of the Platonic material most probably has to do with the rise of Aristotelianism as represented by Abū-Bišr Mattā and his student al-Fārābī; the situation in Byzantium is plausibly to be interpreted in the context of the reaction of Byzantine intellectuals to the Graeco-Arabic translation movement. One may make the observation and ask whether it is merely fortuitous that there is almost no overlap (only some Galen, Dioscurides, and Anatolius) between the inventory of secular works in Photius's *Bibliotheca* and those works that were translated into Arabic, in sharp contrast with the situation concerning the Greek codices copied in the first half of the ninth century. Future research will have to address seriously the question of the dialectic between Arabic scholarship in Baghdad in the ninth century and the renaissance in Constantinople. Provisionally, however, there are sufficient grounds to conclude that the Graeco-Arabic translation movement was causally and directly related to the "first Byzantine humanism" and also, through the Arabic scientific tradition in the Islamic world which fostered it, to the renewal of the ancient sciences in Byzantium after the horrors of the "dark age."

EPILOGUE

Translation is always a culturally creative activity, equally so as the composition of "original" books. Everything that has to do with translation has a relevance and meaning for the recipient culture that are different from those of the donating. The decision *to* translate something and the time when, the decisions what and how to translate, and the reception of the translated piece, are all determined by, and hence meaningful for, the receiving culture. An extreme example, but illustrative because of that, is Galland's translation of the *Thousand and One Nights*, or FitzGerald's translation of ʿUmar al-Ḫayyām's *Rubāʿiyyāt*. These translations mark creative moments in French and English literature, not Arabic or Persian.

From this aspect, the Graeco-Arabic translation movement was as significant a manifestation and as original a creation of early ʿAbbāsid society as, say, *ḥadīṯ* scholarship or Qur'ānic commentary or even the "modern" poetry of that period.[1] Certainly it was based on the Greek texts of the classical tradition, and just as certainly features in *ḥadīṯ*, in Qur'ānic scholarship, and in all the other Islamic sciences have elements from Arab paganism, Judaism, Christianity, Gnosticism, Hinduism, etc. – in short, from prior traditions, religions, and cultures in the area and beyond – as Western scholarship in the last two centuries has been assiduously documenting. But then by the

1 Cf. Sabra, "Greek Science in Medieval Islam," p. 226, where he calls it an "enormously creative act." I would thus hesitate to call the process of transmission from Greek into Arabic as he does, an "appropriation" – a surreptitiously servile term – and prefer to call it what it really was, a creation of early ʿAbbāsid society and its incipient Arabic scientific and philosophical tradition. "Appropriation" is the usual term used by scholars to refer to this process; cf. the word "Aneignung" in the title of the article by Kunitzsch, "Über das Frühstadium der arabischen Aneignung antiken Gutes," and p. 269, without, however, any explicit discussion about the choice of term.

end of the twentieth century one hopes that historical understanding has been sufficiently castigated as to appreciate Said's statement in my epigraph, that "partly because of empire, all cultures are involved in one another; none is single and pure." The question is to explain the particular historical process whereby, through empire, the disparate constituent elements coalesce into the original cultural configuration we are studying. The essence is in the details – both in order to establish the reasons why the coalescence took place in the specific time and place, and, conversely, in order to account for its absence elsewhere despite the seeming presence of the same elements.[2] An excellent illustration of this is the old conundrum that Byzantine society, although Greek-speaking and the direct inheritor of Greek culture, never reached the level of scientific advancement of the early ʿAbbāsids and had itself later to translate *from Arabic* ideas that ultimately go back to classical Greece.[3] In such an analysis, the contribution of individuals is also to be put in perspective. I mentioned at the outset (chapter 1.3) that Sergius of Rēšʿaynā and Boethius, at the two antipodes of Greek cultural spread in early sixth century, conceived of projects to translate and comment upon philosophy and the sciences as presented in the philosophy of Aristotle – and hence all knowledge, as understood in the Alexandrian scholarship of their age.[4] The conception is to their credit as

2 Cf. the methodological reflections of Sabra on the historiography of science, "Situating Arabic Science," pp. 654–61, where he argues for empirical research directed toward specific localities and times. This refines the earlier view of S.D. Goitein, "Islam, the Intermediate Civilization," who asserted that "we have to consider each historical period in its own right" (p. 228), but went on to distinguish only three such periods. The formulation of the goal is correct but the periodization is too schematic and just as reificatory.

3 A static understanding of history that relies on essentialist concepts like race or spirit to explain historical processes can only find itself in the embarrassing situation in which we can observe the Byzantine historian Agathias. In one of those magnificent instances of irony that only history can produce, Agathias ascribed the alleged inability of the Sasanian king Chosroes I Anūširwān to understand Greek philosophy to the irreducible values of Greek culture which, he claimed, could not be translated or preserved "in a primitive and most uncultured tongue" (ἀγρίᾳ τινὶ γλώττῃ καὶ ἀμουσοτάτῃ, in his *Historiae* B 28.3, p. 77 Keydell; cf. Duneau, "La pénétration de l'hellénisme dans l'Empire perse sassanide," p. 18). As the documentation collected in this study indicates, it was the policies precisely of this king, and the invigoration in his court of a translation culture, which constituted an indispensable milestone in the tortuous historical paths that led to the Graeco-Arabic translation movement. It proved Agathias wrong and contributed, in the ninth century, to the revived interest in secular Greek culture by Agathias's very own Byzantine descendants.

4 See the discussion of this point in my "Paul the Persian," section III.

individuals; that they failed indicates the adverse circumstances of their environment.

The Graeco-Arabic translation movement, then, cannot be understood apart from the social, political, and ideological history of the early ʿAbbāsid empire, of which it was an integral element. What were the differentiating factors, in the final analysis and given all the necessary conditions in the background (chapter 1), that made all those policy decisions of the caliphs and the ruling elite (chapters 2–4), and all those social factors and scholarly needs discussed in detail (chapters 5–6), actually function in such a way as to result in an unprecedented translation movement and spur one of the most productive and progressive periods in human history in general and Arab history in particular?

The crux of the matter seems to lie in al-Manṣūr's creation, after the ʿAbbāsid revolution, of a new social configuration in Baghdad through the genial idea of creating a new city. This meant, in essence, granting himself the licence to start everything anew by freeing him from constraints carried over from the previous *status quo*. That is, of course, why revolutions are called revolutions, but al-Manṣūr seems to have grasped this core characteristic and carried it further. He consolidated the gains of the dynastic and social revolution and pre-empted any future opposition by creating a new geographical location in which he could fashion the new *status quo* on his own terms.[5] Being free of the *status quo* meant not only breaking the political power of certain groups and factions over the rest of Muslim society, but also eliminating the ideological constructs which every political group projected as its intellectual underpinning and which, over time and through the consequent entrenchment, could have become opposed to other ideological constructs and impeded progress as al-Manṣūr saw it.

Specifically: the Umayyad state of affairs, based on pre-Islamic Arab tribalism, however useful it may have been for the initial success of the Arab expansion, had, even before the downfall of the dynasty, grown counter-productive by falling back on its pre-Islamic pattern

5 That this realization must have come to him as a result of experience is evident from the ʿAbbāsids' abortive attempts to locate their new capital in at least four different locations before settling on Baghdad. See J. Lassner's article "al-Hāshimiyya," *EI* III,265–6, and cf. further Kennedy, *Early Abbasid Caliphate*, pp 86–8. Van Ess is emphatic about the foundation of Baghdad as a turning point in the intellectual history of Islam: *Theologie und Gesellschaft*, III,3–4, with bibliographical references.

of tribal factionalism: witness the transferral, by the last Umayyad caliph Marwān II (r. 744–50), of the effective capital from Damascus to Ḥarrān, where he could count on the support of the Qays Arabs against his political opponents among the Kalb Arabs in southern Syria and Palestine. The ʿAbbāsid revolution and the move to Baghdad changed all that, not, of course, by eliminating the rivalry between the Qays and the Kalb or, for that matter, Arab tribalism as such, but by removing it from center stage and as the major contradiction of the political and social process. Along with the destruction of the Umayyad political and social configuration, there were consequently eliminated also whatever ideological structures it supported. This does not mean that Umayyad ideologies, however one might specify them, would have been necessarily opposed to a translation movement and its cultural implications (although in chapter 1.2 I suggested that the survival of Byzantine forms of intellectual life in Damascus would have been an inhibiting factor), but that the elimination of Umayyad ideological structures meant the elimination of any power groups (like the Umayyad Byzantine bureaucracy), factions, or classes with vested interests in certain ideological positions which could have opposed new developments such as a translation movement. This left the early ʿAbbāsids – effectively, al-Manṣūr – free to establish his power and fashion his own ideologies. This situation goes hand in hand with al-Manṣūr's policy of creating political coalitions with different groups and balancing the power of one against the other. This was recognized by the geographer Ibn al-Faqīh al-Hamadānī (cf. chapter 5.4) who made explicitly the point around 290/903:

> The good thing about Baghdad is that the rulers can feel secure against any head of (religious) party winning there the upper hand, as the ʿAlids and the Shīʿites frequently do over the people of Kūfa. In Baghdad opponents of the Shīʿites live together with the Shīʿites, opponents of the Muʿtazilites together with the Muʿtazilites, and opponents of the Ḫāriǧites together with the Ḫāriǧites; each group holds the other one in check and prevents it from setting itself up as leader.[6]

6 Ibn-al-Faqīh al-Hamadānī, *(Aḫbār) al-Buldān*, facsimile reproduction of MS Mešhed 5229, F. Sezgin (ed.), Frankfurt, Institut für Geschichte der Arabisch-Islamischen Wissenschaften, Frankfurt am Main, 1987, p. 105; cited by van Ess, *Theologie und Gesellschaft*, III,9.

The only dominant group in Baghdad was thus the ʿAbbāsid family, and this can hardly be accidental. By founding Baghdad and populating it with elements whose ideologies neutralized each other al-Manṣūr eliminated from the political center the paramount Umayyad characteristic of Arab tribalism, gave himself the freedom to fashion his own political and cultural policies, and forestalled any future opposition to them from a socially dominant group. It is difficult to imagine that the master stroke which conferred upon him all these benefits could have been unintentional. But along with the Umayyads out went also *Arab* culture as political and ideological focus: because it excluded by its very nature those not born Arabs, it could not serve the perceived requirements of the ʿAbbāsid dynasty to form coalitions with and please political partners of different ethnic backgrounds; what was substituted was *Arabic* culture, based on the language, in which everybody could participate.

With the stage set in this fashion, all the factors discussed in Part I and Part II become operative and indeed meaningful. In this context, al-Manṣūr's adoption of a Sasanian imperial ideology becomes possible and meaningful, as does the establishment of the attendant translation movement. The process, once set in motion, proceeded for over two centuries on its own for the very concrete and historical reasons discussed in the preceding chapters.

As far as Islam as religion is concerned, and by Islam here I mean the contents of the Qur'ān and the practice of the Prophet Muḥammad as transmitted and understood by all those who considered themselves Muslims at the time of the ʿAbbāsid revolution, it is fundamental to realize that there was *nothing* in the understanding of Islam by *all* of them – despite their very considerable differences regarding the criteria of correct faith and of legitimate leadership of the community – that was incompatible with the larger world-view of Arabic culture that the ʿAbbāsid elite were promoting. The reactions that can be witnessed to the translation movement while it was in process were all socially, politically, or intellectually motivated; they had no doctrinal content (chapter 7.2). If anything, the norm among intellectuals, in terms of percentage, was either a philhellenic attitude or one of indifference to the translated sciences. In subsequent centuries, certain individual scholars and, on rarer occasions, elements of the religious establishment in various Islamic states at some point adopted a position opposing some or most of the translated sciences for very specific reasons that have to be analyzed in each instance. But these elements were especially not unified under a master plan of counter-attack on doctrinal grounds, nor does their opposition define "Islamic orthodoxy" even within their societies, let alone in its totality (see chapter 7.3).

The legacy of the translation movement in Islamic societies was profound and manifold, but it is historically inaccurate to talk about it in isolation from the Arabic scientific and philosophical tradition which fostered it throughout its existence. One should avoid generating the false impression that the translations, once executed in a receptive phase, caused the development of Arabic philosophical and scientific thinking during a subsequent creative phase of this tradition (see chapter 6.3). On the other hand, this book is not about Arabic science and philosophy. With this caveat in mind, it is possible to identify what was specific to the translation movement as such.

The particular linguistic achievement of the Graeco-Arabic translation movement was that it produced an Arabic scientific literature with a technical vocabulary for its concepts, as well as a high *koiné* language that was a fit vehicle for the intellectual achievements of scholarship in Islamic societies in the past and the common heritage of the Arab world today. Its significance for the Greek language is no less spectacular. Not only did it preserve for posterity, in Arabic translation, both lost Greek texts and more reliable manuscript traditions of those extant, but it contributed, through the demand it generated for secular Greek works, to their preservation also *in Greek* by quickening their transcription from uncials into minuscule script copies (see chapter 7.4).

On a broader and more fundamental level, its significance lies in that it demonstrated for the first time in history that scientific and philosophical thought are international,[7] not bound to a specific language or culture. Once the Arabic culture forged by early ʿAbbāsid society historically established the universality of Greek scientific and philosophical thought, it provided the model for and facilitated the later application of this concept in Greek Byzantium and the Latin West: in Byzantium, both in Lemerle's "first Byzantine humanism" of the ninth century and in the later renaissance of the Palaeologoi; and in the West, both in what Haskins has called the renaissance of the twelfth century and in the Renaissance proper.

7 W. Jaeger made this point, calling the period of the translation movement "die erste internationale Wissenschaftsepoche, die die Welt gesehen hat," in his "Die Antike und das Problem der Internationalität der Geisteswissenschaften," *Inter Nationes*, Berlin, 1931, vol. 1, p. 93b. Due to the inaccessibility of this publication, I am citing Endress, *GAP* II,423 and note 48, who is citing Jörg Kraemer.

APPENDIX: GREEK WORKS TRANSLATED INTO ARABIC

A Bibliographical Guide by Subject

Readers of this book may be interested in obtaining more information on the particular Greek works translated into Arabic. Given the relatively arcane nature of the subject and the complexity of the sources, both primary and secondary, the following guide is intended to facilitate further research.

Fundamental for the historical and philological study of the Arabic translations from Greek and Syriac and their legacy in Arabic scholarship is the book-length article by G. Endress, "Die wissenschaftliche Literatur," in *GAP*, vol. II, pp. 400–506, and vol. III (Supplement), pp. 3–152, with a practically exhaustive bibliography. It should be consulted for all subjects listed below. The indices of names and technical terms at the end of both volumes are particularly useful. A first-hand impression of the depth and breadth of the translated works and the literature they inspired can be obtained in English from F. Rosenthal's *The Classical Heritage in Islam*.

Greek works in the following subjects, given below in alphabetical order, were translated into Arabic. Lists of the translated works with full bibliographical references can be found in these sources:

(a) Agriculture: *GAS* IV,301–29; Ullmann, *Geheimwissenschaften*, pp. 427–39.
(b) Alchemy: *GAS* IV,31–119; Ullmann, *Geheimwissenschaften*, pp. 145–91; see also the article "al-Kīmiyā' by Ullmann in *EI* V,110–15.
(c) Algebra: see Mathematics.
(d) Astrology: *GAS* VII,30–97; Ullmann, *Geheimwissenschaften*, pp. 277–302.
(e) Astronomy: *GAS* VI,68–103.
(f) Botany: Ullmann, *Geheimwissenschaften*, pp. 70–4.
(g) Geography: *GAS* X and ff., forthcoming.

(h) Geometry: see Mathematics.

(i) Grammar: F. Rundgren, "Über den griechischen Einfluss auf die arabische Nationalgrammatik," *Acta Universitatis Upsaliensis*, 1976, Nova Series, vol. 2,5, pp. 119–44; review by C. Versteegh, *Bibliotheca Orientalis*, 1979, vol. 36, pp. 235–6; C. Versteegh, *Greek Elements in Arabic Linguistic Thinking*, Leiden, E.J. Brill, 1977; C. Versteegh, "Hellenistic Education and the Origin of Arabic Grammar," *Studies in the History of Linguistics* 20, Amsterdam, 1980, pp. 333–44.

(j) Literature and literary theory: High Greek literature was not translated into Arabic. It is reported that Theophilus of Edessa (see chapter 1.1) translated some Homer into Syriac and that Ḥunayn himself could recite Homer in Greek by heart, but none of this survives in either Syriac or Arabic translation. The extensive Homeric citations in Arabic which do survive are all translations of the passages in the works which cite him, primarily Aristotle and Ps.-Plutarch's *Placita philosophorum.* What was translated of Greek literature was what may be loosely called "popular" and "paraenetic" literature. For literary theory there was, of course, Aristotle's *Poetics.* The following genres can be identified:

[i] Gnomic and paraenetic literature: D. Gutas, *Greek Wisdom Literature in Arabic Translation*, New Haven, American Oriental Society, 1975; F. Rosenthal, *Classical Heritage*, ch. 12; F. Rundgren, "Arabische Literatur und orientalische Antike," *Orientalia Suecana*, 1970–1, vol. 19–20, pp. 81–124.

[ii] Fables and Aesopica: F. Rosenthal, "A Small Collection of Aesopic Fables in Arabic Translation," *Studia semitica necnon iranica Rudolpho Macuch . . . dedicata*, M. Macuch *et al.* (eds), Wiesbaden, Otto Harrassowitz, 1989, pp. 233–56.

[iii] Novels, *1001 Nights:* T. Hägg, "The Oriental Reception of Greek Novels: A Survey with Some Preliminary Considerations," *Symbolae Osloenses*, 1986, vol. 61, pp. 99–131; G.E. von Grunebaum, "Creative Borrowing: Greece in the *Arabian Nights*," in his *Medieval Islam*, Chicago, Chicago University Press, 1946, second edition 1953, pp. 294–319.

[iv] The Alexander Romance: see "Iskandar Nāma" in *EI* IV,127–9; G. Endress, review of M. Brocker, *Aristoteles als Alexanders Lehrer in der Legende*, Bonn, 1966, in *Oriens*, 1968–9, vol. 21–22, pp. 411–16; M. Grignaschi, "La

figure d'Alexandre chez les Arabes et sa genèse," *Arabic Sciences and Philosophy*, 1993, vol. 3, pp. 205–34; S. Brock, "The Laments of the Philosophers over Alexander in Syriac," *Journal of Semitic Studies*, 1970, vol. 15, pp. 205–18.

[v] Poetry, general: I. ʿAbbās, *Malāmiḥ yūnāniyya fī l-adab al-ʿarabī*, second edition, Beirut, 1993.

[vi] Literary theory: W. Heinrichs, *Arabische Dichtung und griechische Poetik*, Beirut, F. Steiner, 1969; G. Schoeler, *Einige Grundprobleme der autochthonen und der aristotelischen arabischen Literaturtheorie*, Wiesbaden, F. Steiner, 1975; D.L. Black, *Logic and Aristotle's* Rhetoric *and* Poetics *in Medieval Arabic Philosophy*, Leiden, E.J. Brill, 1990.

(k) Magic: Ullmann, *Geheimwissenschaften*, pp. 364–82.

(l) Mathematics and geometry: *GAS* V,70–190; review by D.A. King, *Journal of the American Oriental Society*, 1979, vol. 99, pp. 450–9.

(m) Medicine, pharmacology, veterinary science: *GAS* III, 20–171, 349–55; Ullmann, *Medizin*, pp. 25–100 and *passim*. Extremely useful, and with full consideration of the Arabic evidence, are the bibliographies for Hippocrates and Galen compiled by Gerhard Fichtner at the Institut für Geschichte der Medizin (Goethestr. 6, 72076 Tübingen), *Corpus Hippocraticum* and *Corpus Galenicum*; latest revised edition: 1995.

(n) Meteorology, astrometeorology: *GAS* VII,212–32, 308–21.

(o) Military manuals: C. Cahen, article "Ḥarb" in *EI* III,181; V. Christides, "Naval Warfare in the Eastern Mediterranean (6th–14th Centuries): An Arabic Translation of Leo VI's *Naumachica*," *Graeco-Arabica* (Athens), 1984, vol. 3, pp. 137–48.

(p) Mineralogy: Ullmann, *Geheimwissenschaften*, pp. 95–102.

(q) Music: R. d'Erlanger, *La musique arabe*, Paris, 1935, vol. 2, pp. 257–306; H.G. Farmer, *The Sources of Arabian Music*, Leiden, E.J. Brill, 1965, pp. xi–xii, 13–21; A. Shiloah, *The Theory of Music in Arabic Writings*, München, G. Henle Verlag, 1979.

(r) Optics: M. Blay and G. Troupeau, "Sur quelques publications récentes consacrées à l'histoire de l'optique antique et arabe," *Arabic Sciences and Philosophy*, 1995, vol. 5, pp. 121–36.

(s) Pharmacology: see under Medicine.

(t) Philosophy: There is as yet no modern bibliographical survey of the Arabic translations of all the Greek philosophers; Steinschneider's *Die Arabischen Übersetzungen aus dem Griechischen* remains the only single treatment. In general see G. Endress in

GAP III,24–61, and his "Die Arabisch-Islamische Philosophie. Ein Forschungsbericht," *Zeitschrift für Geschichte der Arabisch-Islamischen Wissenschaften*, 1989, vol. 5, pp. 1–47; also in *Contemporary Philosophy: A New Survey*, vol. vi,2, Amsterdam, 1990, pp. 651–702. For philosophical schools other than Platonism and Aristotelianism, see D. Gutas, "Pre-Plotinian Philosophy in Arabic (Other than Platonism and Aristotelianism): A Review of the Sources," in *Aufstieg und Niedergang der Römischen Welt*, Berlin, W. de Gruyter, 1993, Part II, vol. 36.7, pp. 4939–73. For Aristotle in particular see Peters, *Aristoteles Arabus*, its review by H. Daiber in *Gnomon*, 1970, vol. 42, pp. 538–47, and the entries in *DPA*, vol. 1. For Plato see F. Rosenthal, "On the Knowledge of Plato's Philosophy in the Islamic World," *Islamic Culture*, 1940, vol. 14, pp. 387–422, and 1941, vol. 15, pp. 396–8; reprinted in his *Greek Philosophy in the Arab World*, Aldershot, Hampshire, Variorum, 1990, no. II; also F. Klein-Franke, "Zur Überlieferung der platonischen Schriften im Islam," *Israel Oriental Studies*, 1973, vol. 3, pp. 120–39. Further bibliography and discussion in *GAP* II,478–81, III,24.

(u) Veterinary science: see under Medicine.

(v) Zoology:

[i] General: Ullmann, *Geheimwissenschaften*, pp. 8–18; H. Eisenstein, *Einführung in die arabische Zoographie*, Berlin, D. Reimer Verlag, 1991, pp. 117–21 and *passim*.

[ii] Hunting literature: Ullmann, *Geheimwissenschaften*, pp. 43–5.

(w) For Christian Greek works translated into Arabic see G. Graf, *Geschichte der Christlichen Arabischen Literatur*, Vatican, Biblioteca Apostolica, 1944, vol. 1; and P. Peeters, *Le tréfonds oriental de l'hagiographie byzantine*, Brussels, 1950, pp. 165–218.

BIBLIOGRAPHY AND ABBREVIATIONS

The following bibliography lists all the works cited in this study (except encyclopaedia articles), the abbreviations used, and selected items relating to the Graeco-Arabic translation movement. Further references can be found in the bibliography given in the Appendix, and especially in *GAP.* The Arabic article *al-* and the prefixes of titles in Western names (de, von) have been disregarded in the alphabetical order.

ʿAbbās, I., *ʿAhd Ardašīr*, Beirut, Dar Sader, 1967

ʿAbbāsid Belles-Lettres, J. Ashtiany *et al.* (eds), Cambridge, Cambridge University Press, 1990

al-Ābī, Manṣūr ibn-al-Ḥusayn, *Naṯr ad-durr*, Munīr M. al-Madanī (ed.), vol. 7, Cairo, al-Hay'a al-Miṣriyya al-ʿĀmma li-l-Kitāb, 1990

Afnan, S.M., *Philosophical Terminology in Arabic and Persian*, Leiden, E.J. Brill, 1964

Agathias, *Historiarum libri quinque* [Corpus Fontium Historiae Byzantinae II], R. Keydell (ed.), W. de Gruyter, Berlin, 1967

al-ʿAlī, Ṣ.A., "Muwaẓẓafū bilād aš-Šām fī l-ʿahd al-Umawī," *al-Abḥāṯ*, 1966, vol. 19, pp. 44–79

Allen, T.W., "A Group of Ninth Century Greek Manuscripts," *Journal of Philology*, 1893, vol. 21, pp. 48–55

Alon, I., "The Arabic Version of Theophrastus' Metaphysica," *Jerusalem Studies in Arabic and Islam*, 1985, vol. 6, pp. 163–217

Arabic Literature to the End of the Umayyad Period, A.F.L. Beeston *et al.* (eds), Cambridge, Cambridge University Press, 1983

Arnaldez, R., "Sciences et philosophie dans la civilisation de Baġdād sous les premiers ʿAbbāsides," *Arabica*, 1962, vol. 9, pp. 357–73

—— "L'Histoire de la pensée grecque vue par les arabes," *Bulletin de la Société Française de Philosophie*, 1978, vol. 72.3, pp. 117–68

Ashtor, E., "The Diet of Salaried Classes in the Medieval Near East," *Journal of Asian History*, 1970, vol. 4, pp. 1–24, reprinted in his *The Medieval Near East: Social and Economic History*, London, Variorum, 1978, no. III

—— "An Essay on the Diet of the Various Classes in the Medieval Levant," in R. Forster and O. Ranum (eds), *Biology of Man in History. Selections from the Annales*, Baltimore, Johns Hopkins University Press, 1975, pp. 125–62

Avicenna, see Ibn-Sīnā

Badawī, ʿA., *At-Turāṯ al-yūnānī fī l-ḥaḍāra al-islāmiyya*, Cairo, Maktabat an-Nahḍa al-Miṣriyya, 1946

—— *La transmission de la philosophie grecque au monde arabe*, Paris, Vrin, 1968

al-Baghdādī, ʿAbd-al-Qāhir ibn-Ṭāhir, *al-Farq bayna l-firaq*, M. Badr (ed.), Cairo, 1910; reprinted Beirut, Dār al-Āfāq al-Ǧadīda, 1977

Bailey, H.W., *Zoroastrian Problems in the Ninth-Century Books*, Oxford, Clarendon, 1943

Baltussen, H., *Theophrastus on Theories of Perception*, Utrecht, University of Utrecht, 1993

Balty-Guesdon, M.-G., "Le *Bayt al-ḥikma* de Baghdad," *Arabica*, 1992, vol. 39, pp. 131–50

Baumstark, A., *Geschichte der syrischen Literatur*, Bonn, Marcus und Webers, 1922

al-Bayhaqī, Ibrāhīm ibn-Muḥammad, *al-Maḥāsin wa-l-masāwiʾ*, F. Schwally (ed.), Giessen, 1902

(Benakis, L.G.) Λίνος Γ. Μπενάκης, "Ἕνα ἀνέκδοτο Ἑλληνοαραβικὸ λεξιλόγιο Ἀριστοτελικῆς λογικῆς ὁρολογίας τοῦ Βησσαρίωνος Μακρῆ (1670)," Νεοελληνικὴ Φιλοσοφία 1600–1950, Πρακτικὰ τῆς Γ′ Φιλοσοφικῆς Ἡμερίδας Ἰωαννίνων, Μάρτιος, 1988, Thessaloniki, Vanias, 1994, pp. 97–108

Bergé, M., "Abū Ḥayyān al-Tawḥīdī," in *ʿAbbāsid Belles-Lettres*, pp. 112–24

Bergsträsser, G., *Ḥunain ibn Isḥāḳ und seine Schule*, Leiden, E.J. Brill, 1913

—— *Ḥunain ibn Isḥāq über die syrischen und arabischen Galen-Übersetzungen* [Abhandlungen für die Kunde des Morgenlandes XVII,2], Leipzig, Deutsche Morgenländische Gesellschaft, 1925

—— *Neue Materialien zu Ḥunain ibn Isḥāq's Galen-Bibliographie* [Abhandlungen für die Kunde des Morgenlandes XIX,2], Leipzig, 1932

Bidawid, R.J., *Les lettres du Patriarche Nestorien Timothée I* [Studi e Testi 187], Vatican, Biblioteca Apostolica Vaticana, 1956

Biesterfeldt, H.H., *Galens Traktat 'Dass die Kräfte der Seele den Mischungen des Körpers folgen' in arabischer Übersetzung*, Wiesbaden, F. Steiner, 1973

al-Bīrūnī, see Sachau, E.

Bos, G., *Qusṭā ibn Lūqā's Medical Regime for the Pilgrims to Mecca*, Leiden, E.J. Brill, 1992

Bosworth, C.E., "The Ṭāhirids and Arabic Culture", *Journal of Semitic Studies*, 1969, vol. 14, pp. 45–79

—— "The Heritage of Rulership in Early Islamic Iran and the Search for Dynastic Connections with the Past," *Iran*, 1973, vol. 11, pp. 51–62

—— "The Persian Impact on Arabic Literature," in *Arabic Literature to the End of the Umayyad Period*, pp. 483–96

—— *Storm and Stress along the Northern Frontiers of the ʿAbbāsid Caliphate* [The History of al-Ṭabarī, vol. 33], Albany, State University of New York Press, 1991

Bowen, H., *The Life and Times of ʿAlī ibn ʿĪsā, the Good Vizir*, Cambridge, Cambridge University Press, 1928

Bouyges, M., *Averroès. Tafsir ma baʿd at-tabiʿat. Notice*, Beirut, Dar el-Machreq, 1952; reprinted 1972

Boyce, M., "Middle Persian Literature," in *Iranistik II, Literatur I* [Handbuch der Orientalistik I,iv,2.1], Leiden, E.J. Brill, 1968, pp. 31–66

Brentjes, S., "Textzeugen und Hypothesen zum arabischen Euklid," *Archive for History of Exact Sciences*, 1994, vol. 47, pp. 53–92

Brock, S., "From Antagonism to Assimilation: Syriac Attitudes to Greek Learning," in N. Garsoian, T. Mathews, and R. Thompson (eds), *East of Byzantium: Syria and Armenia in the Formative Period*, Washington, DC, Dumbarton Oaks, 1980, pp. 17–34

—— *Syriac Perspectives on Late Antiquity*, London, Variorum, 1984

—— "Syriac Culture in the Seventh Century," *Aram*, 1989, vol. 1, pp. 268–80

—— "The Syriac Commentary Tradition," in C. Burnett (ed.), *Glosses and Commentaries on Aristotelian Logical Texts*, pp. 3–15

Brockelmann, C., *Geschichte der Arabischen Literatur*, 2 vols., second edition, Leiden, E.J. Brill, 1943–9; *Supplement*, 3 vols., Leiden, E.J. Brill, 1937–42

Brugman, J. and H.J. Drossaart Lulofs, *Aristotle. Generation of Animals*, Leiden, E.J. Brill, 1971

Bulliet, R.W., *Conversion to Islam in the Medieval Period*, Cambridge, Mass., Harvard University Press, 1979

Burnett, C. (ed.), *Glosses and Commentaries on Aristotelian Logical Texts*, London, The Warburg Institute, 1993

—— see also Pingree, D., and C. Burnett

Cameron, A., "New Themes and Styles in Greek Literature: Seventh–Eighth Centuries," in A. Cameron and L.I. Conrad (eds), *The Byzantine and Early Islamic Near East*, pp. 81–105

—— and L.I. Conrad (eds), *The Byzantine and Early Islamic Near East* [Studies in Late Antiquity and Early Islam 1], Princeton, Darwin Press, 1992

Caspar, R., "Bibliographie du dialogue islamo-chrétien," *Islamochristiana*, 1975, vol. 1, pp. 125–81

Chejne, A., "The Boon-Companion in Early ʿAbbāsid Times," *Journal of the American Oriental Society*, 1965, vol. 85, pp. 327–35

Christensen, A., *L'Iran sous les sassanides*, Copenhagen, Ejnar Munksgaard, second edition, 1944

Classicisme et déclin culturel dans l'histoire de l'Islam, R. Brunschvig and G.E. von Grunebaum (eds), Paris, Besson-Chantermerle, 1957; reprinted Paris, Maisonneuve et Larose, 1977

Commentaria in Aristotelem graeca, edita consilio et auctoritate academiae litterarum regiae Borussicae, Berlin, G. Reimer, 1882–1909; reviewed by K. Praechter, *Byzantinische Zeitschrift*, 1909, vol. 18, pp. 516–38; English translation by V. Caston in *Aristotle Transformed*, R. Sorabji (ed.), pp. 31–54

Conrad, L.I., see Cameron, A. and L.I. Conrad

Corbin, H., *En Islam Iranien*, 7 parts in 4 vols, Paris, Gallimard, 1971–2

Crone, P. and M. Hinds, *God's Caliph: Religious Authority in the First Centuries of Islam*, Cambridge, Cambridge University Press, 1986

aḏ-Ḏahabī, Muḥammad ibn-Aḥmad, *Duwal al-Islām*, Hyderabad, Dā'irat al-Maʿārif, 1364/1945

Dain, A., "La transmission des textes littéraires classiques de Photius à Constantin Porphyrogénète," *Dumbarton Oaks Papers*, 1954, vol. 8, pp. 33–47, reprinted in D. Harlfinger (ed.), *Griechische Kodikologie*, pp. 206–24

Dallal, A., *An Islamic Response to Greek Astronomy*, Leiden, E.J. Brill, 1995

Degen, R., "The Kitāb al-Aghdhiya of Ḥunayn ibn Isḥāq," *Proceedings of the First International Symposium for the History of Arabic Science*, A.Y. al-Ḥassan *et al.* (eds), Aleppo, Institute for the History of Arabic Science, 1978, vol. 2, pp. 291–9

Dhanani, A., *The Physical Theory of Kalām. Atoms, Space, and Void in Basrian Muʿtazilī Cosmology*, Leiden, E.J. Brill, 1994

Dickinson, E.N., *The Development of Early Muslim* Ḥadīth *Criticism: The* Taqdima *of Ibn Abī Ḥātim al-Rāzī (d. 327/938)*, unpublished Ph.D. dissertation, Yale University, 1992

Dictionary of Scientific Biography, C.C. Gillispie (ed.), 17 vols, New York, Scribner's, 1970–90

Dictionnaire des philosophes antiques, publié sous la direction de Richard Goulet, 2 vols to date, Paris, Centre National de la Recherche Scientifique, 1989–

Dodge, B., *The Fihrist of al-Nadim*, New York, Columbia University Press, 1970

DPA = *Dictionnaire des philosophes antiques*

Drossaart Lulofs, H.J., see Brugman, J. and H.J. Drossaart Lulofs

DSB = *Dictionary of Scientific Biography*

Duneau, J.-F., "Quelques aspects de la pénétration de l'hellénisme dans l'Empire perse sassanide (IVe–VIIe siècles)," in P. Gallais and Y.-J. Riou (eds), *Mélanges offerts à René Crozet*, Poitiers, Société d'Études Médiévales, 1966, vol. 1, pp. 13–22

Dunlop, D.M., "The Translations of al-Biṭrīq and Yaḥyā (Yuḥannā) b. al-Biṭrīq," *Journal of the Royal Asiatic Society*, 1959, pp. 140–50

Duval, R., *La littérature syriaque*, Paris, J. Gabalda, 1907

Eche, Y., *Les bibliothèques arabes publiques et semi-publiques en Mésopotamie, Syrie, Egypte au Moyen Age*, Damas, Institut Français de Damas, 1967

EI = *Encyclopaedia of Islam*, second edition

EIr. = *Encyclopaedia Iranica*

El-Hibri, T., "Harun al-Rashid and the Mecca Protocol of 802: A Plan for Division or Succession?" *International Journal of Middle East Studies*, 1992, vol. 24, pp. 461–80

—— *The Reign of the Abbasid Caliph al-Ma'mūn (811–833): The Quest for Power and the Crisis of Legitimacy*, unpublished Ph.D. dissertation, Columbia University, 1992

—— "Coinage Reform under the 'Abbāsid Caliph al-Ma'mūn," *Journal of the Economic and Social History of the Orient*, 1993, vol. 36, pp. 58–83

Encyclopaedia Iranica, E. Yarshater (ed.), 8 vols to date, London, Routledge and Kegan Paul, and Costa Mesa (CA), Mazda, 1985–

Encyclopaedia of Islam, second edition, 9 vols to date, Leiden, E.J. Brill, 1960–

Endress, G., *Die arabischen Übersetzungen von Aristoteles' Schrift De Caelo*, unpublished Ph.D. dissertation, Frankfurt (am Main) University, 1966

—— *Proclus Arabus. Zwanzig Abschnitte aus der Institutio theologica in arabischer Übersetzung* [Beiruter Texte und Studien 10], Beirut, F. Steiner, 1973

—— "Wissen und Gesellschaft in der islamischen philosophie des Mittelalters," in H. Stachowiak and C. Baldus (eds), *Pragmatik I: Pragmatisches Denken von den Ursprüngen bis zum 18. Jahrhundert*, Hamburg, Felix Meiner, 1986, pp. 219–45

—— "Grammatik und Logik. Arabische Philologie und griechische Philosophie im Widerstreit," in B. Mojsisch (ed.), *Sprachphilosophie in Antike und Mittelalter* [Bochumer Studien zur Philosophie 3], Amsterdam, B.R. Grüner, 1986, pp. 163–299

—— (ed.), *Symposium Graeco-arabicum II*, Amsterdam, B.R. Grüner, 1989

—— "The Defense of Reason: The Plea for Philosophy in the Religious Community," *Zeitschrift für Geschichte der Arabisch-Islamischen Wissenschaften*, 1990, vol. 6, pp. 1–49

—— "'Der erste Lehrer.' Der arabische Aristoteles und das Konzept der Philosophie im Islam," in U. Tworuschka (ed.), *Gottes ist der Orient, Gottes ist der Okzident* [Festschrift für Abdoldjavad Falaturi], Köln, Bühlau, 1991, pp. 151–81

—— "Die wissenschaftliche Literatur," in *Grundriss der Arabischen Philologie*, vol. 2, pp. 400–506, and vol. 3 (Supplement), pp. 3–152
—— "The Circle of al-Kindī," in G. Endress and R. Kruk (eds), *The Ancient Tradition in Christian and Islamic Hellenism*, pp. 43–76
—— and D. Gutas, *A Greek and Arabic Lexicon (GALex). Materials for a Dictionary of the Mediaeval Translations from Greek into Arabic* [Handbuch der Orientalistik, I.xi], Leiden, E.J. Brill, 1992–
—— and R. Kruk (eds), *The Ancient Tradition in Christian and Islamic Hellenism*, Leiden, Research School CNWS, 1997
Eqbāl, ʿA., *Ḫāndān-e Nawbaḫtī*, Tehran, second edition, 1345 Š/1966
van Ess, J., "Ḍirār b. ʿAmr und die 'Cahmīya'. Biographie einer vergessenen Schule," *Der Islam*, 1967, vol. 43, pp. 241–79
—— *Frühe Muʿtazilitische Häresiographie*, Beirut/Wiesbaden, F. Steiner, 1971
—— "Une lecture à rebours de l'histoire du muʿtazilisme," *Revue des Études Islamiques*, 1978, vol. 46, pp. 163–240; 1979, vol. 47, pp. 19–70
—— *Theologie und Gesellschaft im 2. und 3. Jahrhundert Hidschra. Eine Geschichte des religiösen Denkens im frühen Islam*, 6 vols, Berlin, W. de Gruyter, 1991–97
F = Ibn-an-Nadīm, *Kitāb al-Fihrist*
Fähndrich, H. (ed.), *Ibn Jumayʿ: Treatise to Ṣalāḥ ad-Dīn on the Revival of the Art of Medicine* [Abhandlungen für die Kunde des Morgenlandes XLVI,3], Wiesbaden, F. Steiner, 1983
Fahd T., "The Dream in Medieval Islamic Society," in G.E. von Grunebaum and R. Caillois (eds), *The Dream and Human Societies*, Berkeley, University of California Press, 1966, pp. 351–63
Fazzo, S. and H. Wiesner, "Alexander of Aphrodisias in the Kindī-Circle and in al-Kindī's Cosmology," *Arabic Sciences and Philosophy*, 1993, vol. 3, pp. 119–53
Fields, P.M., *The ʿAbbāsid Recovery* [The History of al-Ṭabarī, vol. 37], Albany, State University of New York Press, 1987
Fiey, J.M., *Chrétiens syriaques sous les Abbassides, surtout à Bagdad (749–1258)*, Louvain, Secrétariat du Corpus SCO, 1980
Flügel, G., "Dissertatio de arabicis scriptorum graecorum interpretibus," in *Memoriam anniversariam . . . Scholae Regiae Afranae . . . celebrandam indicit . . . Baumgarten-Crusius . . . Rector et Professor I.*, Misenae (Meissen), M.C. Klinkicht, 1841, pp. 3–38
Frye, R.N. (ed.), *The Cambridge History of Iran*, vol. 4, Cambridge, Cambridge University Press, 1975
Gabrieli, F., "Recenti studi sulla tradizione greca nella civiltà musulmana," *La Parola del Passato*, 1959, vol. 14, pp. 147–60; Spanish translation: "Estudios recentes sobre la tradición griega en la civilización musulmana," *Al-Andalus*, 1959, vol. 24, pp. 297–318
Gabrieli, G., "Nota biobibliographica su Qusṭā ibn Lūqā," *Rendiconti della Reale Accademia dei Lincei*, Classe di Scienze Morali, Storiche e Filologiche, Ser. V, 1912, vol. 21, pp. 341–82
al-Ǧāḥiẓ, ʿAmr ibn-Baḥr, *Rasāʾil al-Ǧāḥiẓ*, ʿA. M. Hārūn (ed.), 4 vols, Cairo, al-Ḫānǧī, 1965–79
al-Ǧāḥiẓ (ps.-), *Kitāb at-Tāǧ*, A. Zakī (ed.), Cairo, al-Maṭbaʿa al-Amīriyya, 1914
GAL = C. Brockelmann, *Geschichte der Arabischen Literatur*
GALex = G. Endress, and D. Gutas, *A Greek and Arabic Lexicon*
GALS = C. Brockelmann, *Geschichte der Arabischen Literatur*, Supplement-bände
GAP = *Grundriss der Arabischen Philologie*

GAS = F. Sezgin, *Geschichte des Arabischen Schrifttums*
Gibb, H.A.R., "The Influence of Islamic Culture on Medieval Europe," *Bulletin of the John Rylands Library*, 1955–6, vol. 38, pp. 82–98
—— "The Social Significance of the Shuubiya," in his *Studies on the Civilization of Islam*, S.J. Shaw and W.R. Polk (eds), Boston, Beacon Press, 1962, pp. 62–73; reprinted from *Studia Orientalia Ioanni Pedersen dicata*, Copenhagen, 1953, pp. 105–14
Goitein, S.D., "Between Hellenism and Renaissance – Islam, the Intermediate Civilization," *Islamic Studies*, 1963, vol. 2, pp. 217–33
Goldziher, I., *Muslim Studies*, C.R. Barber and S.M. Stern (translators), London, Allen & Unwin, 1967 [original German edition 1889]
—— "Neuplatonische und gnostische Elemente im Hadith," *Zeitschrift für Assyriologie*, 1908, vol. 22, pp. 311–24
—— "Stellung der alten islamischen Orthodoxie zu den antiken Wissenschaften," *Abhandlungen der Königlich Preussischen Akademie der Wissenschaften*, Jahrgang 1915, Philosophisch-historische Klasse, no. 8, Berlin, Verlag der Akademie, 1916
Grabar, O., *The Formation of Islamic Art*, New Haven, Yale University Press, second edition, 1987
Griffith, S.H., "Eutychius of Alexandria on the Emperor Theophilus and Iconoclasm in Byzantium: A Tenth Century Moment in Christian Apologetics in Arabic," *Byzantion*, 1982, vol. 52, pp. 154–90; reprinted in his *Arabic Christianity in the Monasteries of Ninth-Century Palestine*, Aldershot, Hampshire, Variorum, 1992, no. IV
Grignaschi, M., "Quelques spécimens de la littérature sassanide conservés dans les bibliothèques d'Istanbul," *Journal Asiatique*, 1966, vol. 254, pp. 46–90
—— "Le roman épistolaire classique conservé dans la version arabe de Sālim Abū-l-ʿAlāʾ," *Le Muséon*, 1967, vol. 80, pp. 211–64
Grundriss der Arabischen Philologie, Wiesbaden, L. Reichert; vol. 1: *Sprachwissenschaft*, Wolfdietrich Fischer (ed.), 1982; vol. 2: *Literaturwissenschaft*, Helmut Gätje (ed.), 1987; vol. 3: *Supplement*, W. Fischer (ed.), 1992
Gutas, D., "Paul the Persian on the Classification of the Parts of Aristotle's Philosophy: A Milestone between Alexandria and Baġdād," *Der Islam*, 1983, vol. 60, pp. 231–67
—— *Avicenna and the Aristotelian Tradition*, Leiden, E.J. Brill, 1988
—— "Aspects of Literary Form and Genre in Arabic Logical Works," in C. Burnett (ed.), *Glosses and Commentaries on Aristotelian Logical Texts*, pp. 29–76
—— review of M. Fakhry's *Ethical Theories in Islam* (Leiden, E.J. Brill, 1994) in *Journal of the American Oriental Society*, 1997, vol. 117, pp. 171–5
—— see also Endress, G. and D. Gutas
Ḥāǧǧī Ḫalīfa, Muṣṭafā ibn-ʿAlī (Kâtib Çelebi), *Kašf aẓ-ẓunūn*, Ş. Yaltkaya and K.R. Bilge (eds), 2 vols, Istanbul, Maarif Matbaası, 1941
Haldon, J.F., *Byzantium in the Seventh Century: The Transformation of a Culture*, Cambridge, Cambridge University Press, 1990
—— "The Works of Anastasius of Sinai: A Key Source for the History of Seventh-Century East Mediterranean Society and Belief," in A. Cameron and L.I. Conrad (eds), *The Byzantine and Early Islamic Near East*, pp. 107–47
Ḥamza al-Iṣfahānī, *Taʾrīḫ sinī mulūk al-arḍ wa-l-anbiyāʾ*, Beirut, Dār Maktabat al-Ḥayāt, 1961
Harlfinger, D., (ed.), *Griechische Kodikologie und Textüberlieferung*, Damstadt, Wissenschaftliche Buchgesellschaft, 1980

Hartmann, A., *An-Nāṣir li-Dīn Allāh (1180–1225). Politik, Religion, Kultur in der späten ʿAbbāsidenzeit*, Berlin, W. de Gruyter, 1975

Hartner, W., "Quand et comment s'est arrêté l'essor de la culture scientifique dans l'Islam?" in *Classicisme et déclin culturel dans l'histoire de l'Islam*, Paris, Besson-Chantermerle, 1957; reprinted Maisonneuve et Larose, 1977, pp. 319–37

Heer, N., *The Precious Pearl. Al-Jāmī's al-Durrah al-Fākhirah*, Albany, State University of New York Press, 1979

ḤḪ = Ḥāǧǧī Ḫalīfa (Kâtib Çelebi), *Kašf aẓ-ẓunūn*

Hinds, M., see Crone, P. and M. Hinds

Hugonnard-Roche, H., "Aux origines de l'exégèse orientale de la logique d'Aristote: Sergius de Rešʿaina (†536), médecin et philosophe," *Journal Asiatique*, 1989, vol. 277, pp. 1–17

—— "Les traductions du grec au syriaque et du syriaque à l'arabe," in *Rencontres de cultures dans la philosophie médiévale. Traductions et traducteurs de l'antiquité tardive au XIVe siècle*, J. Hamesse et M. Fattori (eds), Louvain-la-Neuve/Cassino, Université Catholique/Università degli Studi, 1990, pp. 131–47

—— "Remarques sur la tradition arabe de l'*Organon* d'après le manuscrit Paris, Bibliothèque Nationale, ar. 2346," in C. Burnett (ed.), *Glosses and Commentaries on Aristotelian Logical Texts*, pp. 19–28

—— "La formation du vocabulaire de la logique en arabe," in D. Jacquart (ed.), *La formation du vocabulaire scientifique et intellectuel dans le monde arabe*, pp. 22–38

—— "Note sur Sergius de Rešʿainā, traducteur du grec en syriaque et commentateur d'Aristote," in G. Endress and R. Kruk (eds), *The Ancient Tradition in Christian and Islamic Hellenism*, pp. 121–43

Humphreys, R. Stephen, *Islamic History. A Framework for Inquiry*, Princeton, Princeton University Press, 1991

Ḥunayn ibn-Isḥāq, *Risāla* = Bergsträsser, *Galen-Übersetzungen*

al-Ḫwārizmī al-Kātib, *Mafātīḥ al-ʿulūm*, G. van Vloten (ed.), Leiden, E.J. Brill, 1895

al-Ḫwārizmī, Muḥammad ibn-Mūsā, *Algebra of Mohammed ben Musa*, F. Rosen (ed. and trans.), London, Oriental Translation Fund, 1831; reprinted Hildesheim, Olms, 1986

IAU = Ibn-Abī-Uṣaybiʿa, *ʿUyūn al-anbāʾ fī ṭabaqāt al-aṭibbāʾ*

Ibn-Abī-Uṣaybiʿa, Aḥmad ibn-al-Qāsim, *ʿUyūn al-anbāʾ fī ṭabaqāt al-aṭibbāʾ*, A. Müller (ed.), 2 vols, Cairo–Königsberg i. Pr., al-Maṭbaʿa al-Wahbīya, 1299–1301/1882–4

Ibn-Faḍlallāh al-ʿUmarī, Aḥmad ibn-Yaḥyā, *Masālik al-abṣār fī mamālik al-amṣār*, MS AyaSofya 3422; printed in facsimile as *Routes toward Insight into the Capital Empires*, F. Sezgin (ed.), Publications of the Institute for the History of Arabic-Islamic Science, Series C, vol. 46.9, Frankfurt am Main, 1988

Ibn-al-Faqīh al-Hamaḏānī, *al-Buldān*, facsimile reproduction of MS Mešhed 5229, in *Maǧmūʿ fī l-ǧuġrāfiyya* [Series C-43], F. Sezgin (ed.), Frankfurt, Institut für Geschichte der Arabisch-Islamischen Wissenschaften, Frankfurt am Main, 1987

Ibn-Ǧulǧul, Sulaymān ibn-Ḥassān, *Ṭabaqāt al-aṭibbāʾ wa-l-ḥukamāʾ*, Fuʾād Sayyid (ed.), Cairo, Institut Français d'Archéologie Orientale, 1955

Ibn-Kaṯīr, Abū l-Fidāʾ, *al-Bidāya wa-n-nihāya fī t-taʾrīḫ*, 14 vols, Cairo, Maṭbaʿat as-Saʿāda, 1932

Ibn-Khaldûn, *The Muqaddimah*, translated by F. Rosenthal, Princeton, Bollingen, second edition, 1967

Ibn-al-Murtaḍā, Aḥmad ibn-Yaḥyā, *Ṭabaqāt al-Muʿtazila. Die Klassen der Muʿtaziliten*, S. Diwald-Wilzer (ed.), Wiesbaden, F. Steiner, 1961

Ibn-an-Nadīm, Muḥammad ibn-Isḥāq, *Kitāb al-Fihrist*, G. Flügel (ed.), 2 vols, Leipzig, 1871–2.

Ibn-Nubāta, Ǧamāl-ad-Dīn, *Šarḥ al-ʿuyūn fī šarḥ risālat Ibn Zaydūn*, M. Abū-l-Faḍl Ibrāhīm (ed.), Cairo, Dār al-Fikr al-ʿArabī, 1964

Ibn-al-Qifṭī, ʿAlī ibn-Yūsuf, *Taʾrīḫ al-ḥukamāʾ*, J. Lippert (ed.), Leipzig, Dieterich'sche Verlagsbuchhandlung, 1903

Ibn-Qutayba, ʿAbdallāh ibn-Muslim, *Adab al-kātib*, M. Grünert (ed.), Leiden, E.J. Brill, 1900

—— *Kitāb al-anwāʾ*, C. Pellat and M. Hamidullah (eds), Hyderabad, Dā'irat al-Maʿārif al-ʿUthmāniyya, 1956

—— *ʿUyūn al-aḫbār*, 4 vols, Cairo, 1923–30; reprinted 1973

Ibn-Riḍwān, Abū-l-Ḥasan ʿAlī, *Al-Kitāb an-nāfiʿ fī kayfiyyat taʿlīm ṣināʿat aṭ-ṭibb*, Kamāl as-Sāmarrā'ī (ed.), Baghdad, Maṭbaʿat Ǧāmiʿat Baghdād, 1986

Ibn-Rušd, see Bouyges, M.

Ibn-Sīnā, Abū-ʿAlī al-Ḥusayn ibn-ʿAbdallāh, *aš-Šifāʾ*, *Al-Manṭiq, al-Ǧadal*, A.F. El-Ahwānī (ed.), Cairo, 1965

Irigoin, J., "L'Aristote de Vienne," *Jahrbuch der Österreichischen Byzantinischen Gesellschaft*, 1957, vol. 6, pp. 5–10

—— "Survie et renouveau de la littérature antique à Constantinople (IXe Siècle)," *Cahiers de civilisation médiévale, Xe–XIIe Siècles*, 1962, vol. 5, pp. 287–302, reprinted in D. Harlfinger (ed.), *Griechische Kodikologie*, pp. 173–205

Iskandar, A.Z., "An Attempted Reconstruction of the Late Alexandrian Medical Curriculum," *Medical History*, 1976, vol. 20, pp. 235–58

Ivry, A.L., *Al-Kindi's Metaphysics*, Albany, State University of New York Press, 1974

Jacquart, D. (ed.), *La formation du vocabulaire scientifique et intellectuel dans le monde arabe* [Études sur le Vocabulaire Intellectuel du Moyen Age VII], Turnhout, Brepols, 1994

Jaeger, W., "Die Antike und das Problem der Internationalität der Geisteswissenschaften," *Inter Nationes*, Berlin, 1931, vol. 1

Jones, A.H.M., J.R. Martindale, and J. Morris, *The Prosopography of the Later Roman Empire (260–641)*, 3 vols, Cambridge, Cambridge University Press, 1971–92

Jourdain, C., *Recherches critiques sur l'âge et l'origine des traductions latines d'Aristote et sur les commentaires grecs ou arabes, employés par les docteurs scolastiques*, Paris, 1843

Jürss, F., "Bemerkungen zum naturwissenschaftlichen Denken in der Spätantike," *Klio*, 1965, vol. 43–45, pp. 381–94

Kennedy, H., *The Early Abbasid Caliphate*, London, Croom Helm, 1981

—— *The Prophet and the Age of the Caliphates*, London and New York, Longman, 1986

al-Kindī, Yaʿqūb ibn-Isḥāq, *Fī l-falsafa al-ūlā*, in *Rasāʾil al-Kindī al-falsafiya*, M.ʿA. Abū-Rīda (ed.), 2 vols, Cairo, Dār al-Fikr al-ʿArabī, 1950

Klinge, G., "Die Bedeutung der syrischen Theologen als Vermittler der griechischen Philosophie an den Islam," *Zeitschrift für Kirchengeschichte*, 1939, vol. 58, pp. 346–86

Knorr, W.R., "The Medieval Tradition of a Greek Mathematical Lemma," *Zeitschrift für Geschichte der Arabisch-Islamischen Wissenschaften*, 1986, vol. 3, pp. 230–64

Kraemer, Joel L., "Humanism in the Renaissance of Islam: A Preliminary Study," *Journal of the American Oriental Society*, 1984, vol. 104, pp. 135–64

—— *Philosophy in the Renaissance of Islam*, Leiden, E.J. Brill, 1986
—— *Humanism in the Renaissance of Islam*, Leiden, E.J. Brill, second edition, 1992
Kraus, P., "Zu Ibn al-Muqaffa'," *Rivista degli Studi Orientali*, 1934, vol. 14, pp. 1–20
Kruk, R., see Endress, G. and R. Kruk
Kühn, C.G., *Claudii Galeni opera omnia*, 20 vols, Leipzig, Car. Cnoblochius (K. Knoblauch), 1821–33
Kunitzsch, P., *Der Almagest. Die Syntaxis Mathematica des Claudius Ptolemäus in arabisch-lateinischer Überlieferung*, Wiesbaden, F. Steiner, 1974
—— "Über das Frühstadium der arabischen Aneignung antiken Gutes," *Saeculum*, 1975, vol. 26, pp. 268–82
—— "Zur Problematik und Interpretation der arabischen Übersetzungen antiker Texte," *Oriens*, 1976, vol. 25–26, pp. 116–32
Labarta, A., *Mūsà ibn Nawbajt, al-Kitāb al-kāmil*, Madrid, Instituto Hispano-árabe de Cultura, 1982
Landron, B., "Les chrétiens arabes et les disciplines philosophiques," *Proche Orient Chrétien*, 1986, vol. 36, pp. 23–45
Lassner, J., *The Topography of Baghdad in the Early Middle Ages*, Detroit, Wayne State University, 1970
—— *The Shaping of 'Abbāsid Rule*, Princeton, Princeton University Press, 1980
Lecomte, G., "L'introduction du *Kitāb adab al-kātib* d'Ibn Qutayba," in *Mélanges Louis Massignon*, Damascus, Institut Français de Damas, 1957, vol. 3, pp. 45–64
Lemerle, P., *Le premier humanisme byzantin. Notes et remarques sur enseignement et culture à Byzance des origines au Xe siècle*, Paris, Presses Universitaires de France, 1971; revised translation by H. Lindsay and A. Moffatt, *Byzantine Humanism. The First Phase* [Byzantina Australensia 3], Canberra, Australian Association for Byzantine Studies, 1986
Lettinck, P., *Aristotle's* Physics *and Its Reception in the Arabic World*, Leiden, E.J. Brill, 1994
Levey, M., *Medical Ethics of Medieval Islam, Transactions of the American Philosophical Society*, 1967, vol. 57, part 3
Lohr, C.H., "The Medieval Interpretation of Aristotle," in N. Kretzmann, A. Kenny, J. Pinborg (eds), *The Cambridge History of Later Medieval Philosophy*, Cambridge, Cambridge University Press, 1982, pp. 80–98
McCarthy, J., *at-Taṣānīf al-mansūba ilā faylasūf al-'Arab*, Baghdad, Maṭba'at al-'Ānī, 1382/1962
Madelung, W., "The Origins of the Controversy Concerning the Creation of the Koran," in *Orientalia Hispanica* [Festschrift F.M. Pareja], J.M. Barral (ed.), Leiden, E.J. Brill, 1974, pp. 504–25
—— "Ibn Abī Ǧumhūr al-Aḥsā'ī's Synthesis of *kalām*, Philosophy and Sufism," in *Actes du 8ème Congrès de l'Union Européenne des Arabisants et Islamisants* (Aix-en-Provence, 1976), Aix-en-Provence, 1978, pp. 147–56, reprinted in his *Religious Schools and Sects in Medieval Islam*, London, Variorum, 1985, no. XIII
—— "Mazdakism and the Khurramiyya," in his *Religious Trends in Early Islamic Iran*, Albany, Bibliotheca Persica, 1988, pp. 1–12
Makdisi, G., "L'Islam Hanbalisant," *Revue des Études Islamiques*, 1974, vol. 42, pp. 211–44; 1975, vol. 43, pp. 45–76; translated by M.L. Swartz, *Studies on Islam*, pp. 216–74
—— "The Hanbali School and Sufism," *Boletin de la Asociacion Española de Orientalistas*, Madrid, 1979, vol. 15, pp. 115–26, reprinted in his *Religion, Law and Learning in Classical Islam*, Aldershot, Variorum, 1991, no. V

—— *The Rise of Colleges: Institutions of Learning in Islam and the West*, Edinburgh, Edinburgh University Press, 1981
—— "The Juridical Theology of Shāfiʿī: Origins and Significance of uṣūl al-fiqh," *Studia Islamica*, 1984, vol. 59, pp. 5–47
—— *The Rise of Humanism in Classical Islam and the Christian West*, Edinburgh, Edinburgh University Press, 1990
al-Marzubānī, Muḥammad ibn-ʿImrān, *Muʿǧam aš-šuʿarāʾ*, ʿA.A. Farrāǧ (ed.), Cairo, ʿĪsā al-Bābī al-Ḥalabī, 1960
al-Masʿūdī, ʿAlī ibn-al-Ḥusayn, *Murūǧ aḏ-ḏahab*, C. Pellat (ed.), 7 vols, Beirut, Université Libanaise, 1965–79
—— *at-Tanbīh wa-l-išrāf*, M.J. de Goeje (ed.), Leiden, E.J. Brill, 1894
Mattock, J.N., "The Early Translations from Greek into Arabic: An Experiment in Comparative Assessment," in G. Endress (ed.), *Symposium Graeco-arabicum II*, pp. 73–102
Ménage, V.L., "Three Ottoman Treatises on Europe," in C.E. Bosworth (ed.), *Iran and Islam. A Volume in Memory of Vladimir Minorsky*, Edinburgh, Edinburgh University Press, 1971, pp. 421–33
de Menasce, J.P., "Zoroastrian Pahlavi Writings," in R.N. Frye (ed.), *The Cambridge History of Iran*, vol. 4, pp. 1166–95
Meyerhof, M., "Von Alexandrien nach Bagdad. Ein Beitrag zur Geschichte des philosophischen und medizinischen Unterrichts bei den Arabern," *Sitzungsberichte der Berliner Akademie der Wissenschaften*, Philologisch-historische Klasse, 1930, pp. 389–429
—— "Sultan Saladin's Physician on the Transmission of Greek Medicine to the Arabs," *Bulletin of the History of Medicine*, 1945, vol. 18, pp. 169–78
—— see also Schacht, J. and M. Meyerhof
Miquel, A., *La géographie humaine du monde musulman jusqu'au milieu du 11e siècle*, 4 vols, Paris/La Haye, Mouton, 1967–75
Miskawayh, Aḥmad ibn-Muḥammad, *Taǧārib al-umam*, facsimile edition by L. Caetani [Gibb Memorial Series VII], Leiden, Brill, and London, Luzac, 1909–17
Möller, D., *Studien zur mittelalterlichen arabischen Falknereiliteratur*, Berlin, Walter de Gruyter, 1965; review by F. Viré, *Arabica*, 1966, vol. 13, pp. 209–12
Nallino, C.A., "Tracce di opere Greche giunte agli Arabi per trafila pehlevica," in T.W. Arnold and R.A. Nicholson (eds), *A Volume of Oriental Studies Presented to E.G. Browne*, Cambridge, Cambridge University Press, 1922, pp. 345–63; reprinted in Maria Nallino (ed.), *Raccolta di scritti editi e inediti*, Rome, Istituto per l'Oriente, 1948, vol. 6, pp. 285–303
Nau, F., "Le traité sur les 'Constellations' écrit en 661 par Sévère Sebokht, évêque de Qennesrin," *Revue de l'Orient Chrétien*, 1929–30, vol. 27
Nöldeke, T., "Der Chalif Mansur," in his *Orientalische Skizzen*, Berlin, 1892, pp. 111–51; English translation by J.S. Blake, with revisions by the author, "Caliph Mansúr," in his *Sketches from Eastern History*, London, 1892, pp. 107–45, reprinted in Beirut, Khayats, 1963
Paret, R. "Notes bibliographiques sur quelques travaux récents consacrés aux premières traductions arabes d'œuvres grecques," *Byzantion*, 1959–60, vol. 29–30, pp. 387–446
Pellat, C., "Le traité d'astronomie pratique et de météorologie populaire d'Ibn Qutayba," *Arabica*, 1954, vol. 1, pp. 84–8
—— "Al-Ǧāḥiẓ. Les nations civilisées et les croyances religieuses," *Journal Asiatique*, 1967, vol. 255, pp. 65–90; reprinted in his *Études sur l'histoire socio-culturelle de l'Islam (VIIe–XVe s.)*, London, Variorum, 1976, no. V

—— *The Life and Works of Jāḥiẓ*, Berkeley and Los Angeles, University of California Press, 1969
—— "Al-Ṣāḥib ibn ʿAbbād," in *ʿAbbāsid Belles-Lettres*, pp. 96–111
Peters, F.E., *Aristoteles Arabus*, Leiden, E.J. Brill, 1968
—— *Aristotle and the Arabs*, New York, New York University Press, 1968
—— "Hellenism in Islam," in C.G. Thomas (ed.), *Paths from Ancient Greece*, Leiden, E.J. Brill, 1988, pp. 77–91
Pines, S., "A Tenth Century Philosophical Correspondence," *Proceedings of the American Academy for Jewish Research*, 1955, vol. 24, pp. 103–36
—— "An Early Meaning of the Term *Mutakallim*," *Israel Oriental Studies*, 1971, vol. 1, pp. 224–40, reprinted in his *Studies in the History of Arabic Philosophy* [Collected Works III], S. Stroumsa (ed.), Jerusalem, The Magna Press, 1996, pp. 62–78
Pingree, D., "Historical Horoscopes," *Journal of the American Oriental Society*, 1962, vol. 82, pp. 487–502
—— "Astronomy and Astrology in India and Iran," *Isis*, 1963, vol. 54, pp. 229–46
—— *The Thousands of Abū Maʿshar*, London, The Warburg Institute, 1968
—— "The Fragments of the Works of Yaʿqūb ibn Ṭāriq," *Journal of Near Eastern Studies*, 1968, vol. 27, pp. 97–125
—— "The Fragments of the Works of al-Fazārī," *Journal of Near Eastern Studies*, 1970, vol. 29, pp. 103–23
—— "The Greek Influence on Early Islamic Mathematical Astronomy," *Journal of the American Oriental Society*, 1973, vol. 93, pp. 32–43
—— "Māshā'allāh: Some Sasanian and Syriac Sources," in G.F. Hourani (ed.), *Essays on Islamic Philosophy and Science*, Albany, State University of New York Press, 1975, pp. 5–14
—— "Classical and Byzantine Astrology in Sassanian Persia," *Dumbarton Oaks Papers*, 1989, vol. 43, pp. 227–39
—— and C. Burnett, *The* Liber Aristotilis *of Hugo of Santalla*, London, The Warburg Institute, 1997
Plethon, Georgios Gemistos, see Tambrun-Krasker, B.
Ptolemy, *Geography*, Arabic translation; facsimile reproduction of MS Aya Sofya 2610, F. Sezgin (ed.), Frankfurt am Main, Institut für Geschichte der Arabisch-Islamischen Wissenschaften, 1987
Putman, H., *L'église et l'Islam sous Timothée I (780–823)*, Beirut, Dar el-Machreq, 1975
Q = Ibn-al-Qifṭī
Raby, J., "Mehmed the Conqueror's Greek Scriptorium," *Dumbarton Oaks Papers*, 1983, vol. 37, pp. 15–34 (with 41 figures)
Rashed, R., "Problems of the Transmission of Greek Scientific Thought into Arabic: Examples from Mathematics and Optics," *History of Science*, 1989, vol. 27, pp. 199–209
—— "Al-Kindī's Commentary on Archimedes' 'The Measurement of the Circle'," *Arabic Sciences and Philosophy*, 1993, vol. 3, pp. 7–53
—— *Oeuvres philosophiques et scientifiques d'al-Kindī. Volume I. L'Optique et la Catoptrique*, Leiden, E.J. Brill, 1997
—— "Le commentaire par al-Kindī de l'*Optique* d'Euclide: un traité jusqu'ici inconnu," *Arabic Sciences and Philosophy*, 1997, vol. 7, pp. 9–56
Rosen, F., see al-Ḫwārizmī, Muḥammad ibn-Mūsā
Rosenthal, F., "Al-Kindī als Literat," *Orientalia*, 1942, vol. 11, pp. 262–88

—— *Aḥmad b. aṭ-Ṭayyib as-Saraḫsī*, New Haven, American Oriental Society, 1943
—— "Al-Asṭurlâbî and as-Samaw'al on Scientific Progress," *Osiris*, 1950, vol. 9, pp. 555–64
—— "Isḥāq b. Ḥunayn's Ta'rīḫ al-Aṭibbā'," *Oriens*, 1954, vol. 7, pp. 55–80
—— *Classical Heritage* = *Das Fortleben der Antike im Islam*, Zürich, Artemis, 1965, translated as *The Classical Heritage in Islam*, London and Berkeley, Routledge & Kegan Paul and University of California Press, 1975
—— *A History of Muslim Historiography*, Leiden, E.J. Brill, second edition, 1968
—— *The Return of the Caliphate to Baghdad* [The History of al-Ṭabarī, vol. 38], Albany, State University of New York Press, 1985
—— "From Arabic Books and Manuscripts, XVI: As-Sarakhsī(?) on the Appropriate Behavior for Kings," *Journal of the American Oriental Society*, 1995, vol. 115, pp. 105–9
Rowson, E.K., "The Philosopher as Littérateur: al-Tawḥīdī and His Predecessors," *Zeitschrift für Geschichte der Arabisch-Islamischen Wissenschaften*, 1990, vol. 6, pp. 50–92
ar-Ruhāwī, Isḥāq ibn-ʿAlī, *The Conduct of the Physician by Al-Ruhāwī* [Facsimile of the unique Edirne MS Selimiye 1658], Publications of the Institute for the History of Arabic-Islamic Science, edited by F. Sezgin, Series C, vol. 18, Frankfurt am Main, 1985
Ruland, H.-J., *Die arabischen Fassungen von zwei Schriften des Alexander von Aphrodisias Über die Vorsehung und Über das liberum arbitrium*, unpublished Ph.D. dissertation, University of Saarbrücken, 1976
—— *Die arabische Übersetzung der Schrift des Alexander von Aphrodisias über die Sinneswahrnehmung* [Nachrichten der Akad. der Wiss. in Göttingen, Philol.-Hist. Klasse, 1978, Nr. 5], Göttingen, 1978
Sabra, A.I., "The Andalusian Revolt against Ptolemaic Astronomy," in E. Mendelsohn (ed.), *Transformation and Tradition in the Sciences*, Cambridge, Cambridge University Press, 1984, pp. 133–53
—— "The Appropriation and Subsequent Naturalization of Greek Science in Medieval Islam: A Preliminary Statement," *History of Science*, 1987, vol. 25, pp. 223–43
—— "Situating Arabic Science. Locality versus Essence," *Isis*, 1996, vol. 87, pp. 654–70
Sachau, E., *Alberuni's India*, London, 1888; reprinted Bombay, 1964
Ṣāʿid al-Andalusī, al-Qāḍī Abū-l-Qāsim, *Ṭabaqāt al-umam*, L. Cheikho (ed.), Beirut, Imprimerie Catholique, 1912
Sadighi, G.H., *Les mouvements religieux iraniens au IIe et au IIIe siècle de l'hégire*, Paris, Les Presses Modernes, 1938
Saʿīd, Ǧ., "Muḥammad ibn-ʿAbd-al-Malik az-Zayyāt, al-Wazīr, al-Kātib aš-Šāʿir," *Maǧallat al-Maǧmaʿ al-ʿIlmī al-ʿIrāqī*, 1986, vol. 37.3, pp. 174–221
Salem, E.A., *Hilāl aṣ-Ṣābi', Rusūm Dār al-Khilāfa*, Beirut, American University of Beirut, 1977
Saliba, G., "The Development of Astronomy in Medieval Islamic Society," *Arab Studies Quarterly*, 1982, vol. 4, pp. 211–25; reprinted in his *A History of Arabic Astronomy*, 1994, pp. 51–65
—— *A History of Arabic Astronomy*, New York and London, New York University Press, 1994
Samir, K., and P. Nwyia, *Une correspondance islamo-chrétienne entre Ibn al-Munaǧǧim, Ḥunayn ibn Isḥāq et Qusṭā ibn Lūqā* [Patrologia Orientalis, vol. 40, fascicle 4, no. 185], Turnhout, Brepols, 1981

Sauter, C., "Die peripatetische Philosophie bei den Syrern und Arabern," *Archiv für Geschichte der Philosophie*, 1903, vol. 17, pp. 516–33

Savage-Smith, E., "Attitudes toward Dissection in Medieval Islam," *Journal of the History of Medicine and Allied Sciences*, 1995, vol. 50, pp. 67–110

Sayılı, A., *The Observatory in Islam*, Ankara, Türk Tarih Kurumu, 1960, reprinted 1988

Scarcia Amoretti, B., "Sects and Heresies," in R.N. Frye (ed.), *The Cambridge History of Iran*, vol. 4, pp. 481–519

Schacht, J. and M. Meyerhof, *The Medico-Philosophical Controversy between Ibn Butlan of Baghdad and Ibn Ridwan of Cairo*, The Egyptian University, Faculty of Arts Publication no. 13, Cairo, 1937

Schoeler, G., *Arabische Handschriften*, Teil II, Stuttgart, Franz Steiner, 1990

Séert, Chronique de, A. Scher et R. Griveau (eds) [Patrologia Orientalis XIII,4], Paris, Firmin-Didot, 1919

Sezgin, F., *Geschichte des Arabischen Schrifttums*, 9 vols to date, Leiden, E.J. Brill, 1967–

Shaban, M.A., *The ʿAbbāsid Revolution*, Cambridge, Cambridge University Press, 1970

—— *Islamic History 2*, Cambridge, Cambridge University Press, 1976

Shahid, I., *Byzantium and the Arabs in the Fifth Century*, Washington, DC, Dumbarton Oaks, 1989

Shaki, M., "The Dēnkard Account of the History of the Zoroastrian Scriptures," *Archív Orientální*, 1981, vol. 49, pp. 114–25

Sidarus, A., "Un recueil de traités philosophiques et médicaux à Lisbonne," *Zeitschrift für Geschichte der Arabisch-Islamischen Wissenschaften*, 1990, vol. 6, pp. 179–89

Sorabji, R., *Aristotle Transformed*, London, Duckworth, 1990

Sourdel, D., *Le Vizirat ʿAbbāside de 749 à 936 (132 à 324 de l'Hégire)*, Damas, Institut Français de Damas, 1959–60, 2 vols

Sournia, J.C., and G. Troupeau, "Médecine Arabe: biographies critiques de Jean Mésué (VIII° siècle) et du Prétendu 'Mésué le Jeune' (X° siècle)," *Clio Medica*, 1968, vol. 3, pp. 109–17

Sprengling, M., "From Persian to Arabic," *The American Journal of Semitic Languages and Literatures*, 1939, vol. 56, pp. 175–224, 325–36; 1940, vol. 57, pp. 302–5

Stein, L., "Das erste Auftreten der griechischen Philosophie unter den Arabern," *Archiv für Geschichte der Philosophie*, 1894, vol. 7, pp. 350–61

Steinschneider, M., *Die Arabischen Übersetzungen aus dem Griechischen*, Graz, Akademische Druck- und Verlagsanstalt, 1960, reprinting articles that appeared in the following periodicals: *Beihefte zum Centralblatt für Bibliothekswesen*, 1889, vol. 5, pp. 51–82, and 1893, vol. 12, pp. 129–240; *Zeitschrift der Deutschen Morgenländischen Gesellschaft*, 1896, vol. 50, pp. 161–219, 337–417; and *Archiv für Pathologische Anatomie und Physiologie und für Klinische Medizin*, 1891, vol. 124, series 12, part 4, pp. 115–36, 268–96, 455–87

—— *Die Hebräischen Übersetzungen des Mittelalters und die Juden als Dolmetscher*, Berlin, H. Itzkowski, 1893

Steppat, F., "From *ʿAhd Ardašīr* to al-Ma'mūn: A Persian Element in the Policy of the *miḥna*," in W. al-Qāḍī (ed.), *Studia Arabica & Islamica* [Festschrift for Iḥsān ʿAbbās], Beirut, American University of Beirut, 1981, pp. 451–4

Strohmaier, G., "Homer in Bagdad," *Byzantinoslavica*, 1980, vol. 41, pp. 196–200

—— "Byzantinisch-arabische Wissenschaftsbeziehungen in der Zeit des Ikonoklasmus," in H. Köpstein und F. Winkelmann (eds), *Studien zum 8. und 9. Jahrhundert in Byzanz* [Berliner Byzantinistische Arbeiten 51], Berlin, Akademie Verlag, 1983, pp. 179–83

—— "'Von Alexandrien nach Bagdad' – eine fiktive Schultradition," in J. Wiesner (ed.), *Aristoteles. Werk und Wirkung, Paul Moraux gewidmet*, vol. 2, Berlin, W. de Gruyter, 1987, pp. 380–9

—— "Al-Manṣūr und die frühe Rezeption der griechischen Alchemie," *Zeitschrift für Geschichte der Arabisch-Islamischen Wissenschaften*, 1989, vol. 5, pp. 167–77

—— "'Umāra ibn Ḥamza, Constantine V, and the Invention of the Elixir," *Graeco-Arabica* (Athens), 1991, vol. 4, pp. 21–4

as-Suyūṭī, Ǧalāl-ad-Dīn, *Ṣawn al-manṭiq wa-l-kalām 'an fann al-manṭiq wa-l-kalām*, 'Alī Sāmī an-Naššār (ed.), Cairo, Maktabat al-Ḫānǧī 1947

Swartz, M.L., *Studies on Islam*, Oxford, Oxford University Press, 1981

aṯ-Ṯa'ālibī, 'Abdalmalik ibn-Muḥammad, *Ḫāṣṣ al-ḫāṣṣ*, Beirut, 1966

—— *Laṭā'if al-ma'ārif*, translated by C.E. Bosworth, *The Book of Curious and Entertaining Information*, Edinburgh, Edinburgh University Press, 1968

—— *Yatīmat ad-dahr*, M.M. 'Abdalḥamīd (ed.), 4 vols, second printing, Cairo, 1956

aṭ-Ṭabarī, Muḥammad ibn-Ǧarīr, *Ta'rīḫ ar-rusul wa-l-mulūk*, M.J. de Goeje *et al.* (eds), Leiden, E.J. Brill, 1879–1901

—— *The History of al-Ṭabarī*, English translation, volumes cited individually under the name of the translator

Ṭaha, S., "At-Ta'rīb wa-kibār al-mu'arribīn fī l-Islām," *Sumer*, 1976, vol. 32, pp. 339–89

Tambrun-Krasker, B. with M. Tardieu, *Oracles Chaldaïques. Recension de Georges Gémiste Pléthon* [Corpus Philosophorum Medii Aevi 7], Athens, The Academy of Athens, 1995

Tardieu, M., see Tambrun-Krasker, B.

at-Tawḥīdī, Abū-Ḥayyān, *al-Imtā' wa-l-mu'ānasa*, Aḥmad Amīn and Aḥmad az-Zayn (eds), second printing, Cairo, 1951; reprinted Beirut, n.d.

—— *Maṯālib al-wazīrayn*, I. al-Kaylānī (ed.), Damascus, Dār al-Fikr bi-Dimašq, 1961

Ṭayfūr, Aḥmad Ibn-Abī-Ṭāhir, *Kitāb Baġdād*, H. Keller (ed.), 2 vols, Leipzig, Harrassowitz, 1908

Troupeau, G., "Le rôle des syriaques dans la transmission et l'exploitation du patrimoine philosophique et scientifique grec," *Arabica*, 1991, vol. 38, pp. 1–10

—— see also Sournia, J.C. and G. Troupeau

Türker, M., *Üç tehâfüt bakımından felsefe ve din münasebeti*, Istanbul, Türk Tarih Kurumu, 1956

—— "Fārābī'nin 'Şerā'it ul-yakīn'i," *Araştırma*, 1963, vol. 1, pp. 151–228

Ullmann, *Medizin* = M. Ullmann, *Die Medizin im Islam* [Handbuch der Orientalistik, Ergänzungsband VI,1], Leiden, E.J. Brill, 1970

—— *Wörterbuch der Klassischen Arabischen Sprache*, 4 vols to date (*kāf-lām*), Wiesbaden, Harrassowitz, 1970–

—— "War Ḥunain der Übersetzer von Artemidors Traumbuch?" *Die Welt des Islams*, 1971, vol. 13, pp. 204–11

—— *Geheimwissenschaften* = M. Ullmann, *Die Natur- und Geheimwissenschaften im Islam* [Handbuch der Orientalistik, Ergänzungsband VI,2], Leiden, E.J. Brill, 1972

—— "Ḫālid ibn Yazīd und die Alchemie: Eine Legende," *Der Islam*, 1978, vol. 55, pp. 181–218

—— "Nicht nur . . . , sondern auch . . . ," *Der Islam*, 1983, vol. 60, pp. 3–36

Vajda, G., "Les zindîqs en pays d'Islam au debut de la période Abbaside," *Rivista degli Studi Orientali*, 1938, vol. 17, pp. 173–229

Walzer, R., "New Light on the Arabic Translations of Aristotle," *Oriens*, 1953, vol. 6, pp. 91–142, reprinted in his *Greek into Arabic*, pp. 60–113

—— "Arabische Übersetzungen aus dem Griechischen," *Miscellanea Medievalia*, 1962, vol. 9, pp. 179–95

—— *Greek into Arabic*, Oxford, B. Cassirer, 1962

Watson, A.M., *Agricultural Innovation in the Early Islamic World*, Cambridge, Cambridge University Press, 1983

Wenrich, J.G., *De auctorum graecorum versionibus et commentariis syriacis arabicis armeniacis persicisque commentatio*, Lipsiae (Leipzig), F.C.W. Vogel, 1842

Whipple, A.O., "Role of the Nestorians as the Connecting Link between Greek and Arabic Medicine," *Annals of Medical History*, 1936, n.s., Vol. 8, pp. 313–23

Wiesner, H., see Fazzo, S. and H. Wiesner

Wilcox, J., *The Transmission and Influence of Qusta ibn Luqa's "On the Difference between Spirit and Soul"*, unpublished Ph.D. dissertation, The City University of New York, 1985

—— "Our Continuing Discovery of the Greek Science of the Arabs: The Example of Qusṭā ibn Lūqā," *Annals of Scholarship*, 1987, vol. 4,3, pp. 57–74

Wilson, N.G., "The Libraries of the Byzantine World," *Greek, Roman and Byzantine Studies*, 1967, vol. 8, pp. 53–80, reprinted in D. Harlfinger (ed.), *Griechische Kodikologie*, pp. 276–309

—— "Books and Readers in Byzantium," *Byzantine Books and Bookmen* [Dumbarton Oaks Colloquium, 1971], Washington, DC, Dumbarton Oaks, 1975

—— *Scholars of Byzantium*, London, Duckworth, 1983

WKAS = M. Ullmann, *Wörterbuch der Klassischen Arabischen Sprache*

al-Yaʿqūbī, Aḥmad ibn-Abī-Yaʿqūb, *Taʾrīḫ*, M. Houtsma (ed.), 2 vols, Leiden, E.J. Brill, 1883

Yāqūt ibn-ʿAbdallāh ar-Rūmī al-Ḥamawī, *Iršād al-arīb*, D.S. Margoliouth (ed.), 7 vols, Leiden, Brill and London, Luzac, 1907–26

Zaehner, R.C., *Zurvan. A Zoroastrian Dilemma*, Oxford, Clarendon, 1955

—— *The Dawn and Twilight of Zoroastrianism*, New York, G.B. Putnam's Sons, 1961

Zakeri, M., "ʿAlī ibn ʿUbaida ar-Raiḥānī. A Forgotten Belletrist (*adīb*) and Pahlavi Translator," *Oriens*, 1994, vol. 34, pp. 76–102

Zimmermann, F.W., *Al-Farabi's Commentary and Short Treatise on Aristotle's* De Interpretatione [The British Academy. Classical and Medieval Logic Texts III], Oxford, Oxford University Press, 1981

CHRONOLOGICAL BIBLIOGRAPHY OF STUDIES ON THE SIGNIFICANCE OF THE TRANSLATION MOVEMENT FOR ISLAMIC CIVILIZATION

This subject has been much discussed in secondary literature and constitutes an interesting chapter in the sociology of knowledge and the history of European scholarship. Among the most important contributions are the following, listed in chronological order (cf. Ullmann, *Medizin*, pp. 1–2; Endress, *GAP* II,482–3):

Wenrich, J.G., *De auctorum graecorum versionibus et commentariis syriacis arabicis armeniacis persicisque commentatio*, Leipzig, F.C.W. Vogel, 1842, Pars prima, pp. 3–70

Renan, E., *L'islamisme et la science*, Paris, Calmann Lévy, 1883

Goldziher, I., "Stellung der alten islamischen Orthodoxie zu den antiken Wissenschaften," *Abhandlungen der Königlich Preussischen Akademie der Wissenschaften*, Jahrgang 1915, Philosophisch-Historische Klasse, no. 8, Berlin, Verlag der Akademie, 1916

Troeltsch, E., "Der Europäismus," in his *Der Historismus und seine Probleme* [*Gesammelte Schriften* III], Tübingen, J.C.B. Mohr, 1922, pp. 703–30

Becker, C.H., "Der Islam im Rahmen einer allgemeinen Kulturgeschichte," in his *Islamstudien*, Leipzig, Quelle und Meyer, 1924, vol. 1, pp. 24–53

Ruska, J., "Über das Fortleben der antiken Wissenschaften im Orient," *Archiv für Geschichte der Mathematik, der Naturwissenschaften und der Technik*, 1927, vol. 10, pp. 112–35

Schaeder, H.H., "Der Orient und das griechische Erbe," *Die Antike*, 1928, vol. 4, pp. 226–65; reprinted in his *Der Mensch in Orient und Okzident*, München, 1960, pp. 107–61

Jaeger, W., "Die Antike und das Problem der Internationalität der Geisteswissenschaften," *Inter Nationes*, Berlin, 1931, vol. 1

Becker, C.H., *Das Erbe der Antike im Orient und Okzident*, Leipzig, 1931

Plessner, M., *Die Geschichte der Wissenschaften im Islam als Aufgabe der modernen Islamwissenschaft* [Philosophie und Geschichte 31], Tübingen, J.C.B. Mohr, 1931

Schacht, J., "Über den Hellenismus in Baghdad und Cairo im 11. Jahrhundert," *Zeitschrift der Deutschen Morgenländischen Gesellschaft*, 1936, vol. 90, pp. 526–45
Grunebaum, G.E. von, "Islam and Hellenism," *Scientia* (*Rivista di Scienza*), 1950, vol. 85, pp. 21–7
Paret, R., *Der Islam und das griechische Bildungsgut* [Philosophie und Geschichte 70], Tübingen, J.C.B. Mohr, 1950
Schacht, J., "Remarques sur la transmission de la pensée grecque aux Arabes," *Histoire de la médecine. Numéro spécialement édité en l'honneur du XVe Congrès de la Fédération des Sociétés de Gynécologie et d'Obstétrique de langue française à Alger, le 5 Mai 1952*, Algiers, 1952, pp. 11–19
Nyberg, H.S., "Das Studium des Orients und die europäische Kultur," *Zeitschrift der Deutschen Morgenländischen Gesellschaft*, 1953, vol. 103, pp. 9–21
Spuler, B., "Hellenistisches Denken im Islam," *Saeculum*, 1954, vol. 5, pp. 179–93
Thillet, P., "Sagesse grecque et philosophie musulmane," *Les Mardis de Dar el-Salam*, Paris, Vrin, 1955, pp. 55–93
Walzer, R., "On the Legacy of the Classics in the Islamic World," *Festschrift Bruno Snell*, München, 1956, pp. 189–96; reprinted in his *Greek Into Arabic*, Oxford, Bruno Cassirer, 1962, pp. 29–37
Classicisme et déclin culturel dans l'histoire de l'Islam, Paris, Besson-Chantermerle, 1957; reprinted Paris, Maisonneuve et Larose, 1977; review by D. Sourdel, *Arabica*, 1958, vol. 5, pp. 311–17
Kramers, J.H., "Science in Islamic Civilization," in his *Analecta Orientalia, Posthumous Writings and Selected Minor Works*, Leiden, E.J. Brill, 1956, vol. 2, pp. 75–148
Kraemer, Jörg, *Das Problem der islamischen Kulturgeschichte*, Tübingen, 1959
Gätje, H., "Gedanken zur Problematik der islamischen Kulturgeschichte," *Die Welt als Geschichte*, 1960, vol. 20, pp. 157–67
Ritter, H., "Hat die religiöse Orthodoxie einen Einfluss auf die Dekadenz des Islams ausgeübt?" in G.E. von Grunebaum and W. Hartner (eds), *Klassizismus und Kulturzerfall*, Frankfurt am Main, 1960, pp. 120–43
Dubler, C.E., "Islam" (Erbe des Ostens), *Asiatische Studien*, 1960, vol. 13, pp. 32–54
Benz, E., "The Islamic Culture as Mediator of the Greek Philosophy to Europe," *Islamic Culture*, 1961, vol. 35, pp. 147–65
Dubler, C.E. "Das Weiterleben der Antike im Islam," in *Das Erbe der Antike*, Zürich/Stuttgart, 1963
Goitein, S.D., "Between Hellenism and Renaissance – Islam, the Intermediate Civilization," *Islamic Studies*, 1963, vol. 2, pp. 217–33
Dietrich, A., "Islam und Abendland," *Neue Sammlung, Göttinger Blätter für Kultur und Erziehung*, 1965, vol. 5, pp. 37–53
Gottschalk, H.L., "Die Rezeption der antiken Wissenschaften durch den Islam, *Anzeiger der Philosophisch-Historischen Klasse der Österreichischen Akademie der Wissenschaften*, Philosophisch-Historische Klasse, 1965, vol. 102,7, pp. 111–34
Plessner, M., *Die Bedeutung der Wissenschaftsgeschichte für das Verständnis der geistigen Welt des Islams* [Philosophie und Geschichte 82], Tübingen, J.C.B. Mohr, 1966
Goitein, S.D., *Studies in Islamic History and Institutions*, Leiden, E.J. Brill, 1966
Rosenthal, F., "The Greek Heritage in Islam," *Ventures, Magazine of the Yale Graduate School*, 1967, vol. 7.1, pp. 55–61
Gabrieli, F., "Griechentum und Islam – eine Kulturbegegnung," *Antaios*, 1968, vol. 9, pp. 513–32
Bürgel, J.C., "Dogmatismus und Autonomie im wissenschaftlichen Denken des islamischen Mittelalters," *Saeculum*, 1972, vol. 23, pp. 30–46

Kunitzsch, P., "Über das Frühstadium der arabischen Aneignung antiken Gutes," *Saeculum*, 1975, vol. 26, pp. 268–82

Kunitzsch, P., "Zur Problematik und Interpretation der arabischen Übersetzungen antiker Texte," *Oriens*, 1976, vol. 25–26, pp. 116–32

Ṭaha, S., "At-Taʿrīb wa-kibār al-muʿarribīn fī l-Islām," *Sumer*, 1976, vol. 32, pp. 339–89

Toll, C., "Arabische Wissenschaft und griechisches Erbe. Die Rezeption der griechischen Antike und die Blüte der Wissenschaften in der klassischen Periode des Islam," in A. Mercier, *Islam und Abendland. Geschichte und Gegenwart*, Bern and Frankfurt, 1976, pp. 31–57

Daiber, H., "Anfänge und Entstehung der Wissenschaft im Islam," *Saeculum*, 1978, vol. 29, pp. 356–66

Klein-Franke, F., *Die klassiche Antike in der Tradition des Islam*, Darmstadt, Wissenschaftliche Buchgesellschaft, 1980; reviewed by G. Strohmaier, *Sudhoffs Archiv*, 1981, vol. 65, pp. 200–2

Fück, J., "Hellenismus und Islam," in Manfred Fleischhammer (ed.), *Arabische Kultur und Islam im Mittelalter. Ausgewählte Schriften*, Weimar, H. Böhlaus Nachfolger, 1981, pp. 272–88

Strohmaier, G., " Das Fortleben griechischer sozialer Typenbegriffe im Arabischen," in E.C. Welskopf (ed.), *Soziale Typenbegriffe im alten Griechenland*, Berlin, Akadenie-Verlag, 1982, pp. 39–60

Bausani, A., "L'eredità greca nel mondo musulmano," *Contributo*, 1983, vol. 7.2, pp. 3–14

Goodman, L.E., "The Greek Impact on Arabic Literature," in A.F.L. Beeston *et al.* (eds), *Arabic Literature to the End of the Umayyad Period* [The Cambridge History of Arabic Literature], Cambridge, Cambridge University Press 1983, pp. 460–82

Kraemer, J.L., "Humanism in the Renaissance of Islam: A Preliminary Study," *Journal of the American Oriental Society*, 1984, vol. 104, pp. 135–64

Baffioni, C., "Pensiero greco e pensiero islamico: fonti storiche e problemi metodologici," *Scrinium* 5: *L'Islam e la trasmissione della cultura classica* [Quaderni ed estratti di *Schede Medievali*, 1984, vol. 6–7: Testi del III Colloquio Medievale, Palermo, 19–20 Marzo 1984], Palermo, Officina di Studi Medievali, 1984, pp. 25–41

Daiber, H., "Semitische Sprachen als Kulturvermittler zwischen Antike und Mittelalter," *Zeitschrift der Deutschen Morgenländischen Gesellschaft*, 1986, vol. 136, pp. 292–313

al-ʿAlī, Ṣ.A., "Al-ʿIlm al-iġrīqī, muqawwimātuhu wa-naqluhu ilā l-ʿArabiyya," *Maǧallat al-Maǧmaʿ al-ʿIlmī al-ʿIrāqī*, 1986, vol. 37.4, pp. 3–56

Sabra, A.I., "The Appropriation and Subsequent Naturalization of Greek Science in Medieval Islam: A Preliminary Statement," *History of Science*, 1987, vol. 25, pp. 223–43

Strohmaier, G., "'Von Alexandrien nach Bagdad' – eine fiktive Schultradition," in J. Wiesner (ed.), *Aristoteles. Werk und Wirkung, Paul Moraux gewidmet*, Berlin, W. de Gruyter, 1987, vol. 2, pp. 380–9

Kunitzsch, P., "Ḥarakatā t-tarǧama ilā l-ʿarabiyya wa-min al-ʿarabiyya wa-ahammiyatuhumā fī ta'rīḫ al-fikr," *Zeitschrift für Geschichte der Arabisch-Islamischen Wissenschaften*, 1987–8, vol. 4, pp. 93–105

Peters, F.E., "Hellenism in Islam," in C.G. Thomas (ed.), *Paths from Ancient Greece*, Leiden, E.J. Brill, 1988, pp. 77–91

Rashed, R., "Problems of the Transmission of Greek Scientific Thought into Arabic:

Examples from Mathematics and Optics," *History of Science*, 1989, vol. 27, pp. 199–209

Wasserstein, D.J., "Greek Science in Islam: Islamic Scholars as Successors to the Greeks," *Hermathena*, 1989, vol. 147, pp. 57–72

Goodman, L.E., "The Translation of Greek Materials into Arabic," in M.J.L. Young *et al.* (eds), *Religion, Learning and Science in the ʿAbbasid Period* [The Cambridge History of Arabic Literature], Cambridge, Cambridge University Press, 1990, pp. 477–97

Kraemer, J.L., *Humanism in the Renaissance of Islam. The Cultural Revival during the Buyid Age*, Leiden, E.J. Brill, second edition, 1992

Berggren, J.L., "Islamic Acquisition of the Foreign Sciences: A Cultural Perspective," *The American Journal of Islamic Social Studies*, 1992, vol. 9, pp. 310–24

Sabra, A.I., "Situating Arabic Science: Locality versus Essence," *Isis*, 1996, vol. 87, pp. 654–70

GENERAL INDEX

All diacritical marks and all articles, including the Arabic article *al-* (except in modern proper names), are disregarded in the alphabetization.

based on Arab tribalism 189–91; Mosque 171, 183n.64; reactions to the translation movement 156–7; sciences during 31; secretaries to 131; translation activities during 20–7, 28
Usāma ibn-Zayd 18n.10
Ustād̲sīs 48, 50, 78
Usṭāṯ 143, 145

veterinary science 1, 195
viziers 128–33
Vologases I 36

Wahb family 131–2
Wahhābīs 167
Walzer, Richard 21n.16, 147n.67, 149
Warz-nāma 114
Wāsiṭ 19, 52
al-Wāṯiq 118, 125, 130
Watson, A.M 12n.1
Wenrich, Johann G. xii–xiii
Wilcox, Judith 126nn.11–12
Wilson, Nigel G. 177nn.46–7, 180n.54
wisdom literature (gnomologia) 1

Yāfiṯ 89
Yaḥyā ibn-Abī-Ḥakīm al-Ḥallāǧī 125
Yaḥyā ibn-Abī-Manṣūr 55n.47, 58
Yaḥyā ibn-ʿAdī 61, 72, 98, 100–4, 132, 136, 147, 155, 163
Yaḥyā ibn-Akṯam 100–1
Yaḥyā ibn-Ḫālid ibn-Barmak 114, 137, 156
Yaḥyā ibn-Ziyād 65
al-Yaʿqūbī 46n.34, 114n.12, 126n.12
Yāqūt 56, 127
Yazdiǧird III 113
Yūḥannā ibn-Māsawayh 118–19, 123, 138
Yūnān 88, 165

Zagros mountains 19
Zakeri, Mohsen 27n.30
Zand 36
zandaqa 67, 70, 72n.22, 157
Zanǧ 162
az-Zayyāt: *see* Muḥammad ibn-ʿAbd-al-Malik az-Zayyāt
zīǧ 113–14
Zīǧ al-Arkand 113
Zīǧ al-Harqan 113
Zīǧ aš-Šāh 113
Zīǧ as-Sindhind 114
Zīǧ as-Sindhind al-kabīr 114
Zimmermann, Fritz 142n.56
zoology 1, 145, 165, 196
Zoroaster 36, 39–42; ps.-Zoroaster 37, 41, 45, 49–50, 109
Zoroastrian(s)/-ism 14, 34–41, 43; and astrology 71; imperial ideology 25, 27, 28, 34, 40–6, 55, 60, 66, 75, 78–9, 83, 88, 94; as patrons 134; revivalist movements under early ʿAbbāsids 45–51

INDEX OF MANUSCRIPTS

3089048

Made in the USA